Solemate

Also by Lauren Mackler

Speaking of Success:
World Class Experts Share Their Secrets,
featuring Jack Canfield, Stephen Covey,
Lauren Mackler, and Ken Blanchard;
edited by Insight Publishing

Solemate

Master the Art of Aloneness &
Transform Your Life

Lauren Mackler

HAY
HOUSE

HAY HOUSE
Australia • Canada • Hong Kong • India
South Africa • United Kingdom • United States

Published and distributed in the United Kingdom by:
Hay House UK Ltd, 292B Kensal Rd, London W10 5BE.
Tel.: (44) 20 8962 1230; Fax: (44) 20 8962 1239. www.hayhouse.co.uk

Published and distributed in the United States of America by:
Hay House, Inc., PO Box 5100, Carlsbad, CA 92018-5100. Tel.: (1) 760 431
7695 or (800) 654 5126; Fax: (1) 760 431 6948 or (800) 650 5115.
www.hayhouse.com

Published and distributed in Australia by:
Hay House Australia Ltd, 18/36 Ralph St, Alexandria NSW 2015. Tel.: (61)
2 9669 4299; Fax: (61) 2 9669 4144. www.hayhouse.com.au

Published and distributed in the Republic of South Africa by:
Hay House SA (Pty), Ltd, PO Box 990, Witkoppen 2068.
Tel./Fax: (27) 11 467 8904. www.hayhouse.co.za

Published and distributed in India by:
Hay House Publishers India, Muskaan Complex, Plot No.3, B-2, Vasant
Kunj, New Delhi – 110 070. Tel.: (91) 11 4176 1620;
Fax: (91) 11 4176 1630. www.hayhouse.co.in

Distributed in Canada by:
Raincoast, 9050 Shaughnessy St, Vancouver, BC V6P 6E5.
Tel.: (1) 604 323 7100; Fax: (1) 604 323 2600

© Lauren Mackler, 2009

The moral rights of the author have been asserted.

The author of this book does not dispense medical advice or prescribe
the use of any technique as a form of treatment for physical or medical
problems without the advice of a physician, either directly or indirectly.
The intent of the author is only to offer information of a general nature
to help you in your quest for emotional and spiritual wellbeing. In the
event you use any of the information in this book for yourself, which
is your constitutional right, the author and the publisher assume no
responsibility for your actions.

A catalogue record for this book is available from the British Library.

ISBN 978-1-84850-110-2

Printed and bound in Great Britain by
TJ International, Padstow, Cornwall.

Mixed Sources
Product group from well-managed
forests and other controlled sources
www.fsc.org Cert no. SGS-COC-2482
© 1996 Forest Stewardship Council

I DEDICATE THIS BOOK TO MY HERO
AND FATHER, EDWARD D. MACKLER, M.D.

CONTENTS

INTRODUCTION

This book is about *you*. Mastering the art of aloneness is about having a good relationship with yourself. It's about becoming the person you were meant to be, treating yourself well, and shedding the old beliefs and behaviors that limit your ability to live a healthy, happy, satisfying life—with or without a partner.

When we are born, we are whole, integrated human beings filled with tremendous potential. We feel good about ourselves and are able to experience and express the full range of human emotions. As we grow up, we adapt to the peculiarities—and even pathologies—of our own families by adopting patterns of thought and behavior, some of which erode our innate wholeness. We carry these patterns into adulthood, and they shape our lives, our feelings about ourselves, and our relationships with others.

Mastering the art of aloneness is about reclaiming your innate wholeness, rather than seeking an ideal partner—an outer soul mate—to give you a sense of completeness and well-being. It's a gradual, step-by-step process that involves understanding where your self-defeating patterns come from and how to move beyond them. That means uncovering and retrieving your authentic self—the person you really are beneath the layers of your life conditioning—and living in a conscious and deliberate way so you can achieve the results that you want from life and feel complete and happy on your own.

I first developed the Mastering the Art of Aloneness workshop in 1998—initially as a 12-week series, to allow people ample time to go through the process while receiving ongoing support. When I discovered that a lot of people found it difficult to take time out of their busy schedules to commit to a 12-week program, I began holding intensive weekend workshops. Those early 12-week sessions were particularly gratifying, because not only was I able to give people the tools they needed to begin to make changes in their lives, but as they each went off and used these tools, I could actually witness the dramatic transformations they were experiencing in their own lives from week to week. It's exciting to watch, and just as exciting to experience. This book gives you the same tools I use in my private coaching practice and in my workshops, all of which are designed to help you transform your life.

Throughout *Solemate,* I share my own personal stories as well as those of some of the clients with whom I've worked. I've concealed the identity of my clients, in some cases changing details of their lives to protect their identities while staying true to their underlying experiences. I've made a conscious effort to avoid sexist language, as well as the tedium of referring to all these imaginary people as "he or she" throughout the text. So I've randomly used the word "he" or the word "she" when I provide examples, trying to alternate between them when I'm not referring to particular clients. Other than that, please don't infer anything from where or how I've used these particular pronouns.

My interest in the field of personal development began in the early '80s in California when I attended a series of Insight Seminars. Those personal-development workshops, combined with a growing interest in holistic healing, laid the foundation for my later education in the field. In the years that followed, I underwent training as a workshop facilitator and collaborated with my then-husband, a German physician, on a series of holistic healing workshops in Europe. Inspired in part by a seminar I attended led by Dr. Bernie Siegel, author of *Love, Medicine & Miracles* and a pioneer in integrating emotional and spiritual approaches into the healing of life-threatening illnesses, I created a workshop for cancer patients called *Cancer as a Chance to Live*. I studied breath therapy in India, completed a psychotherapeutic counseling program in Germany, and trained in mind-body modalities such as bioenergetics, voice dialogue, emotional release, and craniosacral therapy. But it wasn't until I returned to the United States in 1995, began a new course of personal-development work, and completed my American degree in psychology that the underpinnings of my approach first began to take shape.

The catalyst was my own struggle with loneliness and depression in the wake of a devastating divorce. That, in turn, led me to begin the personal-development work that helped me transform my life. I had to dig deep into my past to understand my family of origin and the roots of my own dysfunction. Through that process, I came to understand the crucial connection between our life conditioning, the self-defeating patterns that diminish the quality of our lives, and the steps we can take to change those limiting patterns. I've developed what I believe is a unique method for helping others uncover their authentic selves and reclaim their innate wholeness so they can live a fuller, richer life on their own—or with someone else. My hope, in writing this book, is to give you the road map to achieving that life—a road map that I, like most people, never had.

Now, a few notes before you begin. Mastering the art of aloneness is a process. As its name suggests, this is not something that happens overnight. You can't just snap your fingers and make it happen. Here are the three fundamental keys, the must-haves for mastering this art: focus, strategy, and commitment.

First, you need a *focus*. Mastering the art of aloneness is about *living in alignment with your life's purpose and your authentic self*—what you were meant to do and who you were meant to be. That's your *focus*. Finding your focus is central to this entire process. Throughout this book, I'll be giving you the tools you need to define and clarify the life you want and to identify and understand what areas of your life you need and want to focus on. Ultimately, you'll be aligning everything you do—your thoughts, your behaviors, and your actions—in a conscious and deliberate manner to create that life.

Second, you need a *strategy*. This book is your road map. It's designed to enable you to develop a specific strategy *of your own* to get where you want to go, a step-by-step action plan that meets your individual needs. It includes a series of exercises that will help you understand who you are—under all those layers of conditioning—and where you want to go. You'll be exploring your own family of origin to identify the specific thought and behavior patterns that are holding you back from achieving your full potential and the specific steps you need to take to change those deeply ingrained patterns. In addition, I'll provide you with guidance on developing a set of skills that are essential for achieving mastery over your own life and improving your relationship with yourself—and with others.

Finally, this process requires a *commitment.* It involves creating an ideal relationship with yourself. To be fully committed to this process, you have to feel deserving of it and you have to love yourself. After all, you're not going to feel compelled to invest your time and energy in somebody you don't like very much. That's a central theme of this book: providing the guidance you need to build a healthy, constructive, and loving relationship with yourself.

As you take the first steps toward mastering aloneness, recognize that you'll slip up. Imagine how a typical smoker quits smoking. He throws away that first pack of cigarettes. Then he might weaken and buy another pack, then just smoke a few cigarettes, then give it up for another few days or weeks, then start up again. And then, one day, he's just done with it. He's tried to quit, and finally he just stops. That back-and-forth is part of the process. Like quitting smoking, mastering aloneness is about *changing your habitual patterns of behavior.* As you begin the process, it's important to be supportive and gentle with yourself. When you slip up, think of it as simply getting more information about what doesn't work for you.

Making a commitment to mastering the art of aloneness means accepting the fact that you will slip up; treating yourself with love and compassion when you do, and then moving forward. That's the commitment I hope you will make to yourself before you turn the next page.

UNCOVERING YOUR AUTHENTIC SELF

CHAPTER 1

BEGINNING THE JOURNEY

Following the end of my marriage in 1993, I began a profound journey that—combined with my professional training, my experience as a therapist and coach, and my extensive personal-development work—led me to a new approach to recovering the authentic self and mastering aloneness. To help you understand the process and the experiences that inspired it, I'll begin with my own journey and the things I discovered along the way.

My marriage began as a storybook romance, and in the wake of that romance, I started a new life with my husband that lasted for 13 years. We shared an adventurous spirit, a passion for learning, and, ultimately, two beautiful children. A German physician with a penchant for travel, he was vacationing in California in the spring of 1980 when we met. At the time, I was singing in a popular group called *Tuxedo Junction*—struggling financially, working part-time as a cocktail waitress to supplement my singing income, and involved in negotiations for a new record contract. Looking back from where I am today, I see that I was an emotional wreck. Trying to make it in Hollywood as a singer and actress and finding it hard to pay the bills, I was flirting with depression and carrying around a lot of unresolved baggage and pain from my youth. I was drinking too much and jumping from relationship to relationship. I was restless and unsettled. Then along came this stunningly handsome man—smart, sophisticated, and a good ten years older than me—my Prince Charming. I was attracted to the fact that he was a physician like my father, but with a twist that made him particularly intriguing—he was a true adventurer with an exciting lifestyle; he would work for a while and then travel for months at a time.

By the end of that summer, I had dropped everything to return to Germany with him. Inseparable and ecstatically happy, we became engaged at a little pub in Hamburg the evening of my 22nd birthday. We'd known each other only six months. I see now that I was a "damsel in distress" and he was my rescuer. I was seduced by the travel, by his attention, by the idea of being taken care of.

Not long after the night of our engagement, my new fiancé and I left Germany to set up house together in California. He secured a fellowship at a clinic in Los Angeles, while I enrolled in The Lee Strasberg Theatre & Film Institute as a full-time student. We married on June 27, 1981, only one year after becoming a couple. From the secure vantage point of my marriage, I began exploring the field of personal development. I'd always been a natural "seeker," searching for the deeper meaning I felt was missing from my life. And I was something of a rebel, raging against the system and the status quo.

During our early months in California, I became drawn to Buddhism and enamored with the idea of replacing the anger and rebellion inside me with love and compassion. I went on a health-food kick and stopped drinking alcohol and caffeine. I swore off refined sugar and white flour. For the first time in my life, my mood stabilized and I felt emotionally balanced. When I attended my first personal-development workshop, it opened a new door for me. *This makes sense,* I said to myself. *This is what I want to do with my life.* A few days after attending that first workshop, I decided to quit show business. Disillusioned with the superficiality of Hollywood and longing to be near my family, I convinced my husband to move back with me to my hometown on the East Coast. I knew I wanted to pursue the personal-development path, but, in truth, it would be years before I realized that I would have to fix what was going on inside of me before I would be able to be truly productive in any field.

My husband was a brilliant physician, a pioneer in his field, and after the move, his career really took off. But I was floundering. I was certain that I wanted a career of my own, but I'd never attended college and had no qualifications to speak of. Lacking experience outside the performing arts, I was lucky to find a job appearing on a weekly segment of a TV show called *PM Magazine.* Yet, within a few months, I decided I wanted a baby. At the age of 26, I got pregnant and quit my job. Happier than I'd ever been in my life, I immersed myself in having the healthiest pregnancy possible and planned to be the best mother I could be. My daughter was born in 1983, followed two years later by my son. I threw myself into motherhood. Both my husband and I were determined that our children would receive the time and attention that our own parents had been unable to give to us. We shifted our focus off each other and entirely onto our children—to the detriment of our marriage.

Looking back on the gradual demise of our relationship, there were plenty of red flags. Our way of handling them was, for the most part, to simply ignore them. I remember being panic-stricken one day when my husband expressed the fact that he was unhappy in our marriage. Instead of responding to his feelings and dealing with the increasing distance between us, I remember denying that anything was wrong between us and pointing out that all couples with little children face these same issues. Acknowledging that we had real problems as a couple terrified me—probably because, for years, I'd seen my own parents sweep their problems under the rug.

Instead of dealing with our eroding marriage, I immersed myself deeper in living the American dream. We purchased our first home and then moved on to another, bigger one. I became a full-time mother and homemaker. As a young woman, I'd been fearless and independent. I had grand dreams of becoming a famous singer and actress. But, instead, I ended up doing exactly what my own mother had done. She, too, had given up her career to marry and raise a family. I see now that I was unconsciously following in her footsteps. And, as much as I loved my children, I was starved for adult connection. I felt extremely lonely in my big house in the suburbs. It was as if Betty Friedan had never existed or the '60s and '70s had passed me by.

Unfortunately, I had built my life on a very shaky foundation. As I entered my 30s, my old restless spirit began to break through. By then, we had left the United States to settle in Germany. First, we went to Hamburg, the city where my husband had grown up. Then we moved to a small village, 20 miles from the nearest city. For my husband, the move represented a new job opportunity, but for me, it was an isolating experience. By then, both my children were in school. Unable to speak the native language, I was now living in a town where no one spoke English. Alone for large blocks of time with nothing on which to focus my interests, I grew increasingly restless and depressed. Over the next several years, we would move again and again as my husband's career continued to flourish. All the while, our marriage would continue to unravel.

Early on in our marriage, I'd collaborated with my husband on a series of holistic healing workshops. With my children in school, I felt compelled to start pursuing my career again. In 1990, I traveled to Los Angeles to complete my training as a workshop facilitator, followed by a series of various workshops and seminars. It was an invigorating experience. I felt infused with a renewed sense of purpose and creativity. Back in Germany, I began facilitating workshops for cancer patients with my husband. The work we were doing was groundbreaking, and we began to receive national media attention. My husband recognized my ability to facilitate deep, transformational work with the people attending our workshops and asked me to start counseling some of the patients in his medical practice. Eager to follow this path, I pursued my studies in Europe, India, and the United States. I was on a steep learning curve, moving in exciting new directions, but my marriage was falling apart. As the distance between us continued to grow, my husband and I decided on a trial, live-in marital separation. It was an unusual arrangement; we agreed to lead separate lives but continue to share the house and to raise our children together. Ultimately, instead of bringing us closer or motivating us to work on the problems in our marriage, the arrangement only served to pull us further apart.

There had been signs all along that our marriage was unraveling, but neither my husband nor I had the awareness, capabilities, or resources to halt its collapse. It was only years later, through my personal-development work, that I recognized the underlying problem: we had come together for all the wrong reasons. We had been drawn to each other because of voids within ourselves. To me, my husband was a smart, successful physician (like my father) who made me feel safe and protected. He represented safety and security. At the time, of course, I didn't know this; I was madly in love and oblivious to my underlying motivations. Meanwhile, to him, I possessed a passion and spontaneity he had never known. In his eyes, I was exotic and exciting. In short, we were attracted to our own projections of each other—not to each other's true selves.

When our marriage finally ended, I was in tremendous pain, feeling a deep sense of loss, loneliness, and fear. Not long after the children and I moved out, my husband's girlfriend moved into what had been our home, exacerbating an already difficult situation. As we moved forward with plans to divorce, the situation spiraled out of control, becoming a nasty and grueling parting that spanned four years. For two of those years, I struggled to make ends meet in Germany as my relationship with my estranged husband worsened and his financial support declined. Within a year of the separation, my children and I had gone from living in relative luxury and security to struggling to make the rent in a fourth-floor walkup permeated by the noxious odor from a chemical storage facility next door. Professionally, I went from facilitating workshops and counseling patients in my husband's medical practice to waiting tables at a local pub.

Living alone with virtually no support system in Germany, I was terrified of what our future would hold. Feeling alone, filled with despair, and, finally, reduced to using our security deposit to pay the rent, I sold everything the children and I had, bought three plane tickets to the United States, and returned home.

Hitting Bottom

The day the children and I arrived in the United States from Germany was probably the worst day of my life. It was July 14, 1995. We flew into Boston during the early stages of the Big Dig, a massive highway and tunnel reconstruction project. The city looked like a war zone. It seemed as if everything around us was torn up, a cruel metaphor for our own situation. It was steamy hot—hovering somewhere above 100 degrees—and there was no air conditioning in the van my parents had hired to pick us up from the airport. But I didn't just feel hot and uncomfortable; I felt defeated and guilt-ridden and scared. I was 37 years old. I'd been married at the age of 23, when I hardly knew who I was. My husband had been my source of safety and security, and now my safety net was gone. Here I was with a 9-year-old boy and an 11-year-old girl to raise on my own, and no way to take care of myself—or them.

It would be two months before I really hit bottom. My parents, generously, took us in. But the situation wasn't workable for very long. Their condominium was way too small for the five of us. The TV was blaring constantly. My parents both smoked and my mother, who had a history of poor health and undiagnosed depression, continued to decline. Wracked with guilt over the tremendous pain and loss my children were experiencing, feeling like a complete failure, and unable to see a glimmer of hope for the future, I was sinking deeper and deeper into depression myself.

I can still remember the feelings of despair I experienced on the Friday before Labor Day in 1995, a moment when it felt like the rest of America was heading off to the beaches with their intact families for the long weekend. I went into my parents' den and told them that I needed help—now. "If I don't get to a doctor or a hospital, or get some medication," I announced, "I'm going to have a mental breakdown." I had reached the breaking point, and, although I didn't realize it at the time, that moment would prove to be a major turning point in my life.

Rebuilding My Self, Rebuilding My Life

Today I'm an independent, self-sufficient woman. I own my own home and have a successful business coaching individuals, consulting to corporations, writing, and teaching. My children are grown up and realizing their own dreams. My son just graduated from college and has been accepted to Harvard Law School. My daughter, who is about to receive her M.B.A. in sustainable development, plans to help companies become more socially and environmentally responsible. I, too, have grown and changed. I bear little or no resemblance to the young woman who struggled with depression, the restless soul who couldn't quite manage her life, or the defeated 37-year-old who flew into Boston from Germany that day in 1995. It took me more than ten years to get where I am today. Looking back, I recognize the wisdom of the famous line from Nietzsche: What doesn't kill you makes you stronger. Everything I've been through makes me the person that I am today. All my experiences give me the depth of compassion and understanding that I bring to my work, and they have taught me the lessons I'm passing on in this book.

That Labor Day weekend in 1995, I found a doctor who prescribed an antidepressant as a short-term solution to manage my depression and keep me from complete mental and emotional collapse. That, in turn, led me to a wonderful woman named Terry Kellerman, who became my therapist and coach, and served as a loving guide through an eight-year journey that changed my life and informs my work today.

Once I began to emerge from the throes of depression, my priorities began to crystallize. I had to find a way to support myself and take care of my kids. I decided I had to complete my American bachelor's degree and then go on and get a master's degree. At that point, my parents really stepped up to the plate, offering to pay for my return to college and help with the bills while I was in school. I had no idea how to manage money, so that, too, became a priority.

My children were struggling with all the changes occurring in their lives and they needed me more than ever. It's always traumatic for a child when the family is torn apart, but many children stay in the same school and keep their friends, or they remain in the same house or community. They see both parents and have a sense of continuity. For my children, life as they knew it was completely destroyed. When we left Germany, they gave up their school, their neighborhood, and their friends to move to the United States—what was, for them, a foreign country. Their economic circumstances and lifestyle changed dramatically. Their father was no longer a presence in their lives, and that was an enormous loss for them. For me, it meant the responsibility for their well-being fell completely on my shoulders—and I knew I'd have to rise to the challenge.

As my mental and emotional health began to improve, and I began my personal-development work with Terry, my attitude began to change. I saw that I had been presented with a rare opportunity. I was living in a sleepy little town. I didn't know anyone, and there was really nothing much to do. Instead of being restless and bored and lonely, instead of digging myself into an emotional hole, I began to see things from a different perspective. I took long, meditative walks by myself in the mornings when my kids were in school. Without the distractions of a relationship or an active social life, I could focus on fixing what was ailing me and helping my children cope with their new life. I could concentrate on taking good care of them and good care of myself—by eating right, getting enough exercise, and focusing on my mental and emotional health. I could begin to live more deliberately.

I also began to see my divorce—and my relationship with my ex-husband—in a different light. Instead of feeling like a victim, I began to see myself as an active participant in our marriage and its undoing. I began to take responsibility for what had happened to me, to my marriage, and to my children—and I stopped blaming others. I took an important first step when I started taking responsibility. In my personal-development work, I asked myself: *What role did I play in the breakdown of my marriage?* Only as the answer became clear was I able to begin to replace my feelings of anger and bitterness with compassion and forgiveness for myself and for my ex-husband.

These are all elements of the process of mastering the art of aloneness that I will share with you in this book. But the cornerstone of my experience is this: I began to understand and address the roots of my lifelong restlessness and unhappiness—the patterns I had developed long ago that originated in my childhood and family.

Working with Terry, I began to look deeper into my family of origin—and the relationship between my experiences growing up and my self-defeating patterns of behavior. I began to differentiate between my conditioned self and who I really am. Only then did I begin to recover my wholeness. I learned that I am an incredibly strong and independent person, and yet I had built this illusion that I was incapable of taking care of myself— that I was helpless and that I needed a man to rescue and take care of me. And at its root, that's a belief I had adopted long ago in my family of origin.

Where I Come From

I grew up the youngest of four children in the old whaling city of New Bedford, Massachusetts. My earliest memories include feelings of extreme loneliness, a feeling of being unwanted, of being invisible. My mother was 38 when I was born, with three boys ages two, seven, and eight. I was unplanned, and she was overwhelmed and depressed following my birth. A cousin was brought into the house to take care of me during the first few years of my life, followed by a series of other caretakers. I had raging colic as an infant. When I started nursery school at the age of three, my parents hired a driver—a man in his 50s—to drive me back and forth to school, which was about a mile from our house. I can remember feeling frightened and alone in the back seat of his car, coming home and being set in front of the television to eat my lunch alone, then being sent upstairs for a nap.

My strongest memories from early childhood were of my mother—or, rather, of her absence. In the morning, she had difficulty getting up and would lie in bed with a facecloth over her head and her sunglasses on. She'd say she had a migraine and needed to rest. She'd finally get up around four o'clock in the afternoon and start cooking dinner and drinking Canadian Club whiskey. Although it's never been acknowledged within my family, she was clearly an alcoholic.

If I were to describe my family's outward appearance, you'd get a very different picture. My mother was a beautiful, articulate, and highly intelligent woman who had a successful career prior to her marriage. To the outside world, she appeared to be a sophisticated and affluent doctor's wife who had it all—a successful husband, four healthy children, and an immaculate, beautiful home. My father was a doctor, an active and beloved leader in the community. He was a charming, successful man and a model citizen. He'd worked his way through medical school and then married my mother, a southern belle from Chattanooga, Tennessee, and a head nurse at the hospital in Florida where they had met. They had been married for 56 years when my mother died in 2004. For the first few years of their marriage, my father's mother lived with them. Eventually they bought a new home with my father's office attached to our house—all of which calls to mind the picture of an active, engaged family.

But, in fact, like many families, we were the picture of dysfunction. For one thing, my grandmother, who despised my mother for marrying her only son, was hardly the model of a loving, nurturing grandparent. I remember her sitting on our living-room sofa with a bottle of Scotch in her lap, getting drunk and berating my mother, who was always trying to win her approval. I barely remember my father as a presence. He was so involved with his work and civic activities that he was largely absent. As I got older, I recall coming home from school to find my mother lying down in bed watching soap operas. If I wanted to spend time with her, I had to sit in front of the television and be silent. She often had crying fits. She'd lock herself in her room while I stood outside the door trying to get in, confused and scared, wanting to be able to console her, to fix it, but I never could. Her depression went untreated, just as her alcoholism went unacknowledged.

We were a family of disconnected people. In the evenings, during dinner, we'd sit down in front of the television while we ate. We didn't talk to one another. I think, growing up, my brothers—especially the older two—had each other. The youngest of the three was very introverted and kept to himself in his room. But I was extroverted, with a sensitive, artistic, and inquisitive personality. I had no one in the family with whom to connect. At the time, I thought that life as I knew it was normal. Looking back, I realize that as a child I didn't feel nurtured, supported, cared for, or wanted.

In my early adolescence, all hell broke loose. I started to act out. I became angry, depressed, resentful, and moody. When I was 11, I had my first alcoholic drink at a friend's house. At 12, I was smoking and experimenting with drugs—uppers and downers I found in the family medicine cabinet, samples from my father's medical practice. At 13, I was hanging out with a rough crowd in the public parks of New Bedford, with kids three or four years older who were shooting heroin. And, at the age of 14, I ran away from home—and never really went back until I was an adult.

In retrospect, it was a strong survival instinct that drove me to leave. And, while running away led to a series of self-destructive and even dangerous situations, I believe it helped me hold onto an important piece of my authentic self. Throughout my young adult life, I kept repeating self-defeating patterns, which I continued throughout my marriage. If I hadn't met Terry Kellerman and begun the personal-development work that took me to the root of my problems, more likely than not I would be repeating those patterns today.

Connecting the Dots

In one way or another, just about every family is dysfunctional. As writer Sue Grafton once said: "People talk about 'dysfunctional' families; I've never seen any other kind." Everyone emerges from their family of origin with a distinctive set of issues. Within some families, children grow up experiencing extreme dysfunctions such as physical, verbal, or sexual abuse. In others, they experience subtler dysfunctions that shape their core beliefs and behavior—maybe taboos that impede their ability to express their feelings, constant criticism that erodes their self-esteem, or rigid rules that inhibit self-expression. We are all products of our families' unique patterns and dysfunctions. We all take the core beliefs and behaviors learned in childhood with us into adulthood. Some of these beliefs and behaviors are like viruses, infecting our lives, our relationships, and our sense of well-being. And, until we become aware of what they are and how to move beyond them, none of us is truly whole.

If you don't feel like a whole and complete person on your own—someone capable of expressing the full range of human emotions and achieving your full potential— you're always going to be seeking someone else to complete you. Take the example of a man who grows up in a family where he's never allowed to express joy or enthusiasm or excitement; he'll be looking for someone else to bring those expressions into his life. Or a woman who never feels safe or secure on her own—she'll spend her life seeking safety and security from others. That's the kind of dynamic I saw in my own marriage. It created a relationship that was built, not on our strengths and who we really were, but on our individual pathologies.

In my coaching practice, I'm amazed by the number of people who come to me with little understanding of the human conditioning process and how it holds them back in their lives. Many people invest countless hours, dollars, and resources in self-help approaches focused on changing their behavior—but they still struggle with the same issues over and over. I strongly believe that it's because they've failed to address these family-of-origin issues. Others spend years in therapy talking about their family-of-origin issues. They may come away with an intellectual understanding of their families and patterns of dysfunction, but they don't know how to move past them. They lack the strategies to change their habitual patterns. The challenge is to connect the dots. With *Solemate,* that's what I'm endeavoring to do: help you connect the dots. That means focusing in on the core beliefs and behavioral patterns you adopted in your family of origin *and* developing workable strategies that will help you change them. Once you begin to understand the patterns that are creating negative results in your relationships and in your life, you begin treating yourself very differently. Your attitudes and outlook begin to change. You begin to live more consciously and deliberately. And you can accomplish things you never dreamed possible. The transformation can be dramatic. That's the journey on which you're about to embark.

To begin, you're going to need a journal. That's one of the first things I tell my clients to do at the start of every coaching program, and it's the first step to mastering the art of aloneness: Go out and buy yourself a journal. Buy a beautiful card to go with it and write a loving message on the card. It's a way of thanking yourself for investing time, money, and energy in *yourself.* Have your journal gift-wrapped and bring it home; then consciously allow yourself to receive it and enjoy the gift. This journal represents your commitment to mastering the art of aloneness, and it will become indispensable on your journey. It's where you'll watch your self unfold. It's where you'll keep your notes and the results of the exercises you'll find in this book. It will become your reference for achieving an understanding of who you are and where you want to go.

CHAPTER 2

EMBRACING YOUR ALONENESS

Today, in one out of four American households, someone is living alone.[1] In 2005, America reached a milestone. According to the American Community Survey released by the U.S. Census Bureau in 2006, for the first time in history fewer than half of all American households—just shy of 50 percent—consisted of married couples.[2] And, for the first time, more American women were living without a spouse than with one.[3] This means, on average, Americans now spend half of their adult lives outside of marriage.[4] These are major shifts that have been brewing for decades, and yet people's attitudes about being alone have changed remarkably little during those years.

Aloneness is still associated with a variety of negative emotions. As an example, at the start of every *Mastering the Art of Aloneness* workshop, I ask participants what they think of when they hear the word "aloneness." What words and feelings come to mind? I hear the same responses over and over. "Lonely." "Depressed." "Unwanted." "Afraid." "A loser." It's no surprise that most people think of aloneness as a negative state, something to avoid rather than embrace. From early childhood, we're conditioned to associate aloneness with emotional pain. We're taught that it's a condition to pity, something to be ashamed of. That attitude manifests itself in all kinds of ways. Parents become anxious when their children don't have enough play dates. Teenagers base their self-esteem on how many friends they have. And, all too often, adults measure each other's well-being according to whether or not someone is married or in a committed relationship. For most people, being alone means being unhappy.

With this book, I'm not suggesting that being alone is something we should aspire to or that it's the ideal lifestyle. Mastering the art of aloneness doesn't mean living in isolation or never needing the love, support, and involvement of others. It means creating and living a life in which you feel whole and content as an individual on your own; a life in which you can take care of yourself emotionally and financially. Mastering the art of aloneness is a process. It involves developing the self-awareness, life skills, and emotional intelligence you need to share healthy relationships—and to live a rich, full, gratifying life whether you're living it alone or with someone else. That process involves thinking about aloneness in a radically different way—making a conscious and deliberate change in the way you think and the way you live.

Strength in Numbers

The simple truth is: if you live alone, you are not alone. More and more American adults live single lives. In the United States today, there are 95.7 million single adults.[5] That number has risen steadily over the past 30 years, and it now represents 43 percent of all U.S. adults.[6] Of course, these figures include couples living together outside of marriage. But a large proportion of these people are divorced, widowed, or never married, and living alone.

This shift reflects a number of trends, including the cultural changes catalyzed by the women's movement. For one thing, people are marrying later. Thirty years ago, 64 percent of American women ages 20 to 24 had already married. Today, most American women in that age group (73 percent) have *never* married, and among women ages 30 to 34, 22 percent have never married—up from only 6 percent 30 years ago.[7]

These trends aren't restricted to the United States. In 2002, researchers in the United Kingdom reported that more people were living alone or as single parents than in traditional nuclear families.[8] And throughout the European Union, by the year 2000, a growing proportion of all private households were reportedly one-person households—representing at least 30 percent of all households in most northern European countries.[9]

Given the high divorce rate and the fact that women outlive men by an average of seven years,[10] it's likely that a married adult will go back to being single at some point in his or her life. Roughly 50 percent of U.S. marriages end in divorce. Nearly one-quarter of all single adults in the United States are divorced, and another 14 percent are widowed.[11] Yet, whether they've never been married or are going back to life on their own after a committed relationship, many people find being single a source of loneliness, shame, and distress.

Society and the Media

Although living life as a single is more widely accepted than it was 30 years ago, there is still a pervasive mindset that if you don't find a mate—especially by the time you're in your 30s—there must be something wrong with you. Most people still believe that marriage is the favored lifestyle, and we're barraged by media messages reinforcing this notion. I find it curious that, in television commercials, most adults wear wedding rings; that in TV ads for nighttime cold medicines, couples are typically shown in a double bed, while in ads for sleep aids, singles are shown struggling to find their way to sleep. In her book *Singled Out: How Singles Are Stereotyped, Stigmatized, and Ignored, and Still Live Happily Ever After,* Bella DePaulo shares a litany of examples—ads for everything from luggage (How to solve the pesky problem of "Which bag is *ours?*") to home improvements ("Is your husband good with tools?"). DePaulo also reminds us that in *Sex and the City,* a show devoted to the subject of four strong, independent females living on their own in New York, the final season ends with four romantic couplings.[12]

Popular music and movies all tell the same story: Romantic love is the answer. Without love, we have nothing. All you need is love. Although some contemporary songwriters write songs about standing strong and happy on one's own—particularly female artists such as Sarah

McLachlan, Paula Cole, and Alanis Morissette—the market is dominated by songs that tell us you can only find true happiness when someone loves you and wants to be with you. It's difficult to even imagine a movie or story that ends with the hero or heroine living joyfully and contently alone instead of living the fairy tale version of happily-ever-after with a mate. The classic line in the film *Jerry Maguire*—"You complete me"—reinforces what many singles believe: If I could only find my soul mate, I would feel whole and my life would come together. And if I can't, I'm in deep trouble.

Romance sells. It's fun. It's entertaining. What's troubling, though, is the pervasive message that a romantic relationship is a cure for whatever ails you. Of course, many people don't have to look beyond their immediate families to get that message. Many of my clients complain that they're pressured by their parents to find a mate, marry, and have children. Once they hit their 30s, people who remain single often experience feelings of abandonment, sadness, low self-worth, and shame as their single friends dwindle in number. They feel increasingly surrounded by married couples—many of whom, they find, no longer extend invitations to them simply because they don't have partners. It's not surprising that people who are alone feel bad about it.

Gender Differences

Despite the classic stereotypes of the swinging bachelor and the old maid, my experience suggests that both men and women find it difficult to create happy and satisfying lives on their own. Although more women than men participate in my Mastering the Art of Aloneness workshops and coaching program, I suspect it's because women are just more comfortable reaching out for professional help. From infancy, boys and girls are treated very differently when it comes to asking for and getting help. Boys are conditioned to be more self-sufficient, to pick themselves up by their bootstraps, and to avoid expressing their vulnerability and feelings.[13] In contrast, girls are conditioned to rely more on others. As a result, it's less threatening for a woman to reach out for support.

It's important to recognize that, while men may be less inclined to share their feelings of insecurity and emotional pain with others, that doesn't mean they're not experiencing the same feelings and situations as their female counterparts. When men attend my workshops, they describe the very same frustrations and challenges that women face: feeling lonely and unhappy in their single life, continually picking the wrong people for relationships, a fear of growing old or sick with no one to rely on, and the feeling that their inability to sustain a healthy and lasting relationship is a sign that they are somehow defective or a failure.

A Vicious Cycle of Negativity

If you're alone and you believe, either consciously or unconsciously, that "there must be something wrong with me because I'm alone" or "I can only be happy if I'm in a committed relationship," it will have an enormous impact on how you see yourself, how you feel, and how you live your life. You may actually be setting yourself up for loneliness and rejection. How? First of all, when people feel bad about themselves, they tend to project that onto others. Just as confidence inspires confidence, negativity invokes negativity. Other people *are* less likely to be attracted to someone who lacks a sense of well-being. If you're walking around slump-shouldered, feeling sorry for yourself, it's easy for other people to be put off by your demeanor. To make matters worse, feelings of low self-worth may cause you to withdraw from the world, cutting yourself off from the very people and activities that can enrich your life. If you avoid other people, withdrawing into yourself because you're afraid of being judged or rejected, loneliness becomes a self-perpetuating and self-fulfilling prophecy.

Even more important, if you feel bad about yourself, you're much less likely to take good care of yourself, which can take many shapes and forms. When you're feeling depressed, you're less motivated to exercise regularly and you may not sleep well. People with a low sense of self-worth often seek comfort in ways that are unhealthy. Some overeat, indulging in food to ward off their bad feelings. Others try to numb their feelings with alcohol, drugs, or nicotine. Still others escape from their emotional pain through distractions like compulsive shopping, sexual promiscuity, or workaholism. Everyone is different. But the bottom line is: if you believe that you can only be happy if you have a partner, you inevitably fail to fully live your life, waiting instead for someone to come along and rescue you from what you see as a miserable existence. The challenge is to break these patterns—of thought and behavior—that are holding you back from living your life to the fullest.

A New View of Aloneness

If you want to live a more satisfying, happier life alone, first you have to start believing that you can. You have to *decide* to think differently about aloneness. And, at the same time, you have to start doing things differently.

So the first step to mastering the art of aloneness is changing your perceptions of aloneness. Instead of viewing it as a shameful condition associated with loneliness, pain, and emptiness, you need to begin to think of it as one of freedom, growth, and opportunity. At first, this isn't easy. Changing these deeply ingrained preconceptions about aloneness—especially before you've changed your reality—is the hardest part of the process. It requires a leap of faith and relentless perseverance. But, simultaneously, you're going to start changing your behaviors.

Here's why: Our perceptions produce our emotional responses. Our emotional responses drive our behavior, and our behaviors create our reality—the quality of our lives and the circumstances in which we live. Put another way, we are what we think. If you think of aloneness as a source of loneliness and misery, then the simple fact that you're alone can make you feel sad and lonely, and that can lead to inertia and depression. So, instead of having the energy to go out and do something that will make you feel good, energized, and inspired by the world around you, you end up sitting around and feeling sorry for yourself. Your life becomes a self-fulfilling prophecy—because you do the things that produce the very results you *don't* want to achieve. That, in turn, continually reinforces your belief that aloneness is a source of pain instead of joy and opportunity. You're trapped in a vicious cycle. Your negative thinking is producing negative behavior, which in turn is reinforcing your negative thinking. You've got to break the pattern—by thinking differently about aloneness, acting in ways that reinforce your new attitude, and focusing on the opportunities inherent in your situation.

Let me give you an example of how changing my own perceptions of aloneness after my divorce helped me transform my experience of pain, failure, and depression into one of tremendous opportunity.

Turning Obstacles into Opportunities

When I returned to the United States from Germany, I believed that any possibility of a happy, successful life was shattered forever by my divorce. I was convinced that I would be struggling emotionally and financially for the rest of my life. These feelings were rooted in the deeply ingrained belief that my happiness depended on having a husband who would love me and take care of me financially, and that without this, I had and was nothing. Although a part of me was determined to go back to school, get my American degrees, and be able to earn my own living, for several years the belief that I needed a man to take care of me prevailed.

As a first step toward changing my own negative perception of aloneness, I made a conscious effort to identify the good things that could come from my being on my own. I started focusing on those opportunities instead of constantly ruminating about the downside. I decided to go back to school and commit to my studies. Though I had to single-handedly care for my two children, who were facing the challenge of living nearly

4,000 miles away from their father and adjusting to a completely new life in the United States, I was free to raise them however I saw fit. Plus, unlike many divorced families with shared-care arrangements, my kids didn't have to navigate two different households and two different sets of rules. I had lived away from my parents since I was 14 years old. Being back in my hometown gave me the chance to spend time with my parents, both of whom were now in their 70s. The meager income the children and I had to live on each month enabled me to learn to become a disciplined and resourceful money manager. Having the sole responsibility for running a household gave me the opportunity to develop greater self-sufficiency and confidence.

The diminished conditions of my post-divorce life hadn't changed, but my way of looking at it certainly had. And, gradually, things started to get better. Any time I found myself reverting to my old, negative way of thinking about my situation, I'd consciously redirect my mind to focus on the opportunities inherent in our new life. When my children wanted something I couldn't afford or complained about the shabbiness of our apartment, I'd encourage them to focus on how they could use the current situation to their benefit, instead of as a limitation. For example, when they complained that all their friends had Nintendos and we couldn't afford one, I'd explain that kids who spend all their time playing electronic games often lose their creativity and ability to focus. ("You'll be more creative and focused if you spend your free time drawing or painting.") Here's another example: We moved nine times after my marriage ended. When my children complained about all the moves, I'd say: "You're going to build a sense of security from the inside out. You're going to be very adept at managing change in your lives." Of course, they were kids. Sometimes they'd balk or argue with me when I turned these negatives into positives. But, ultimately, this approach seems to have had a profound effect on them. Today, both of my children are resourceful, strong, and successful young adults. They have learned to consistently rise to meet the challenges of their lives instead of allowing themselves to be defeated by them.

By looking at my life in terms of opportunities and putting this approach into practice, I became more self-sufficient and was better able to manage my life. The entire process enriched my life in unexpected ways. My aloneness catalyzed a deep commitment to working on my own personal development. With no romantic partner or relationship issues to distract me, I was able to focus intently on learning about who I really was, where I came from, where I'd been in my life, the choices I'd made, and the impact those choices had on my life and those of my children. Aloneness itself became my great opportunity.

Creating Healthier Relationships
Through Personal Development

Mastering the art of aloneness will not only enhance the quality of your relationship with yourself and improve your life, it will dramatically change your relationships with others. Instead of seeking another person to make you whole, you engage in relationships with a sense of being complete and whole on your own. Learning greater self-sufficiency builds your self-esteem and confidence. It also allows you to participate in relationships with others out of *conscious choice,* rather than from a place of neediness or of fear that you won't be able to take care of yourself.

Relationships that are based on neediness and fear tend to be conflict-ridden and stressful. The emotionally needy people in relationships—the "Pursuers"—are continually fighting for closeness and feel a sense of panic when their partners want to do something or go somewhere without them. The partners of these emotionally needy people—"Distancers"—are always fighting for their space. They may feel overwhelmed and trapped by the feeling of being overly responsible for the other person's happiness and/or sense of security. Such relationships turn into battlefields, breeding jealousy, insecurity, resentment, and contempt.

In contrast, in a healthy, conscious relationship, rather than being stuck in the rigid roles of the Pursuer and Distancer, partners make these roles fluid and interchangeable. One week one person may express the need for more time alone, and the next week he or she may feel a need for a greater sense of connectedness than the other person, and vice versa. At times, their need for togetherness may be virtually the same. A healthy relationship means a healthy acceptance of and respect for each other's needs and a recognition that those needs are always changing.

Personal development allows you to learn how to respond to the world and the people around you in constructive ways—and break the limiting patterns you've carried with you from childhood into adulthood. The process involves deep self-examination and awareness of who you are, how you behave, and the results your actions generate. With greater awareness comes more *conscious choice*—so you can begin to consciously align how you think, behave, and relate to others with the results you long to have in your life. For example, anger is a normal and very human emotion. But few people have been taught how to effectively express and manage anger. You may have been taught to rationalize your anger away, blame or verbally attack the person who's made you angry, or withdraw from and avoid the other person—and your feelings—altogether. An emotionally mature and constructive approach to anger involves understanding what's upsetting you and communicating your feelings effectively.

Development work helps you acquire the practical skills that are essential to building and maintaining a healthy and fulfilling relationship with yourself and others. These include the ability to:

- Develop strong interpersonal and communication skills

- Identify and set healthy boundaries with others

- Feel and effectively express the wide range of human emotions, such as sadness, anger, fear, and joy

- Negotiate and manage differences and conflict with others

- Take responsibility for and care of yourself emotionally, mentally, physically, and financially

When two people have mastered the art of aloneness, they come to relationship from a place of wholeness and personal responsibility, with the life skills needed to share and sustain a joyful, conscious relationship based on healthy *interdependence*. They come together out of *conscious choice* as opposed to *desperate need*. Instead of providing each other with their life sustenance, each partner enriches and enhances an already fulfilling life.

Having a Healthier Relationship with Yourself

I've been talking about mastering the art of aloneness as a prerequisite for a healthy partnership or marriage. But what if the dream of meeting a soul mate remains an elusive ideal that never comes to fruition? What if the dream does indeed become a reality, but the relationship ends or your partner dies? If you make finding a soul mate the main focus of your life—and many people do—then if he or she fails to show up, you may spend many days or months or years *waiting for* a happy and fulfilling life instead of *living* it.

The benefit of mastering the art of aloneness is its focus on creating and living a joyful life *now* rather than waiting around for someone to come along and provide it for you at some immeasurable point in the future. Mastering aloneness allows you to:

- Discover and focus on what interests you— your passions and life goals; the kinds of people with whom you can share supportive, uplifting, and fun relationships; and day-to-day activities and actions that motivate and inspire you

- Actively engage in your own life and with others

- Take action to create the physical and emotional well-being, career, financial security, experiences, relationships, and life circumstances you want to have in your life

- Build a strong and solid inner and outer foundation that *you* have created, that no one can take away from you, and that will sustain you whether you're in a relationship or living on your own

Getting You There

Throughout this book, I'll be giving you the tools you need to work through the process of mastering the art of aloneness. At some points, you may want to enlist professional support—the help of a good therapist or coach to guide you through some of the steps that you might find particularly challenging. I'll address that subject later in the book. But much of this work will draw on your own inner resources.

The exercises at the end of this chapter are designed to jumpstart this process. You'll evaluate where you are today, and you'll begin to change the way you think about aloneness. Simultaneously, you'll start changing your actions and behavior so you begin to reinforce a more positive attitude about being alone. I talked earlier about breaking the vicious cycle of negative feelings and negative behaviors. This is where it begins. Recognize that the more you *engage in new behaviors,* the more you will *create the new results* to which you aspire. Here's an example: Let's say you have a free Saturday. You can look at it from two perspectives. You can stay at home feeling sorry for yourself because you're alone with no plans and nothing to do. You can sit around in your sweatpants and a T-shirt watching television, eating chips, and feeling lousy. Or you can look at it a different way: "I have a free day all to myself, and I can do anything I want. I can go to the gym and work out. I can call a friend and go to the movies. I can work in my garden, make myself a delicious lunch, and read a great novel." Then do something. Do something gratifying. Do something productive. Or do something that truly engages you. But make a conscious effort to avoid doing something that will make you feel isolated and sad. By being more active and more positive, you'll reinforce and solidify your new perspective on aloneness and begin to create a new reality.

This same approach can infuse every aspect of your life—not just your plans for an open Saturday, but your plans for your future, where to focus your energies, and how you approach the challenges you routinely face. Instead of being trapped in negative feelings about aloneness and the conditions those feelings invoke, you can begin to see opportunities you may never have seen before.

Assessing Where You Are Today

We're all different. Each of us faces a unique set of challenges and confronts a unique set of obstacles to mastering our aloneness. The following questionnaire will help you assess where you are today and which areas of your life require further development as you move forward.

Mastering the Art of Aloneness:
A Self-Assessment Exercise

The following areas include the core components of mastering the art of aloneness. Check those areas that are going very well in your life—areas where you are experiencing a high level of satisfaction. Check all boxes that apply.

❏ Physical Health and Well-Being:

- I am in optimal physical health and rarely get sick.

- I'm physically fit and energetic.

- I consistently practice self-care by eating a healthy diet, exercising regularly, and maintaining a healthy and balanced lifestyle.

❏ Relationship with Yourself:

- I feel good about who I am on the inside and about my physical appearance.

- I have a strong sense of self-esteem and self-respect.

- I enjoy emotional and mental balance, health, and well-being.

- I consistently honor myself by expressing my feelings and needs and setting healthy boundaries with others.

❑ Professional Life:

- My work is enjoyable and meaningful to me.

- My work activates my full potential and leverages my skills and strengths.

- My work provides me with the level of success and compensation I want to have.

❑ Personal Development:

- I have a strong sense of who I am and what I want in my life.

- I have a clear understanding of my strengths, weaknesses, passions, and values.

- I'm able to set and follow through on goals and commitments to myself and others.

- I can effectively communicate my thoughts, feelings, and needs to others and manage conflict in an effective and resourceful manner.

❑ Social Relationships:

- I share healthy, supportive, and joyful relationships with others and actively engage in the world around me.

- I feel connected to a community that uplifts and supports me.

❏ Spiritual Life (if it's important to you):

- I have a connection to a higher power or energy and draw from it in my daily life.

- I'm able to be fully present in each moment and take time to appreciate the blessings I have.

❏ Financial:

- I have the financial resources I need to provide the life quality and experiences that I want to have.

- I am financially self-sufficient and feel in control of my financial security.

Identifying Your Challenges and Opportunities

Now we'll take a closer look at the areas you didn't check. Identifying the specific areas of your life that are not satisfying, and the opportunities inherent in improving them, will help you to develop a more positive view of aloneness.

Exercise: Challenges and Opportunities

Step One

Take out your journal and write "The Challenges in Mastering My Aloneness" at the top of a new page. Referring back to the items you did not check on the questionnaire above, make a list of all the challenges and obstacles you face in moving toward your mastery of aloneness—the areas on which you feel you need to focus to move forward. These will serve as benchmarks as you go through this process. For example, if you didn't check *Relationship with Myself,* what are the reasons? Your list might include: "I'm out of shape and feel self-conscious about the way I look," or "I make other people's needs more important than my own," or "I feel shy and insecure when I'm around people I don't know." Identify anything you feel is holding you back from reaching your fullest potential—such as negative emotions (feelings of sadness, loneliness, hopelessness) and negative behaviors (overeating, smoking, drinking too much).

Step Two

Now write "The Opportunities in Mastering My Aloneness" at the top of a new page. Based on the challenges you've identified, list the opportunities inherent in these challenges—those things you can focus on to begin changing your perception of aloneness from a negative situation to one that's full of opportunities. Based on the challenges I listed as examples in Step One, your list might look something like this:

- Get in great physical shape

- Learn how to set healthy boundaries with people and better meet my own needs

- Develop greater self-confidence and feel more at ease around people

This list can be as general or specific as you like. It might include such opportunities as: "Become more independent." "Learn how to manage my finances." "Uncover new interests and passions." "Engage in social activities that will inspire and fulfill me." "Find more meaningful work." "Increase my self-esteem." Or it might include more specific goals and actions, such as: "Join Weight Watchers and lose 15 pounds." "Go through a Human Resources certification program so I can increase my income." "Find a coach or therapist and focus on developing a better relationship with myself and increasing my self-esteem." What's most important here is to develop a list that inspires you to begin to turn your own challenges into new opportunities.

CHAPTER 3

Uncovering Your Conditioned Self

Think of a new baby or a very small child. That child can express all her feelings. One minute, she's sad. The next minute, she's angry. A few minutes later, she's laughing with joy or excitement. A toddler is just as likely to reach over and lovingly stroke her new baby brother's head as she is to whack him on the leg in a jealous rage. All are within the range of perfectly normal human emotions.

What happens next depends on the family. In one family, a parent might pick that toddler up and gently encourage her to kiss her brother. Or explain that, if you hit your brother, it will hurt him and he will cry. Or simply separate the children. In another, a parent might fly into a rage and send the toddler off to her room. Or, worse still, hit her. In yet another family, no one is even paying attention.

When we're born—if we're born healthy—each of us is a whole, integrated human being, capable of expressing the full range of natural human emotions. We have no inhibitions, so we have the ability to feel and express all of our feelings in a very spontaneous and natural way. Then along comes this thing called family. Your family of origin—that is, the family you grew up in—plays an enormous role in determining whether you're able to sustain this innate wholeness throughout your childhood and into adulthood. There are all kinds of circumstances that can disrupt that continuum. Tolstoy once said, "Happy families are all alike; every unhappy family is unhappy in its own way." Put another way, there are constructive, well-functioning families where children learn to express all their feelings in a healthy way. And then there's everybody else—families with a variety of dysfunctions, each one unique.

In truth, very few adults escape from childhood unscathed. Most families have some form of dysfunction, running the gamut from mild to extreme. Consider these statistics: 63 percent of Americans are affected by substance-use disorders, and, of these, 72 percent are affected by the disorder of a family member.[1] Roughly one in four children in the United States is exposed to alcohol abuse and dependence within the family.[2] Between 40 and 60 percent of marriages now end in divorce, a number that's up to 10 percent higher for second and subsequent marriages. The majority of divorces occur in families with children under the age of 18.[3] But dysfunction occurs even in homes that aren't experiencing the consequences of divorce or substance abuse. As psychologist J. Bailey Molineux recently wrote in a column titled "Dysfunctional Families Can Be Loving":

The way I figure it, 90 percent of families are dysfunctional, if by that I mean that they have suffered some emotional pain. I can interview just
about anyone and find some dysfunctions in
their family histories—premature death, divorces,
business failures, serious accidents or chronic illnesses, secrets, emotional cutoffs, alcoholism,
parental abandonment, marital problems. To be
alive is to be part of a dysfunctional family. It is
built into the fabric of life.[4]

In this chapter, you're going to begin to explore the
dysfunctions in your own family and start to connect
the dots—by making a connection between your family
of origin and the core limiting beliefs and behaviors that
run your life. This is not easy work. It can be uncomfortable and emotionally demanding, and it requires that
you be completely honest with yourself as you examine your weaknesses, your limitations, and the areas of
your life that present challenges. That means setting
your ego aside, which in itself can be difficult. You also
have to look back at pieces of your childhood and revisit
events that you may find painful. That's not easy either.
Some people find it hard to look at the choices their own
parents made and to evaluate those choices. As you go
through this process, it's important to keep in mind that
this work is not about blaming your parents, or anyone else for that matter. It's not about being a victim.
The purpose of this family-of-origin work is to gain an
understanding of how you behave and why, so you can
change your limiting behaviors into a new set of behaviors that can propel you forward. This is one of the most
important steps in mastering the art of aloneness.

The Family as a System

Every family is a system. Like a colony of ants, a football team, or an exclusive tennis club, every family has its own set of rules and the family members play various roles to keep the system going. General systems theory was first developed by an Austrian biologist named Ludwig von Bertalanffy. When his concepts were applied to the field of psychology by a number of prominent theorists, they became a valuable tool for understanding the dynamics of the family. Popularized in the United States in the 1980s by author John Bradshaw with his book *Bradshaw On: The Family*,[5] family systems theory plays an important role in my coaching work and in mastering the art of aloneness. It provides a powerful framework for understanding the roots of the self-defeating patterns of thought and behavior that we take with us into adulthood. In my work, I've drawn from the fields of psychology, physiology, sociology, holistic healing, and strategic business practices to develop a unique model for achieving mastery over one's life. It's a very practical approach that helps you cut right to the core of what I refer to as the *default operating system*—the internal operating system rooted in the unconscious that automatically drives your thoughts and behaviors. It's designed to help you understand how your early life experiences within your family of origin shape your internal operating system in ways that can inhibit your sense of well-being and impede your ability to achieve your innate potential.

Here's the problem: As a child, you internalized beliefs and adopted behaviors that enabled you to adapt to and function within your own unique family system. But when you take those beliefs and behaviors with you into adulthood, they often don't make sense anymore. You're

operating in a different environment—the adult wor\
and the relationships that come with it. Your world, your\
needs, and your goals have changed, but your habitual
perceptions and behaviors haven't. As an example, let's
say you grew up in a family in which your mother's love
was conditional. When she approved of your behavior,
she was loving and affectionate—you were her good little girl. But she chastised or criticized you whenever you
did something she didn't like, withdrawing her affection
or rejecting or punishing you. Then you were a bad girl.
Growing up, in order to avoid the pain of her disapproval,
you might have developed a habit of behaving in ways
that were designed to please her—at the expense of your
own needs. If Mommy wanted you to be quiet, you'd be
quiet. If Mommy wanted you to stop crying, you stopped.
If Mommy wanted you to be a cheerleader or wear your
hair long or go without makeup, that's what you did. You
learned to suppress your own wants and needs to win her
approval. How does that translate into adult behavioral
patterns? When you become involved in an adult relationship, you have no idea how to articulate your needs,
because you're so used to suppressing them. You might be
terrified of making the other person unhappy. While your
overriding goal—that of seeking approval—made sense
during your young life, because pleasing that demanding
mother made you feel loved, it is counterproductive to
hold on to that pattern as an adult.

Our Fundamental Human Needs

The family exists to meet certain fundamental human
needs. In fact, every human system—whether it's an individual,

r a society—must meet these fundamen-
thrive. Psychiatrist Jerome Bach, M.D.,
it demonstrated that a family system—
ᵧstem—has four very basic requirements:
⸬ional maintenance, relationship, and productivity.⁶
⸬sed on Bach's work and the work I've done with my clients,
I've identified what I believe are the requirements for a family
to function as a healthy system and effectively meet the needs
of its individual members:

- *A sense of safety and stability.* A healthy family system feels physically safe and provides a
  sense of stability. In a healthy family system,
  people aren't throwing things at each other.
  You don't have to worry about whether
  you're going to be hurt; you don't have a
  parent who's screaming at you and scaring
  you. It's a system that meets your most basic
  human needs—for food, shelter, and physical safety—and provides consistency and
  predictability. You know from one day to the
  next that your family is going to be there
  for you; that there's a routine in place; that
  home is a safe, stable place.

- *Interpersonal connectedness.* Members of
  the family are involved with each other.
  There's a sense of intimacy. You interact. You
  communicate. You take an interest in one
  another and share your thoughts, feelings,
  and experiences. You're involved in each
  other's lives in a healthy way.

- *Support and nurturance.* Each individual gets a
  sense of support from the other family members. You feel nurtured and cared for. You're
  encouraged to be yourself and to pursue your
  own path. Family members express affection
  for each other both physically and verbally.
  As a result, everyone in the family feels valued and cared for.

- *Emotional release.* Family members feel free
  to express whatever they're feeling. If you're
  feeling angry or sad, you can express it. You
  don't have to hold it in and internalize it. The
  same holds true for happiness or excitement.
  Because nobody's putting a lid on your feelings, you're free to express them in ways that
  are healthy and respectful of others.

- *Self-expression.* This means being able to
  express the uniqueness of who you are. For
  example, one child might be artistic and be
  allowed to freely express that part of himself
  through dance, music, art, or whatever else
  he is inspired to pursue. Another child might
  be a natural athlete. No one's insisting that,
  instead, she should be book-smart. It's safe to
  be and to express yourself as the person you
  really are—your *authentic self.* Family members are free to express their thoughts and
  feelings, their talents and abilities, and their
  passions and interests.

- *Esteem.* When we're born, we naturally feel
  good about ourselves. We have no reason
  not to. Have you ever noticed that a very
  young child will wave to everybody on the
  street, say goodbye to everyone at the super-
  market, and walk up to people and just say
  hello? That's a reflection not only of trust,
  but also of self-confidence. Esteem means
  feeling good about yourself—feeling capable,
  feeling like you're a good person, feeling a
  sense of pride in who you are and in what
  you can accomplish.

Constructive and Dysfunctional Family Systems

A healthy, constructive family system operates differently from a dysfunctional one in three important
respects. A constructive family embraces the differences
between individual family members, allowing each person to flourish. The family system itself is able to thrive
because people take on different roles at various times
to meet the family's overall needs. As an example, when
the father needs emotional support, the mother takes on
the supportive role, and vice versa. It's a far more fluid
and open system than the typical dysfunctional family
system. Below are the core characteristics of a healthy,
constructive family system:

- *Rules and structures are flexible.* They're
  designed to serve both the needs of the
  system and the members of the system. The
  full range of human emotions is accepted.

Your parents or primary caretakers guide you in a constructive manner, so that you can develop healthy behavioral styles and use them in your day-to-day interactions in the world.

- *Differences are respected.* Not everyone in the family is expected to think or behave in the same way. There's a healthy respect for dis-similarities—for each person's individuality and unique personality.

- *Family roles are fluid and flexible.* People aren't locked into a specific role. Roles are inter-changeable, depending on circumstances. For example, one day, one child might be the center of attention because she's got a softball game; the next day, another child, who needs help with schoolwork, might take center stage. Or, on one occasion, one parent might be providing counsel and support to the other; then those roles will reverse. It's all in response to the natural flow of events. And since freedom of self-expression is encouraged, people are free to express all parts of themselves and take on different roles at different times.

In contrast, here are the core characteristics of a *dysfunctional* family system:

- *An absence of rules and structures, or very rigid ones.* Either there are no rules or structures—and chaos prevails—or rules are extremely rigid and everyone is expected to conform, leaving no room for mistakes or flexibility.

- *Suppression of emotions and behavior.* Thoughts, feelings, and behaviors that threaten the prevailing norms of the system are suppressed, which results in the erosion of each person's innate wholeness.

- *Sameness is the rule.* Any deviation from the acceptable norms—as defined by the particular family system—is considered crazy, sick, or bad.

- *The roles of family members are rigid and inflexible.* Family members take on and become locked into distinct roles to keep the whole dysfunctional family machine running. This is the result of the system's need for balance or homeostasis, a subject I'll talk more about later.

Like Tolstoy's unhappy families, all dysfunctional families are different. The level and character of the dysfunctions are determined by the parents—by the extent to which they have each retained their innate wholeness, and by the relationships they have with themselves and with each other. The parents bring to the family the dysfunctions from their own families of origin, which are passed on like a legacy to the next generation. Let me give you an example of how this works. If a mother grew up in a family system in which feelings and expressions of anger were forbidden, in order to survive in that system, her innate ability to express anger is diminished. In order to feel safe within her family system, she had to suppress her anger. Her family was dysfunctional, because it made no room for the natural expression of anger. Let's say she marries someone who grew up in the same kind of family—where anger was unacceptable. As a result, in their relationship, this couple will have difficulty dealing with conflict—because, in order to deal with conflict, you have to have a way of expressing your anger. There will also be issues around anger in the new family they create.

How does that play out? Let's call their son Tommy. When Tommy has his first temper tantrum—which is a perfectly natural early expression of frustration or anger—his parents' dysfunctions come into play. If Tommy takes a toy and throws it against the wall, they might have any number of reactions. They might shame Tommy and say: "That's bad. You're a bad boy" or "That's naughty. We don't raise our voices in this house." Or reject and humiliate him with: "Go to your room and think about what you did." They might abandon the child: "I'm not going to stay here in this room and talk to you. I don't talk to bad boys who break their toys."

It's also quite possible that, in response to her own parents' taboos, rather than suppress her anger, Tommy's mother could have rebelled against her family norms and developed a hair-trigger temper. In that case, she might scream at Tommy—"You stupid idiot, you broke the toy"—or even strike the child. No matter which of these responses greets Tommy's tantrum, over time he learns that anger is bad and that he's bad because he experiences anger. By receiving the same message over and over, Tommy will learn through conditioning that he has to disenfranchise the part of him that expresses anger. That anger has to go underground, compromising his innate wholeness.

Before we move on to how this plays out later for Tommy, and what the full range of possible family dysfunctions is, it's only fair to share with you an example of what might go on in a healthy family when Tommy has a temper tantrum and breaks his toy. One possibility is that Tommy's parents will validate his experience. They might say: "You're feeling angry!" or "Boy, you're really mad." The underlying message is: This is normal. This is a valid experience. Anger is a normal feeling. Maybe Tommy's broken his toy and there's a clear opportunity for a lesson in cause and effect. "Honey, when you throw your toy against the wall, it gets broken. When you get really angry, you can go punch a pillow. But if you throw your toy, you'll break it." So the child learns to release his anger in another way that's more constructive. And, as he gets older, he learns to use his words.

In a healthy family, the parents accept anger as a normal emotion that needs to be discharged. But in a dysfunctional family where anger is repressed, those emotions can't be discharged and released. So when Tommy grows up, he may continue the habit of internalizing his anger. Since he's unable to express it freely, he could turn his feelings of anger inward, which can lead to depression and other emotional and physical consequences. Or he may react by outwardly expressing it in destructive ways—maybe through an explosive temper or through passive-aggressive behavior in which he expresses anger by being critical, sarcastic, judgmental, or oppositional.

The anger has to find expression somehow; he's going to either direct it at himself or direct it at others.

Keep in mind that these patterns of behavior are the result of consistent patterns within a family. All parents make mistakes; even the healthiest parent has been known to scream in the face of a tantrum. Unfortunately, some parents make the same mistakes over and over, because that's what they learned in their own families. When you uncover dysfunctional patterns in your own parents' behavior, it's important to remember: Your parents are only human. Through their experiences as children, they too have suffered pain and the erosion of their self-esteem and wholeness. Try to be empathetic and forgiving, recognizing that your parents were doing the best they could with the emotional resources and knowledge they had available to them at the time. Again, the purpose of this process is not in finding fault with or blaming your parents. The purpose is to gain a deeper understanding of yourself, so that you can reclaim your own lost parts and live in alignment with who you really are and where you want to be in your life. As you go through the process of examining the dynamics of your family of origin, you may experience some difficult feelings; you might feel sad, disloyal, resentful, conflicted, upset, or even furious. Although processing and moving through your feelings is an important part of personal-development work, there's no value in staying stuck in a victim role or playing the blame game. The value of this process lies in uncovering constructive changes you can make in yourself and in your own life.

The Erosion of Wholeness

Anger is just one example of the constellation of normal human emotions, and repressing anger is just one family experience that interferes with your sense of wholeness and well-being. Below is a list that covers the range of conditions and experiences that can erode a person's innate wholeness:

- *Verbal, sexual, or physical abuse.* This can take the most obvious extreme forms—verbal and physical battering, sexual abuse, or witnessing these forms of abuse within your family. But it also includes less overt forms of abuse—for example, having a parent who's critical and judgmental and talks to you in a demeaning way, or having a parent who sexualizes the parent-child relationship with flirtations or inappropriate comments.

- *Parental alcoholism and other addictive behavior.* Addictions lead to a variety of family dysfunctions, from denial and abandonment to physical abuse and unpredictability. Children who grow up in households where there is an addiction come away with all kinds of patterns of behavior that enable them to adapt and survive, including addictions of their own. This category extends to families where there is habitual drinking—a daily cocktail hour, for example. Even though parents aren't falling-down drunk, they may drink enough to diminish their ability to effectively meet

their children's needs for parental involvement and attention.

- *Neglect.* This can range from severe, overt
physical neglect—not feeding a child, changing his diapers, or putting him to bed at
night—to milder or more covert forms of
neglect. Maybe a parent is a workaholic and
just isn't around very much; maybe a parent is very self-absorbed and consistently
puts his or her needs ahead of the child's;
there could be a sick family member or child,
which causes a parent to neglect the other
children.

- *Betrayal.* Betrayal involves trust, and acts of
betrayal can run the gamut from the extreme
to the mundane. At one end of the spectrum,
say you adore your parents and you find out
your father is cheating on your mother; your
family falls apart and you experience tremendous loss. At the other end of the spectrum,
maybe your father has promised to take you
to a ball game, but it never happens. Or your
mother never remembers to pick you up on
time. Or one minute your mother is telling
you what a smart little girl you are, and the
next minute she says you're getting fat. That
feels like a betrayal.

- *Physical or emotional abandonment.* I have
a friend whose mother just up and left the
family when he was 12 years old. That's the

most obvious and extreme form of abandonment. But there are subtler forms. If parents
are always out with friends and leave you
home alone or with a babysitter all the time,
that's another form. Or maybe your parents
are physically in the house, but they don't
talk much with you or express any interest
in you; that's a form of emotional abandonment. Over and over, you end up feeling
unwanted and uncared-for.

- *Oppression of self-expression.* If you're unable
  to freely express your feelings or who you
  really are, your self-expression is oppressed.
  This is what I touched on with the example
  of Tommy and his tantrum—his parents
  couldn't deal with his anger. Another common example: Let's say your feelings were
  hurt at school. Someone called you stupid,
  and you came home and started to cry,
  and your father said, "Stop crying, that's
  for sissies." Or you were listening to music,
  twirling in circles, and singing along, having a grand old time, and your mother
  told you to calm down, remarking, "You're
  always too loud." This also extends to your
  personal interests and passions. A mother
  tells her daughter: "You don't want to be a
  dancer. You'd have to be thin." Or a father
  pushes his son to play football when what
  the teenager really wants to do is spend his
  afternoons at the chess club. That father is
  suppressing his son's own innate nature,
  interests, and needs.

- *Being shamed or humiliated.* How many children haven't heard the expression "You
  should be ashamed of yourself"? At one
  extreme, parents can say profoundly deflat-
  ing things to a child that shame and humiliate him: "You're an idiot." "I wish I'd never
  had you." "That's just plain stupid." "I can't
  stand the sight of you." They can tease in
  humiliating ways: "Bobby wet his pants
  today at school." But shame and humilia-
  tion come in subtler forms. "Why can't you
  get the grades your sister gets?" "You're not
  wearing *that,* are you?" "Aren't you eating a
  little too much again?" Comments that are
  overly critical and judgmental all fall into
  this category. So do actions. When you're sitting in a car at the foot of the driveway with
  your date, and your mother comes out and
  knocks on the window and screams at you,
  that's humiliating—or when you miss that
  last pitch at a baseball game and your father
  gives you a public dressing-down.

Core Limiting Beliefs

When you're a very young child, all you have to go
on is your immediate environment. You're like a sponge;
your parents are like gods. You don't yet have the capacity to intellectualize or rationalize. You take the world
at face value—and the world your family creates is your
reality. From that reality you draw what I call your *core
beliefs*. If you grew up in The Brady Bunch—with parents

who were caring, loving people, where conflicts were resolved through discussion, and where you were loved unconditionally for who you are—you would probably come away with the core belief that the world is a safe, predictable place and that you are a person worthy of love. But if you grew up in an environment in which you were neglected or abused, your core beliefs might include a very different set of beliefs about yourself and the world around you.

I have a client, Peter, whose mother had borderline personality disorder. She was verbally and physically abusive; she would lock Peter in a closet as a punishment—or on an emotional whim. Peter grew up terrified; he spent his young life walking on eggshells for fear that he would set his mother off. He adapted by not talking; he wouldn't say anything; he endeavored to be invisible. The core beliefs he took with him into adulthood were these: *The world is not a safe place. I'm powerless over my environment. Life is unpredictable—the bottom could fall out at any time. People will hurt me and can't be trusted.*

Another of my clients, Harry, grew up in a big family during the '60s in a small Midwestern town. He was dyslexic, but the problem was never diagnosed and he really struggled in school. Afraid that people would find out he was stupid, he compensated for his feelings of helplessness by becoming an intimidating bully. His core beliefs: *I am unworthy. I'm bad. I'm stupid.*

Based on my work with clients, here is a list of the most common *core limiting beliefs* that people adopt as truths about themselves and the world around them, then take with them from childhood into adulthood:

- I'm not safe.

- I'm powerless and have no control.

- There's no one there for me.

- Life is unpredictable; the bottom can fall out anytime.

- People will hurt me and can't be trusted.

- I'm unworthy/unlovable/unwanted/ bad/invisible.

- I'm not good enough.

- I'm stupid.

- I'm ugly.

- If I meet others' needs/expectations, I'll be safe/accepted/loved.

- Others' needs are more important than my own.

- I'm responsible for others.

- Success/status equals recognition/ security/love.

- I have to be perfect at all times.

- I'm incapable of taking care of myself.

- If I express my feelings and needs to others, I'll be judged and rejected.

- I'm entitled to have whatever I want.

Seeking a Natural Balance

Let's step back and, again, think of the family as a system. Like many systems, the family seeks a balance or equilibrium. In nature, the process of maintaining that balance is called *homeostasis*. For example, the human body is a self-regulating system that seeks to maintain its temperature, among other things. When it gets too hot outside, the body tries to compensate by sweating; when it gets too cold, the body tries to restore its equilibrium by shivering, which produces heat. Based on the laws of homeostasis, when one element of a system is off kilter, it triggers a reaction as the entire system tries to adjust.

When family systems theory borrows from the biological concept of homeostasis, it presumes that a family, too, has a natural equilibrium and that the family system strives for balance. As an example, let's say a family member dies who played a certain role within the family. The system will be disrupted and will automatically adjust to seek a new balance. Say the mother dies, and she was the primary wage earner; someone will have to step in and pick up the slack. Or say a new baby comes into the family, drawing the mother's near-complete attention for the first weeks of its life; the rest of the family has to adjust to find a new balance.

In thinking about relationships, homeostasis provides an explanation for why opposites tend to attract. A shy person might be drawn to an outgoing person because they balance one another. Similarly, in relationships, there's always a tension between closeness and distance. I talked earlier about the fluidity of that process within healthy relationships: at one moment, one person has a greater need for closeness; at another moment, the other person needs more of an emotional connection. Couples are always jockeying for a balance in the unconscious pursuit of homeostasis.

Within a family system—with all its complex relationships—homeostasis helps explain why family members take on certain roles. As you'll recall, in a healthy family, roles are fluid and flexible. One day, Annie gets all the attention; the next, Jennifer. One moment, the father plays the role of comforter in a crisis; the next day, for whatever reason, that role falls to the mother. I saw this process at work when my own children were growing up. When my daughter was an adolescent, challenging my parental rules and boundaries, my son was cooperative and easygoing. But a few years later, when he went through adolescence, the roles switched. All these examples relate to homeostasis—the natural tendency for the family system to seek balance.

Both constructive and dysfunctional family systems are subject to the law of homeostasis. As a general rule, the more dysfunctional the family, the more rigid the family roles will be. For example, say one parent is addicted to alcohol or drugs, and the other is busy providing for the family and seldom home. The children will automatically pick up the unmet needs of the system and will tend to get stuck in specific roles. For example, one child will take on the role of caretaker; another will act out the unexpressed anger of the system; a third might become the family hero—the one who strives to do everything perfectly. The conditions simply won't exist for the fluid expression of the different parts of each family member.

In my work, I've found that the four roles listed below—originally identified by professionals working in the substance abuse and recovery field—tend to be the most prevalent among people who grow up in dysfunctional families:

- *Hero.* The Hero seeks self-validation and esteem through accomplishments, money, success, and prestige. Heroes always work hard to prove themselves.

- *Mascot.* Holding a special place within the family, the Mascot may be the baby or the clown. Mascots may be unusually beautiful or handsome, or possess some other trait or circumstance that draws special attention from other family members. With this role there's often a strong sense of entitlement, a desire to be taken care of, and/or a strong need for attention.

- *Lost Child.* This is the child who tends to be insecure and/or self-doubting. Lost Children look to others to provide self-validation and esteem. They're often approval-seekers who try to please other people by saying and doing what they think others want them to do or by taking care of others.

- *Rebel.* Viewed by other family members as
  sick, crazy, or bad, Rebels are oppositional,
  angry, critical, hostile, and/or self-righteous
  and may be verbally or physically abusive.

My reaction to my family of origin provides a perfect example of this dynamic. I took on the role of Rebel,
expressing my family system's anger and frustration,
becoming a living expression of its darkest dysfunctions.
As a young child, I felt largely ignored and invisible. I had
no one with whom to connect within my family, and I
found my mother's withdrawal from me—and the outside world—painful and frustrating. Many of my natural
human needs went unmet, including a deep need for self-
expression. I was a very creative person, and I needed a
safe place where I could express my creativity. At home,
nobody paid much attention. But at the end of third grade,
I was admitted to an enrichment program for gifted students. It was challenging and interesting. In fourth grade,
I won my first part in a school musical. I loved it. And,
given that I was later to pursue a career as a singer, it was
a turning point for me. My elementary school experience
was very positive, which helped offset the erosion of my
self-esteem that was occurring at home.

With the end of sixth grade and the enrichment program, things took a turn for the worse. On top of the
normal challenges of adolescence, I was beginning to feel
the impact of my home life. I started to come apart emotionally, acting out my frustration, alienation, and need
for attention. One incident really captures the essence of
my experience. Early in the seventh grade, I went over
to a friend's house and we broke into the liquor cabinet.
By the time we were finished, I was extremely drunk.

When I arrived home, drunk as can be, I settled into the television room, making intermittent trips to the bathroom to throw up. My mother didn't notice. Before dinner, I retreated to my upstairs bedroom and passed out, fully clothed, on top of my bed. Yet no one expressed any concern when I missed dinner and slept into the night. The following day, I was so sick that my mother had to come pick me up early from school. Even then, she made no effort to find out what was wrong. During that 24-hour period, no one had noticed I was drunk; no one expressed concern about my health; no one made an effort to figure out what was going on.

That attitude prevailed as I continued my downward slide. Before long, I was smoking, experimenting with drugs, and hanging with an older crowd. At 13, I sought refuge in a group of kids who hung out in the public park. Like me, they were alienated and disenfranchised, but they were older. My boyfriend was 16 and addicted to heroin. In elementary school, I'd had outlets for my creative energy and curiosity; not so in junior high. In an effort to express a part of my authentic self—the artistic, creative part of me—I started writing poetry and playing guitar. I began to see myself as an artist, a free spirit.

I was attending a tough urban public school, and there were several stabbings while I was a student there. I was viewed as an outsider, physically threatened, and, at one point, actually beaten up. At the age of 13, my world was falling apart. At home, I was ignored or criticized; at school, I was terrified. My parents were essentially disengaged. I was screaming for help, but they weren't hearing me. And, by the end of my freshman year of high school, I was flunking out.

Two weeks before the school year ended, a friend told me she was running away from home. I jumped at the opportunity, and together we hitchhiked to Provincetown, Massachusetts. Eventually we parted ways, and I went on to Key West, Florida. I was 14 years old, and I didn't really go home again until I was an adult. I took incredible risks. I ended up, at one point, living homeless on the streets; at another, sharing a summer house with ten other out-of-control teens—all the children of parents who weren't doing much active parenting. After six months had passed, my parents sent my brother after me to bring me home. Finding life on the streets terrifying, and feeling lost and disillusioned, I agreed immediately. But I'd already had a taste of independence, and living at home just didn't feel like a viable option. My parents agreed to send me to an alternative high school in Boston and to help pay my living expenses. At the age of 15, I was living on my own in a rented apartment near Kenmore Square and working after school as a waitress for pocket money. I doubled up on course loads to make up for lost time, worked hard, and graduated in less than two years. It was as if I'd sped through my youth and rushed into adulthood to escape my unhappy childhood. After that, I took a menial job and worked just long enough to earn the money for a plane ticket to Los Angeles, where, at the age of 17, I began to pursue my dream of becoming a singer.

By the time I left home at 14, the core limiting belief that I had internalized about myself was: *I'm worthless, unwanted, unlovable, and bad.* I raged at the world. My authentic self—smart and creative with a strong, independent spirit—was still in there somewhere but had no room to grow. To this day, I believe I left in an unconscious attempt to preserve my innate wholeness, a fearless move inspired by my survival instinct. I see it as evidence of my inner strength.

I spent my entire teenage life on the run. Looking back, I recognize that I took on the role of the Rebel within my family system. I was the one with an attitude, the nonconformist, the angry one. I railed against the status quo. I broke all the rules. When I was living at home, my parents were unaware of my experimentation with alcohol and drugs, but my foul moods and temper tantrums did attract my family's attention. Through a combination of my acting out and my family's negative reactions, I continually reinforced my core belief that I was unlovable and worthless. In a family like mine, it's not uncommon for a rebel to emerge.

Core Limiting Beliefs and Family Role Exercises

The three exercises that follow are designed to help you gain greater awareness of the attributes and dynamics of your family of origin, the core limiting beliefs you developed in response, and your primary role within the family.

Exercise: Family System Dysfunction

This quiz measures the degree to which your family of origin fits with the attributes of a dysfunctional family system. Before you begin, I want to encourage you again not to judge or blame your parents as you go through this exercise. It's designed to provide you with some insight into the nature of the family system you come from and, ultimately, help you connect the dots between your family of origin and the limiting patterns you experience in your life.

Respond to each of the statements listed below, rating each item based on how you predominantly experienced your family from your earliest memories as a child until the time you left home. If you were not raised by your parents, substitute primary caretakers where the word *parents* appears. If your parents were divorced and you were raised in two different environments (for example, one household was more dysfunctional than the other), complete the quiz twice, once for each household.

Scoring Key

1 Completely untrue
2 Mostly untrue
3 Slightly more true than untrue
4 Moderately true
5 Mostly true
6 Describes my experience perfectly

Score   *Description*

_____   I was the victim of, or saw another family member subjected to, one or more of the following: verbal abuse, physical abuse, sexual abuse, physical neglect, emotional neglect.

_____   There was a stated or unstated rule that family members should think, feel, and behave in the same way. Any deviations were considered "bad," "crazy," or "sick," or met with disapproval.

_____ There was a stated or unstated rule that one or more of the following feelings were not to be openly expressed: anger, fear, sadness, love, joy.

_____ There was a stated or unstated rule that one's needs were not to be expressed.

_____ I did not feel a solid sense of security and/or support.

_____ I often felt one or more of the following: worried, anxious, sad, lonely, depressed, abandoned, overly responsible for others, fearful, angry, ashamed, unwanted, guilty, defective, insecure, separate/different from others, powerless, frustrated.

_____ One or both of my parents had diagnosed or undiagnosed mental and emotional problems and/or habitual dependency on alcohol or drugs.

_____ There was a stated or unstated rule that one should be perfect at all times.

_____ Family members were expected to keep family matters secret and not reveal them to people outside of the family.

_____ One or both of my parents had a volatile temper that often made me feel afraid and/or upset.

_____ TOTAL SCORE

Interpreting Your Score

10–19	Very low level of family dysfunction
20–29	Fairly low level of family dysfunction
30–39	Moderate level of family dysfunction
40–49	High level of family dysfunction
50–60	Very high level of family dysfunction

Exercise: Core Limiting Beliefs

Check all of the core limiting beliefs below that resonate for you. Check any limiting beliefs that you think you may have internalized in response to overt and covert messages from your parents growing up or from the environment and circumstances you experienced throughout your childhood. Add any other core limiting beliefs you may have internalized that aren't listed here.

When you're finished, take out your journal and write "My Core Limiting Beliefs" at the top of the page. Then transfer your list to your journal by writing all the checked items under that heading.

❏ I'm not safe.

❏ I'm powerless and have no control.

❏ There's no one there for me.

❏ Life is unpredictable; the bottom can fall out anytime.

❏ People will hurt me and can't be trusted.

❏ I'm unworthy/unlovable/unwanted/invisible.

❏ I'm bad/not good enough.

❏ I'm stupid.

❏ I'm ugly.

❏ If I meet others' needs/expectations, I'll be safe/
accepted/loved.

❏ Others' needs are more important than my
own.

❏ I'm responsible for others.

❏ Success/status equals recognition/security/love.

❏ I have to be perfect at all times.

❏ I'm incapable of taking care of myself.

❏ If I express my feelings and needs to others, I'll
be judged and rejected.

❏ I'm entitled to have anything I want.

❏ Other(s): List any other core beliefs you may
have internalized.

Exercise: Identifying Your Family Role

Scoring Key

1   Completely untrue of me
2   Mostly untrue of me
3   Slightly more true than untrue of me
4   Moderately true of me
5   Mostly true of me
6   Describes me perfectly

A.

____ Whatever I do, I have to be the best.

____ Success, money, and status are very important to me.

____ I often feel that nothing I do seems to meet my high standards.

____ I often strive to keep things in perfect order and organized.

____ TOTAL SCORE

B.

____ I enjoy feeling special and/or being the center of attention.

____ I often get upset and/or frustrated when I don't get what I want.

____ I often feel that I shouldn't have to follow the rules that others go by.

____ It's often hard for me to follow routines and be self-disciplined.

____ TOTAL SCORE

C.

____ I worry that my faults and flaws will be revealed to others.

____ I often judge and criticize myself.

____ I tend to make other people's needs more important than my own.

____ It's difficult for me to let others know what I need and/or set boundaries with others.

____ TOTAL SCORE

D.

____ I often feel angry, critical, and/or resentful toward others.

____ I often feel misunderstood and/or misjudged by others.

_____ I am often controlling and dominating
      around others.

_____ I often challenge and/or oppose the status
      quo.

_____ TOTAL SCORE

Interpreting Your Score

The section in which you received the highest score
(A, B, C, or D) indicates the *primary role* you played within
your family system. In small or single-child families,
it's not uncommon for the child or children to assume
more than one role. Other roles where you scored high
would be the *secondary roles*. In general, lower or more
evenly balanced scores are an indicator that your family
system was relatively healthy, or that you've done a lot
of personal-development work to help you override the
patterns from your family or origin.

A: Hero
B: Mascot
C: Lost Child
D: Rebel

Now, in your journal, write your primary role (or
roles) under the heading "My Family Role.

CHAPTER 4

Managing Fear
So It Doesn't
Manage You

When I decided to leave my marriage but hadn't yet moved out, I imagined a new kind of life—a life of freedom and independence. I envisioned new opportunities through which I could express my full potential and rekindle my passions. Faced with a deteriorating marriage that was causing me a great deal of pain, I romanticized a future where I was, once again, on my own. But when my husband and I physically separated, I experienced something else altogether. I was gripped by fear. I started having panic attacks. I'd wake up in the middle of the night in my new apartment, unable to breathe, my heart pounding. What was going on? What was I so afraid of? I was swept up in the fear that, without my husband, I would perish. Interestingly, I'd experienced this kind of panic only once before in my life, when I was four months pregnant with my first child. I've never forgotten it. One afternoon, I had a mental image of being abandoned by my husband and left destitute. I imagined myself huddled in a broken-down tenement with my baby, living in poverty. At the time, I believed this fear was evoked by my pregnancy, which made me feel incredibly vulnerable and accentuated my dependency on my husband. When he came home that evening, I was sobbing and shaken, still terrified. When I shared my fears with him, he was very supportive, consoling me and offering assurances that I was imagining the impossible.

I didn't have any idea where this feeling came from, this fear of abandonment and destitution, but it resurfaced again when our marriage ended. In truth, I had no reason at the time to think that I'd have any financial difficulties. We'd worked out an amicable agreement involving joint custody. I'd moved with my children to a nice apartment, a few houses down from our old home, where my husband remained. And, at first, my husband provided ample financial resources. But ultimately, in the months that followed, as if I'd willed it into being through my imagination, my greatest fear came to fruition. His financial support declined, and I found myself struggling to pay the bills.

Where had it come from, this fear? Over time, through my personal-development work, I was able to trace it directly to my old conditioning. As far back as I can remember, I had believed that I needed a man to take care of me. Only then could I feel safe in the world. My brothers were conditioned to go to college and get good jobs. They were conditioned to be providers. In contrast, the message I received—through my parents' comments, their role modeling, and our culture—was a very different one. Not only was my mother completely dependent on my father, financially and emotionally, but she made it very clear to me through her advice about how to dress, act, and behave that it was important to catch a man, to find a husband to provide for me. I still remember her words: "You need to lose some weight. Men don't like women who are fat." "Don't you think you should get a padded bra? Men like a woman with a little more than you have on top." "You talk too much. Men don't like that." In retrospect, such advice seems bizarrely inappropriate since I left home at the age of 14. More to the point, these messages contributed to one of my most deeply held core limiting beliefs: that I needed a man to take care of me. By imagining that I could make it on my own with two children to raise, I was violating that core belief. In my own mind, I had translated my conditioning into the idea that, quite literally, I needed a man to survive.

Fear is a curious beast. Any number of situations, both real and imagined, can evoke fear. One of them is violating your core limiting beliefs, because those beliefs are all about survival; they're all about keeping ourselves safe, about self-preservation. A little boy learns that it's his job to take care of his alcoholic mother. Another learns that feelings of sadness and anger are taboo. Still another learns that the best way to escape an abusive parent is by keeping very quiet and staying out of the way. These children emerge from their families of origin with a mix of core limiting beliefs: *Other people's needs are more important than my own. My feelings are something I must hide. The world is not a safe place.* Whatever the core limiting belief, going against it produces feelings of fear and anxiety.

The Power of Fear

I've devoted an entire chapter to the subject of fear, because it's one of the biggest obstacles people face in moving forward in their lives and reaching their fullest potential. Through my work with many clients, I've come to believe that most people live their lives from a place of fear. If you're living your life based on avoiding the things that you fear most, you're not free to take risks, or to pursue your dreams and goals. We each have a certain amount of life energy. If your energy is being expended in staying safe—in avoiding failure, rejection, physical harm, and emotional pain by avoiding the people, places, and situations that trigger your fears— then that energy is tied up in your vigilance to stay safe instead of in fulfilling your potential.

Managing fear is crucial to mastering aloneness. To manage it effectively, you first have to understand the nature and physiology of fear. Through evolution, we're hard-wired to respond to fear with intensity. Hence, that panic I felt following my separation manifested itself physically in palpitations and shortness of breath. I experienced a classic fight-or-flight response, a physical response that's been with us as a species from our earliest beginnings. For our evolutionary precursors out in the wild, the fight-or-flight response was a valuable survival mechanism. It's not as useful when triggered by modern-day fears. Here's how it works: When a person or animal senses a threat, the autonomic nervous system, which regulates involuntary body functions—including heart rate, digestion, respiration rate, salivation, perspiration, and dilation of the pupils—moves into action. One part of that system—the sympathetic nervous system—controls our response. When it's activated by something such as motion, sound, light, or images that signal a potential threat, the body goes into a state of heightened alert so that we can react by either fighting or fleeing. A neurotransmitter releases the hormones norepinephrine and adrenaline. Once we're able to discern whether we're actually in danger, that we're actually going to have to *do* something, the body's response intensifies, kicking in more of these powerful hormones. Heart and lung action accelerates; pupils dilate; the blood vessels in parts of the body we don't need for fighting or fleeing—say, the gastrointestinal tract—constrict; the vessels that feed crucial muscles for running and jumping and fighting dilate, and nutrients are released to fuel those muscles. In addition, cortisol, known as the "stress hormone," is released in higher quantities than normal in response to the stress invoked by this fear. Cortisol helps the system react and then helps the body return to its normal resting state once the threat has passed. However, constant, chronic stress causes elevated levels of cortisol, which has all kinds of adverse physical effects, including:

- Impaired cognitive performance (you don't think as clearly)

- Suppressed thyroid function (which affects your metabolism, among other things)

- Blood-sugar imbalances (which can cause everything from a sense of fatigue to diabetes)

- Higher blood pressure (which puts you at risk for heart disease)

- Increased abdominal fat (which nobody
  wants, because it not only looks bad but is
  associated with all kinds of health problems)

In addition, chronic stress can compromise your immune system, making you more susceptible to illness. Ultimately, living with chronic states of fear and stress is unhealthy for our bodies and for our spirits.

Fear can be paralyzing. That's a big reason why our core limiting beliefs have such a hold over our behavior. As an example, I had a client, Casey, a young woman in her early 30s. She was making just under $100,000 a year in a financial-services job that she hated, but she was unable to make a career change because she was gripped by fear. She'd grown up in a family where both her parents were children of the '60s. They'd taken the habit of recreational drug use with them into adulthood and were unable to hold down jobs. Her reaction to growing up in the face of their dysfunctions involved taking on the role of the responsible one in the family, the caretaker, the provider. Casey started babysitting at the age of 12 to earn money. By the time she came to me for help as an adult, she was supporting her father, who was suffering from Alzheimer's disease, and periodically sending money to her mother, who lived in another country. She was romantically involved with a man who was divorced, but still supporting his ex-wife and son. He'd made it very clear that he didn't want to support Casey, and he was unsupportive of her desire to switch careers. She had replicated her relationship with her parents in her romantic relationship. Her core limiting belief: *Other people's needs are more important than my own. I have to be responsible for others.* Her fear: *If I make my own needs*

*more important than everyone else's, I'll be rejected and I'll
end up alone.* When she came to me, she was struggling
with her desire to start her own photography business.
She wanted to have more balance in her life and to be
able to set her own hours. But without her boyfriend's
approval, Casey couldn't make the move. She couldn't
put her own desires ahead of his. Fear was the predomi-
nant emotion that kept her frozen in place.

Trance States

How do our core limiting beliefs exercise such power
over us? How does our conditioning rule our lives?
Reichian therapist Stephen Wolinsky's work on trance
states provides some interesting clues to this process.
Although I was first introduced to the concept of childhood trances during my psychotherapist training in Germany in 1993, it wasn't until I studied Wolinsky's work
several years later that I was struck by how our childhood experiences and subsequent trance states drive the
fears that hold us back as adults.

In his book *The Dark Side of the Inner Child*,[1] Wolinsky describes the trance state as the mechanism through
which we disconnect from our current reality and allow
the emotions from our old reality—from our childhood
or earlier life—to take over. A trance state is a situation in
which we experience that emotional disconnect. It's as
if our emotions are hijacked by our unconscious minds.
According to Wolinsky, age regression is the most common trance state.

Trances explain why many of us react or behave in
ways that seem out of our control, without understanding

why. There is a part of us—which Wolinsky refers to as the observer—that creates and uses trance states as a way to protect ourselves and to survive difficult childhood experiences and traumas. When something happens in our adult life that reminds us of a past event—a trigger—we unconsciously recreate memories and emotions that relate to the past event rather than the present reality. That can cause us to react in ways that are often inappropriate to the here and now.

Trance states can be invoked by all kinds of situations and events. Not long ago, I was working with a client, Marybeth, on issues related to her aloneness. We talked about trance states, and a few weeks later, during one of our sessions, she recounted this story. That week, Marybeth had gone to an unfamiliar church where her son was singing with the choir as part of a school-related event. When she arrived alone at the Episcopal service, she found herself seeking out fellow parents with whom to sit. She said hello to an acquaintance and asked if she could share a seat, but the woman was saving the entire pew for aunts, uncles, and grandparents who were scheduled to arrive shortly. So Marybeth found a seat next to someone she didn't know. Since the two of them were seated alone together, Marybeth reached out her hand and introduced herself; they exchanged a brief hello and the names of their children. The family in the pew in front of her was very well dressed and sitting stiffly, whispering barely audibly among themselves. Suddenly, Marybeth had an intense feeling that something was terribly wrong. Within moments, she was filled with anxiety. She was gripped with a fear that she'd been behaving inappropriately. Anxiety and embarrassment swept over her; she felt an overwhelming sense of confusion. She started to sweat; her mind racing. It took a few minutes for her to collect herself. "What was going on?" she wondered, recognizing that her reaction was out of proportion to what, if anything, might have occurred. Because of the work we'd been doing together on trances, she realized that she was in a trance state. It wasn't her aloneness that was the issue. She was experiencing emotions that sprang from her early life. Raised in a very proper family, she'd grown up in the Episcopal Church, which she had long since abandoned. She'd been taught to be very quiet when entering the sanctuary. By talking so openly and moving from pew to pew when she'd first entered the church, she'd broken the rules; she'd behaved, she thought, inappropriately.

Marybeth was disconnecting from the present. Somehow, the combination of events had taken her back to her early years in church, which, from her perspective, had not been about worshipping, but all about appearances: how you dressed, how you looked, how you behaved. Her core limiting belief: *If I don't behave appropriately, I'll be rejected and humiliated.* Recounting the experience to me as something of an epiphany, Marybeth reported that, during church services growing up, her mother would repeatedly shush her, along with her brother and sister, reprimanding them with stony glares if they spoke at all. Being in an Episcopal sanctuary, sitting behind a whispering family dressed to the nines—just like the people who had surrounded her in church so many years before—had triggered the sensation of shame and confusion she'd experienced as a child. In fact, she noted, issues around behaving appropriately at all kinds of events were emotional triggers for her because of her mother's intense preoccupation with appearances.

For Wolinsky, the dark side of the inner child is the shadow self that produces such reactions. These trances bring our pathologies from childhood into our everyday experiences, ultimately creating patterns of behavior driven by our core limiting beliefs. In *The Dark Side of the Inner Child,* he defines a trance as "the means by which symptoms are created and maintained and become a source of pathology as they are integrated in our habitual mode of response to the world."[2] In other words, trance states are reactions based on the past. They trigger habitual behaviors that are grounded in our core beliefs and conditioning. In adulthood, those trance states surface again and again.

Here's another example. I have a client, a man in his mid-30s, who played the piano as a child. Every time his parents had guests, they'd try to get him to perform. It made him feel uncomfortable, and he would make a lot of mistakes, which humiliated and embarrassed him. As an adult, any time he's in a situation where he is put on the spot or is the center of attention, he gets very anxious. His core belief: *If people notice me, I'll be humiliated.* Any situation he associates with performance—from speaking out at a meeting to delivering a toast—triggers fear. So his habitual response is to avoid the limelight.

To experience the power of a trance state, take a moment to do the following exercise. Have someone guide you through the process, or record the instructions first and then follow along to the sound of your own voice reading them. That will allow you to close your eyes and focus on the exercise itself.

Exercise: Entering a Trance State

Close your eyes and sit back in your chair. Think of a situation or environment that caused you to react in fear. It can be something from your present life or a situation from the past. It might be a situation involving another person, a conversation, or a conflict you had with someone, or it might be an experience or a place in which you felt afraid or in physical danger. Recreate the situation in your mind with as much detail as possible. Notice the physical surroundings. What do you see? Who, if anyone, else is there? What are you doing? What is happening around you? What physical reactions do you have? How do you feel? What thoughts are running through your head? Notice your breathing and your body posture. Notice how recreating this situation in your mind makes you feel, physically, emotionally, and mentally.

Now slowly allow that memory to fade and, keeping your eyes closed, observe what effect the exercise has had on your breathing, the way your body feels, and any emotions or other reactions you might be having. Take out your journal and spend a few minutes recording what you remember and all your reactions to it.

Trance States and Fear

"Our minds are vast storehouses of information," writes Harville Hendrix, Ph.D., in *Getting the Love You Want*. Our unconscious mind holds our pleasurable and painful experiences, our deepest memories even from infancy, and all the lessons from our family of origin that shape our core beliefs and habitual behaviors. When a person or event taps into that storehouse, located in what Hendrix calls the "dark, convoluted recesses of our brains," it can trigger a trance state. Although most people tend to be unaware of the power of the unconscious mind, it is a very active and functioning part in each one of us, and it plays a crucial role in how we experience fear.

Again, to override your fears—to move past them by managing them—you have to first understand the link between the unconscious mind and your behavior. So bear with me. I've drawn on Hendrix's writing to clarify this process. It's helpful to think of the brain as being divided into three main layers: the brain stem, the limbic system, and the cerebral cortex. Let's take them one at a time.

- *The brain stem.* The brain stem and its related structures (the medulla, thalamus, hypo-thalamus, cerebellum, reticular formation, and pons) are collectively referred to as the *old brain.* This is the part of the brain we talked about earlier, where the fight-or-flight response originates. It's the oldest part of the brain and the most primitive, existing in fishes, amphibians, and mammals. This area of the brain automatically regulates blood pressure, heart rate, respiration, digestion, body temperature, and blood sugar. It over-sees basic human functions such as eating, sleeping, posture, and balance.

- *The limbic system.* The limbic system is involved in the regulation of emotions.

It includes the hippocampus and the
amygdala, and it covers the upper brain stem
like a protective sheath. The limbic system
coordinates information delivered to and
from the cerebral cortex, which is the outer
layer of brain matter.

- *The cerebral cortex.* Generally referred to as the
  new brain, the cortex is the most evolved area
  of the brain. This is the area of the brain that
  differentiates us from other species. It's the
  part that governs speech, motor and sensory
  skills, problem solving, and information processing. The cortex makes up about 80 percent of our brain matter, and it's what gives
  the brain its wrinkled appearance. This is the
  part of the brain that's most responsible for
  the development of our intellectual achievements, our civilization, and our history.

The new brain is the part of us that's aware of, and
involved in, our present daily activities—this is the home
of the *conscious mind.* In contrast, what goes on in the old
brain goes on behind the scenes; it's the *unconscious mind.*
The new brain is involved in the business of perceiving
and processing external phenomena in the present, while
the main task of the old brain is basic self-preservation.
As we go about our lives, the old brain and new brain are
busy communicating with one another. As an example,
when a person comes into view, the old brain and the new
brain exchange and interpret information to determine
whether that person is safe or a threat to our survival.
The new brain's job is to send an image of the person to

the old brain, where it is scanned and compared with old images and impressions. All this happens within a fraction of a second. If someone appears whom you know, with whom you have positive associations—your beloved grandmother, for example—a signal goes from your old brain to your new brain through the limbic system, your emotional center. You're filled with good feelings; you might reach out for a nice warm hug.

But what if it's not your beloved grandmother? What if it's someone with whom you have an unpleasant or negative association? Then the limbic system sends a very different signal, one of fear, anxiety, or apprehension. Most importantly for our purposes, the old brain has no sense of time and is not always precise in its interpretations. If you see someone who, unconsciously, reminds the old brain of something terrible that happened to you—even if it happened 20 years ago—the limbic system still sets off an alarm signal, and the fight-or-flight response kicks in. The old brain taps right into that storehouse of information to generate your emotional responses, without discriminating between then and now, present and past. To the old brain, Hendrix notes, "Today, tomorrow, and yesterday do not exist; everything that was, still is."[3]

FEAR

The truth is, most of our fears are not based on our current reality. They are the product of imagined fears that we conjure up in our minds. Put another way, most of our fears are the product of our own fantasies. The acronym FEAR has been floated around in the personal-development field a lot and interpreted in many different ways to make a point about fear. I refer to FEAR as "Fantasized Events As Real," because that's precisely the process that takes place. Marybeth experienced symptoms of fear when she was sitting in a church pew during a school event. What was she afraid of? Of getting in trouble for talking too loudly; of inspiring her mother's wrath; of making people think badly of her for talking out loud in a sanctuary; of behaving inappropriately. The entire emotional reaction was grounded in something that had no basis in reality—except in her reality as a small child; except in her old brain; except as a violation of a core limiting belief she'd brought with her from childhood, based on a rule about how to behave in church that hadn't been tested in 20 years. Such is the nature of our emotions.

When I was a little girl, I often had to choose between spending time with my parents in the den watching television or not spending time with them at all. Since I wanted to be with them, I ended up watching a lot of things that were inappropriate for a young child, particularly scary shows. I developed strong fears about things that go bump in the night. I can remember waking during the night, lying in bed with my heart pounding. If I needed to get up, it took every ounce of my nerve to get out of bed and walk ten feet to the bathroom. I imagined bandage-wrapped mummies or glassy-eyed vampires in my closet, under my bed, and around every corner. Then, I'd jump back into bed, my heart racing, my palms sweating. My point: the body can't differentiate between the real and the imagined, between fantasy and reality.

Of course, if you're walking alone to your car in a dark parking lot at 2 A.M., you may have every reason to experience fear. You're concerned about self-preservation. That fear is going to propel you to your car, key at the ready, as fast you can get there. However, the other kind of fear—the fear that has no basis in reality—is one of biggest things that holds people back from moving forward in their lives. Fear of meeting new people or trying something new. Fear of success and fear of failure. Fear of leaving a job you hate, getting out of a relationship that isn't working, or moving to a new city. Fear of defying convention. Fear of being alone. Fear of change.

Fear tends to rear its head when people attempt to move beyond their comfort zones. Each of us has a comfort zone—a set of boundaries within which we live and maintain a sense of comfort and familiarity. These are the situations and circumstances that we know and that give us a sense of security because they represent what's familiar. Your comfort zone encompasses all that you've known and experienced in your life, and all your life circumstances—your job, your education, the way you dress, how much money you earn, your relationships, the car you drive, how much money you have in the bank, the home you live in, and how you spend your leisure time.

To master the art of aloneness, you have to be able to move outside of your comfort zone. Some people's comfort zones are more expansive than others. For example, a woman with a high-powered job who travels a lot, meets with high-level executives and government officials, has a penchant for trying new restaurants and international foods, and skydives for the thrill of it has—compared to many people—an expansive comfort zone. She might be as comfortable at an Udon Festival in Japan as she is in her own living room. But a trip to her daughter's kindergarten class to help with the Halloween party may be outside her comfort zone because she doesn't spend a lot of time at school compared to some of the other parents or doesn't know what's expected of her—or even because of a negative experience she had in kindergarten. Similarly, a residential architect who meets regularly with affluent clients and interacts with construction workers and contractors every day might be just as comfortable at the country club as he is at the local diner; he talks easily with all kinds of people and is relaxed and confident. But if he's in his mid-40s, works all the time, and is out of shape, going to a new gym may fall outside his comfort zone. We've all had the experience of walking into a situation that feels completely alien. Generally, if it throws us off kilter, it means we've left our comfort zone.

Staying within your comfort zone doesn't necessarily mean you're happy there. It's just what you're used to. Some people have expansive natures and a great sense of adventure; others have very narrow comfort zones. Your willingness to deliberately and continually expand your comfort zone allows you greater experiences and freedom. As you master the art of aloneness, the ability to move outside your comfort zone comes into play, and to do that you have to be able to manage fear. We'll get into how to actually do this later in the chapter.

Whether your fear has been activated by the eruption of old, unconscious memories or by violating one of your core limiting beliefs (like the church pew incident or the terror I experienced immediately following my separation)—or simply by the prospect of moving outside your comfort zone—the result is essentially the same: FEAR. That is, your fear is being triggered by a fantasy, an imagined threat. Your fear is not based in reality. It's based on dangers you're imagining. Stephen Wolinsky calls this process futurizing, which he defines as "our bodies being in the present time, but our minds being in the future." When the results we imagine are negative or catastrophic (which is often the case), that triggers a feeling of fear. Since most people have never learned effective strategies for managing their fear, their only means of escape is to back away from the edge of their comfort zone and remain stuck in their status quo.

Moving Beyond Your Fear

After two years in my own business, I was ready to move my office into a beautiful professional building in an upscale part of the city. I signed the lease and committed to the office build-out and renovations. The day I signed the lease, I woke up during the night and started to worry about what I had done. As I thought about the lease commitment and the money I was about to spend, I felt like the bottom was falling out of my stomach. My heart raced, and I felt short of breath. Again, I was exhibiting the classic symptoms of fear. When I looked closely at what was causing my fear, I realized I was playing a gloom-and-doom movie in my head. It went something like this: I was sitting in my nice new office and I'd spent all this money on the renovations, but I had no clients. I was going to have to give up my office because I didn't have any money coming in. Once again, I saw myself as destitute. Of course, none of this had happened. And, when I thought about it carefully, I saw that this movie had no basis in reality. I was already running a very successful company. I had no reason to believe my business would fail. To manage my fears, I realized I was going to have to change that gloom-and-doom movie. I started, quite consciously, playing a new movie in my head. I imagined my phone ringing off the hook. I imagined a six-month wait to get on my client list. I imagined a line of clients that reached around the block. My new movie was more like the film *Field of Dreams:* If I build it, they will come.

Here, step by step, is the process I followed to manage my fear. First, I recognized and acknowledged it. Then I asked myself: *Where is this fear coming from? What am I imagining will happen?* I became aware of the movie I was playing in my mind. Then I took another crucial step by asking myself: *Is this movie based in reality?* I did a reality check, just to make sure my goals and expectations were in line with the facts. I asked myself: *Am I capable of doing what I plan to do? Will I be able to sustain myself and my business? Will my coaching and consulting practice support this office? Will I be able to provide for my children and myself? Do I have the skills I need? The clients? Are my clients getting good results?* The answer to all these questions was "Yes." I had a viable action plan. I'd been in my own business for two years with a strong track record of success. I already had an extensive client list. By doing a reality check, I grounded my goals and expectations in the here and now, instead of in the gloom-and-doom movie of failure. Then I consciously changed my inner movie to one that supported my moving beyond my comfort zone. I replaced the picture of failure and destitution with a picture of resounding success.

But I didn't stop there. I asked myself: *Why am I playing this movie? What is the underlying core belief that's invoked a trance state?* I searched within myself and arrived back at the age of 13. I remembered sharing my life aspirations with my mother, announcing that I wanted to be a singer. If you'll recall, early in my life, when I lived in California, I was singing professionally. The reality is I have a great singing voice. What was my mother's reaction when I shared my dreams with her? She unintentionally shot them down by saying, "Before you get your hopes up, I think you should get your voice evaluated to see if you have any talent." The underlying message that I got from her response was: *I don't think you're good enough.* Throughout my life, that message resonated through my unconscious mind every time I put myself out there and tried to achieve my professional dreams. The same fear would surface again and again— that I might not have what it takes to be successful. My core limiting belief: *I'm not good enough.* By signing the lease on my new office, I had violated that old belief and set off a trance state that originated from that experience with my mother nearly 33 years before.

When you experience the sensations associated with fear, when you're fantasizing events as real, here are five steps you can take to help you manage it and move beyond it.

The Five Steps to Managing Fear

Step One

Instead of resisting it, honor the fear by acknowledging it. For example, "I'm afraid I will fail" or "I'm afraid I'll be rejected" or "I'm afraid I won't be good enough."

Step Two

Identify the movie you're running—the image you're playing in your mind. Ask yourself, *What am I imagining will happen?*

Step Three

Do a reality check. Figure out if your fears have any real basis in fact. Be as methodical as you need to be.

Step Four

Change the movie you're running in your head. Replace it with a movie that supports your goals rather than undermines them.

Step Five

Identify the core limiting belief that you may be violating by pursuing your goal. Which limiting belief set the FEAR dynamic in motion? In my own example, it was: *I'm not good enough.*

Moving Beyond Your Comfort Zone

Because they lack the skills to do so, many people never have the opportunity to face and move beyond their deepest fears. In order to master aloneness, you have to be willing to move out of your comfort zone. Many people never leave their comfort zones unless a new life situation demands it; it simply requires too much effort. What pushes them out of their comfort zone? Usually it's a crisis of some kind: an emotional crisis that leaves them so distraught that they may have trouble functioning; an illness that requires them to change the way they live;

a setback that forces them to rethink their future or priorities. Major life changes, such as divorce, the death of a loved one, job loss, or a major move all are catalysts that can push you out of your comfort zone. But because most people don't understand the dynamics of FEAR and how to move beyond it, without a major life change or crisis forcing them to do so, many people remain stuck in the status quo, unable to realize their dreams.

One of the greatest challenges is this: when you're standing on the edge of your comfort zone, you don't know what lies ahead. You're forced to imagine what lies beyond those boundaries. Just as I did when I signed the lease for my new office, most people will tend to imagine the worst-case scenario, and that induces fear. At worst, FEAR can be paralyzing; at best, it's uncomfortable. It takes a lot of courage to step outside your comfort zone and into the jaws of discomfort. So we procrastinate, rationalize, make excuses, and find ways to talk ourselves out of moving forward. We're all masters at talking ourselves out of a change that will take us into the unknown.

The future can be a scary place. But, in truth, every moment of every day, we are facing the future. As actor Anthony Hopkins said so beautifully on TV's *Inside the Actors Studio:* "Today is the tomorrow I was so worried about yesterday." The unknown becomes a lot less frightening if you do your research and then your reality check. Whenever you're making a major decision that will take you out of your comfort zone—ending a relationship, making a commitment to something new, taking a new job, moving to a new city, making a major financial investment—the more information you can bring to the process, the better you'll feel about it. You want to make sure it's a grounded decision—that it's not based on an immediate emotional reaction, which can be fleeting and spring from unconscious fears and trance states. How do you gather information about the unknown? By knowing yourself and effectively evaluating your situation or goal. Below are three things you can do when faced with a new life decision and to help you to move beyond the boundaries of your comfort zone.

1. *Weigh the pros and cons.* Make a list of all the pros and cons related to making the change and evaluate them carefully. This helps you alleviate confusion and enables you to distinguish between fantasy and reality. Once you have all the pros and cons listed, go back and rate each item listed on the pro side, using a scale of 1 to 10, based on its importance or value to you (1 is the lowest importance or value to you and 10 is the highest). Now rate each item listed on the con side, using a scale of 1 to 10, based on its degree of negative impact (1 is the lowest negative impact and 10 is the highest—a deal-breaker). Now add up the total in each column and compare them. Are there more pros or cons? Are there any 10s (deal-breakers) on your con side?

2. *Check in with your intuition.* Ask yourself: *How does this sit with me? How does it feel?* Your intuition is an instinctive knowing—or gut feeling—about whether or not something is right for you. It's not a conclusion you

reach based on reasoning or emotions. Emotions and intuition are very different. Your emotions can change from day to day, even moment to moment. Your intuitive feeling about something, on the other hand, tends to remain pretty consistent. If you're making a big decision that takes you out of your comfort zone, you need to feel certain that it's the right one. So you'll want to check in with your intuition over a period of time—over days or weeks or even months—to see how that decision sits with you. Later in the book, we'll be focusing more intently on developing your intuition, which is an important tool for living in alignment with your authentic self.

3. *Do a reality check.* Ask yourself: *Is this a decision that's aligned with my capabilities, with my goals, with who I really am?* Drill down as far as you need to go, hitting all of the relevant points. For example: *Is this something I can afford? How will it affect other aspects of my life? What are the logistics? What am I hoping to gain? Is that goal within my reach?*

Taking Manageable Steps

Not every step forward has to be a big one. Sometimes you have to take baby steps when moving beyond your comfort zone. For some of my clients who are alone, issues related to meeting new people, going to social events, trying new things, and doing things by themselves can produce fear. If you're alone and your fears keep you isolated, then aloneness can turn into loneliness. Your fears are cutting you off from people and activities that can substantially enrich your life.

For example, it's not uncommon for women to be afraid of dining out alone, or going to the movies, the theater, or an art exhibit by themselves. It falls so far outside of their comfort zones that they just don't do it. Let's say you have a fear of going out to dinner by yourself. The idea of it scares you. When you imagine going to a restaurant by yourself, what do you see? Where is your fear coming from? If you're a woman, it might be coming from a limiting belief that a woman who goes out by herself is a loser, a belief that's tied to the spinster myth. It might be coming from a lack of self-esteem, a feeling of not being good enough, of being unworthy. It could spring from a limiting belief that a woman should only go out to dinner with a date. Maybe it's a fear of meeting new people and not having a buffer in the form of another person—a fear that someone may talk to you and you won't know what to say. It might be a fear that other people will be watching you; that you'll be uncomfortable with everyone's eyes on you. To manage the fear, I encourage my clients to become aware of their gloom-and-doom movie—to see what they're *imagining* is going to happen. Then I tell them to dig deeper and figure out what limiting belief may be invoking their fear.

Here, again, are the Five Steps to Managing Fear:

- Name the fear.

- Identify the movie.

- Do a reality check.

- Change the movie.

- Identify the limiting belief.

The next step is to take action to create a new reality. When I have clients with a fear of going somewhere by themselves, I ask them if they're willing to make a commitment to going out to dinner alone. I suggest that they go to a restaurant that has a bar area and sit at the bar. That allows contact with other people. When you're sitting at a table, you don't have an opportunity to connect with other people. In Europe, people who dine alone often share a table with strangers. That's not generally true in the United States. So I suggest a restaurant with a nice bar and assign my clients the action step of initiating a conversation with at least one new person. If that person isn't receptive, then they have to wait and start up a conversation with someone else. I suggest that they bring a book or magazine to occupy themselves while they eat and to help relieve any discomfort or self-consciousness. I encourage them to order a lovely dinner and to focus on enjoying the experience.

When you're grappling with fears that relate to meeting new people or trying new experiences, the attitude you project to others becomes important. You'll want to project confidence and self-assurance. When you feel fearful and uncomfortable, that's what you'll project. It sends a message to other people to steer clear. But once you replace your fearful fantasy with a new movie, it will be easier for you to project a positive image that's more aligned with reality.

I had a female client who wanted to expand her circle of friends and have a more active social life. She loved to dance, but she was uncomfortable going to a dance venue by herself. She lived in Boston, so I gave her an assignment: go to *Dance Free,* a big music hall in Boston where all kinds of people go to dance by themselves or with others. I also asked her to initiate contact with at least one new person. On her first attempt, she went to the dance hall but didn't talk to anyone and was uncomfortable dancing by herself. Instead, she stood off to the side, exuding the energy of a classic wallflower, feeling alone in the crowd. So we did some more coaching around how she could project a more open attitude, identifying the specific new behaviors that would produce her desired outcome of meeting new people. For example, rather than waiting for people to approach her, she could initiate contact by starting a conversation. If her fear of rejection kicked in, I encouraged her to change her gloom-and-doom movie to one in which people were warmly receptive. I reminded her that at first she wouldn't feel more confident on the inside, but by consciously changing her thoughts and old behaviors, she would generate the new outcomes that, over time, would boost her confidence in social situations. On her second trip to *Dance Free,* she introduced herself to and connected with a new group of people. At the close of the evening, they invited her to join them for a glass of wine at a local pub, and she ended up enjoying the whole experience.

When you start to manage your fear and move out of your comfort zone, the results can be astounding. You gain heightened self-esteem and greater self-trust. You build on your track record of success, which makes it easier to step out again. Not only does your comfort zone get bigger, but you open up a world of new opportunities for yourself.

When you're focused on mastering aloneness, the movie to play in your mind is one full of love, abundance, joy, and health—a movie in which you're living the life you were born to live. I'll help you to create that movie in detail in Chapter 8, "Creating Your Life Vision." But before you can make your new life movie a reality, it's important to identify the fears that hold you back and the limiting beliefs that drive them. The following exercise is designed to help you do this.

Exercise: Fears and Core Beliefs

Step One: Identifying your Fears

In your journal, write down all the fears that hold you back in your life, that keep you from moving forward and into the life to which you aspire. These can run the gamut from everyday fears to deeper ones. Try to be as specific as you can. Here are some examples:

- I'm afraid to go to a party by myself.

- I'm afraid to confront people when there's a problem.

- I'm afraid to speak in front of a group of people.

- I'm afraid I can't manage my money.

- I'm afraid of sounding stupid.

- I'm always afraid I'm going to make a mistake.

- I'm afraid of spending the rest of my life alone.

- I'm always afraid I'm going to embarrass myself.

Step Two: Linking Your Fears and Core Beliefs

Now, dig a little deeper. Think carefully about each fear on your list, and consider what you're really afraid of—what the underlying fear is. For example, if you're afraid of going to a party by yourself, what are you *really* afraid of? Being judged? Being rejected? Appearing foolish? In your journal, work through each fear until you find the underlying fear. For example, if you are afraid of being judged, the underlying fear might be: *Others will think there's something wrong with me.* If you're afraid of making conversation, your underlying fear might be: *I'll say something stupid and embarrass myself.*

Now open your journal and write "My Fears and Core Beliefs" at the top of the page. Make a list of all your fears, and then write down the core limiting belief associated with each fear. You might find it helpful to refer to the Core Limiting Beliefs exercise you completed in Chapter 3, "Uncovering Your Conditioned Self" (see page 69). Here are some examples:

Underlying Fear	*Core Limiting Belief*
I'll fail.	I'm not good enough.
I'll be rejected.	I'm unworthy.
I'll get hurt.	People are untrustworthy and hurtful.
I'll become destitute.	I can't provide for myself.
Others will judge me.	There's something wrong with me.
No one will ever love me.	I'm unlovable.

Step Three: Exploring One of Your Fears

Now pick one of the fears you put on your list and go through the following five steps to gain greater awareness of the fear and the core limiting belief that drives it.

1. *Instead of resisting it, acknowledge the fear by identifying it.* For example, "I'm afraid I will fail" or "I'm afraid I'll be rejected" or "I'm afraid I won't be good enough."

2. *Notice the movie you're running*—the image you're playing in your mind. Ask yourself: *What am I imagining will happen?*

3. *Do a reality check.* Figure out if your fears have any real basis in fact. Be as methodical as you need to be.

4. *Change the movie that you're running in your head.* Replace it with a movie that supports your goals, rather than undermines them.

5. *Identify the core limiting belief you're violating by pursuing your goal.* Which old belief set the FEAR dynamic in motion? In my own example, it was: *I'm not good enough.*

Step Four: Taking It to the Next Level

As you go through your daily life over the next week, be observant and become aware of any old trance states, fears, and reactive behaviors that may emerge, as well as the inner movie you're playing that produces those trance states or fears. Write down what you observe in your journal. This will help you gain insight into the role fear is playing in your life and begin to change the patterns at work.

CHAPTER 5

LIVING DELIBERATELY VERSUS BY DEFAULT

As I was winding my way through my own personal-development work, I came to a point where I looked back and thought: *If I had known then what I know now, my life would be very different.* But no one ever sat me down and explained that everything I did or would do in my life would have consequences. I wish my parents had been able to do that. In truth, it's not a lesson most people learn until late in life—if at all.

The law of cause and effect is one of life's great truisms. Newton's third law of motion says it this way: To every action there is an equal and opposite reaction. In common usage, that idea most often translates into: *For every action, there is a reaction.* In philosophy, the concept can be traced back to the ancients. It was Cicero who said: "As you have sown, so shall you reap." The same idea can be found in both Christianity and Judaism— in the New Testament and the Old. In Eastern religions, the idea of karma, found in the Hindu, Jain, Sikh, and

Buddhist faiths, embraces the concept of cause and effect. Karma encompasses all that an individual has done, is doing, and will do—the effects of which are believed to create all that a person experiences. What you sow is what you reap. Your chickens come home to roost. What goes around comes around.

When applied to human behavior, the law of cause and effect translates into the idea that through our actions, we generate outcomes. And it applies to every one of us. Mastering the art of aloneness involves recognizing that your actions have consequences, and by those actions, you create your own life experiences. You are born with the willpower to make choices: to choose your words, your actions, and even your own thoughts. Those choices, in turn, affect every aspect of your life.

Most people behave as if cause and effect didn't exist. They go through their lives on autopilot, acting and reacting to events without thinking carefully about—or understanding—the possible results of those actions or the role they've played in creating the circumstances of their lives.

All of us make major life decisions without consciously understanding that these decisions will affect our future in immeasurable ways. For example, by getting married at the age of 23 in the wake of a whirlwind romance and foregoing a career, I was making a choice that would have an enormous impact on my future life and security and that of my children. But I never saw it that way. I was on autopilot. I was in love. I was escaping from one reality into another. I was acting on the core beliefs I had internalized as the result of a difficult childhood. And I was looking for something to fill a void in myself—based on underlying motivations of which I was unaware.

Just as importantly, many of us go through each day oblivious to the connection between the actions we take and the results they produce. Every minute of every day, you're faced with choices. What should I eat? Yogurt? A Big Mac? Nothing at all? How should I spend my leisure time? Working in the garden? Taking a bike ride? Watching TV? How should I respond to this crisis? To someone's rudeness? Or someone's generosity? How should I treat my co-workers? My friends? My children? All of these day-to-day decisions ultimately add up to the life you have today and the life you'll have in the future.

This chapter is about living more deliberately. That means living consciously in every moment so that you can begin to make changes in your life and take full responsibility for your actions, your choices, and your decisions. Only by living more deliberately can you begin to generate the results you want and begin to live the life you desire. Only by living deliberately can you begin to master the art of aloneness.

The Three Levels of Creation

At the beginning of every Mastering the Art of Aloneness workshop, I tell people that aloneness is a choice. People come to my workshops and individual coaching programs feeling very lonely and believing that they don't want to be alone. I challenge that idea by telling them: "If you truly didn't want to be alone, there are plenty of people you could choose for a relationship. But on some level you're choosing to be alone instead." Of course, being alone is not usually a conscious choice. You may believe you want to be in a relationship, but on an unconscious level, there's a part of you that's holding you back. It may be that some part of you feels unworthy of a relationship or is afraid of being intimate for fear of being rejected, or you may simply be unwilling to settle for someone who isn't right for you. Whatever your reason, at some level, *it is a choice.* That can be a pretty empowering thought. It moves you out of the role of victim and into the role of creator. It moves you out of the role of blaming and into the role of taking responsibility.

Things don't just happen to you. You are the creator of nearly all of your life experiences—although you may not be fully conscious of the role you are playing in their creation. The work in this chapter involves a number of steps. The first involves the process of understanding how the laws of cause and effect come into play in your life—of simply recognizing that by your actions you produce results. This means looking closely at your behavior and taking responsibility for the results that behavior generates. It means becoming conscious of everything you do.

There are three levels at which we participate in generating our own experience: *creating, promoting,* and *allowing.* This is a powerful concept I first learned at the Insight Seminar I attended in 1982—although I failed to truly incorporate this understanding into my life until many years later. It is a valuable tool for helping you understand and recognize the role you play in creating your own life. By looking at events in your life through this lens, you can begin to take greater responsibility. It helps you see that, even in subtle ways, your behavior and actions influence the outcomes you experience.

Here's an example. Let's say you're going to a ball game with a friend, and you're both standing in line to get your tickets at the box office. Someone steps in at the front of the line—a teenage boy—and it turns into a confrontation. Here are the various roles you might play:

- *Creating.* You call out something hostile to the teenager. "Hey, kid, this is a line. Step to the back." And his father, who was holding his place, turns around and screams at you: "Hey, buddy, shut up!" It escalates into a physical scuffle and you get hurt. You initiated that situation through your words—you *created* the situation.

- *Promoting.* Your friend, who's standing in line with you, is the one who gets upset and says, "Hey, kid, this is a line. Step to the back." The father, who was holding his place, turns around and screams at your friend: "Shut up, you idiot!" Your friend threatens to punch him and you say to your friend, "Yeah, smack him! He deserves it!" It turns into a physical scuffle and your friend gets hurt. You *promoted* that situation by encouraging your friend to attack the other person, thereby helping to create it.

- *Allowing.* Another bystander steps up to the teenager, pushes him out of line and says, "Hey, kid, you broke into this line." A scuffle ensues and the teenager gets badly hurt. You stand by and take no action to stop it. By doing nothing, you're *allowing* that situation to unfold.

Take any situation in which you felt like a victim; let's say something happened to you but you didn't cause it or have any responsibility for it. If you look carefully and honestly at how the situation unfolded, most of the time you'll find it relates to something you did or said—or failed to say or do. Your actions created the situation or promoted it or allowed it. These three levels of creation become valuable tools for taking responsibility—for understanding your past, moving forward, and recognizing how the laws of cause and effect play a major role in your life.

Let me share an example that actually happened in my own life. In the early '80s, I was living in Los Angeles with my husband and I'd recently bought a brand-new car. Back then, I was a very pushy and angry person. As a Rebel, I was always on the offensive; that was my default operating style. One afternoon, I was on my way to meet my husband for lunch at a restaurant. First I'll describe what happened that day from the perspective of being a victim, then from a more accountable perspective that draws on the concept of creating, promoting, and allowing.

Here's the victim story: I was about to pull into a space in a parking lot when this car came out of nowhere. The man in the driver's seat started blasting his horn at me. I parked my car and was just minding my own business, when he climbed out of his car in a rage and started screaming at me. He accused me of taking his parking space. So I just walked away and went into the building to meet my husband. When I came back out, I saw that this crazy guy had keyed both sides of my brand-new car!

Here's what actually happened, from the perspective of taking responsibility: The truth is, I didn't really know whose parking space it was. It was a parking lot. I had no idea whether he'd been there before me, waiting to get into the parking space, or not. I saw the spot, and I squeezed into it very quickly, not caring whether anyone was waiting for the space. He said he was there first. And, the truth is, I had actually seen him out of the corner of my eye and zipped into the space anyway. I saw a parking spot and decided it was my space. That was my operating style. My behavior had actually *created* the situation. When he started yelling at me, I yelled right back—so I *promoted* the escalation of the confrontation by invoking more of his rage. Finally, as I turned to walk into the building, I used foul language, audibly cursing him under my breath. And, as I walked away, I had this strong intuitive feeling that he might do something to my car, and I ignored my intuition. By not listening to my intuition, I *allowed* him to key my car.

That's an example of the three different levels of creation at work. When we're in the victim mode, we conveniently omit pieces of the story. We spin it. We spin the truth to ourselves and to others so we don't have to take responsibility. We tell ourselves: *It wasn't my fault.*

If you consider my parking-lot example, you'll see that there were many different ways I could have responded. I could have behaved in a considerate, respectful, and less aggressive manner on the front end—aware that there was another driver nearby, ceding the parking space when I saw him. Once the other driver emerged in a rage, I could have responded calmly and apologized, or even moved my car. I could have made an effort not to escalate the situation. By adopting a conciliatory posture, you can generally defuse most situations.

In order to see the role you played in a situation, you have to break it down and look at it from a position of responsibility by asking yourself: *What did I do to create the situation, to promote it, or to allow it?* Once you start looking at the world this way, you'll be amazed by what you see. You begin to get a much clearer picture of the role you play in every situation of your life. You can then use this as a powerful tool to live more deliberately. As events in your life unfold, be more conscious of your actions. With everything you do, ask yourself: *What is the result I want to achieve?* One note: as you go through this self-evaluation process, don't judge yourself. Don't beat yourself up for situations you've created, promoted, or allowed. Remember, we're all doing the best we can at any given moment. By understanding your actions and taking greater responsibility for your behavior as you move forward, you'll begin to see that you are, indeed, the creator of your own life.

Exercise: Creating, Promoting, and Allowing

Think of a past situation in which you felt like a victim. In your journal, write the story out from the victim perspective (playing the blame game and taking no responsibility for how you created, promoted, or allowed it). Then write it out again, this time from a place of responsibility, including what you did or said (or failed to do or say) that created, promoted, or allowed the situation to unfold. Now write down what you could have done or said (or not done or said) that could have produced a better outcome.

Make this exercise a tool for moving your life in a new direction. Instead of blaming others, view the events in your life as an opportunity to take greater responsibility for yourself and your life. When something goes wrong, ask yourself:

- What was my role in this situation? How did I create, promote, or allow it?

- How could I have created, allowed, or promoted a different outcome?

- What can I learn from this experience?

- How can I create a better outcome in a similar situation going forward?

Deliberation Versus Default

When you're living by default, you're automatically reacting to life in habitual ways, many of which may be limiting you and your life. In contrast, living deliberately means making more conscious and constructive life choices. When you're living deliberately, you're living from a position of responsibility; you're making choices with greater awareness. You've taken yourself off autopilot, so you're better prepared to align your actions with the results you want to achieve.

This is an important step in mastering the art of aloneness because, as you move through this book, you're going to get a clearer sense of the direction you want your life to go. If you start to live more deliberately now, you'll be better prepared to make the choices you need to make down the road—every day—to keep your actions in alignment with that direction. By moving through life in a state of consciousness, you have the opportunity to improve your health and enjoy greater emotional and physical well-being. When your actions are aligned with your conscious intentions, you'll find that life is smoother, less conflicted.

When you're not living deliberately, you're living from your *default operating system.* As you'll recall, your default operating system is made up of the core beliefs and habitual behaviors you adopted during your formative years. Living by default is, in one sense, the path of least resistance, because it's what you already know; it's part of your comfort zone. But, because most people grew up in dysfunctional families, their default operating systems are often based on patterns that limit them. Their operating systems were designed to help them adapt to life within their families, not to produce effective results as adults. Living by default gives you less control over the results you generate. You're stuck with whatever you get— and you might not like whatever it is you're getting.

Here's an example of how living by default can trip you up. Let's say you want to have a healthier lifestyle, but you're an approval-seeker. Your operating style is driven by the core limiting belief: *Other people's needs are more important than my own.* You're always putting your needs on the back burner to take care of everyone else's. You never say no. And you're so busy trying to make everyone else happy that you neglect yourself. People who live that way tend to be overwhelmed; they're under constant stress. Living under stress is associated with all kinds of issues, including health problems. Maybe making other people's needs more important than your own helped you avoid conflict in your family growing up. But, as an adult, your operating style is interfering with the results you desire.

Here's another example. Let's say that you believe people can't be trusted—that they're out to get you. If that's one of your core limiting beliefs, you may have a confrontational and/or defensive behavioral style. You might be difficult and anger easily. As a result, you create conflicts at every turn. You're living ineffectively because you consistently alienate people around you. Maybe you have trouble keeping a job and getting along with co-workers because you're always challenging everything and blaming everyone else. Your oppositional style seeps into your personal life, wreaking havoc in your relationships. Your behavior is counterproductive—and it's driven by an underlying belief that's been inside of you since childhood.

No matter what your core limiting beliefs are, you pay a high price for letting them run your life. In my own life, I count my divorce among those costs. Many times I've thought that if my husband and I had been aware of the dysfunctional patterns we each brought from childhood into our marriage, perhaps we could have transformed it into a healthier relationship and provided an intact family for our children.

A crucial step in mastering the art of aloneness is identifying and shedding those core limiting beliefs and putting a new operating system in place. But that's something that takes a great deal of work, including the exploration of your family of origin. That's the work of mastering the art of aloneness. Until you have a new operating system in place that's based on a more constructive set of beliefs, you'll need to work consciously and diligently to monitor and redirect your behavior. By living deliberately, you gradually begin to think and behave in new ways that override the default operating system that's been derailing you.

Aligning Your Actions with Your Desired Results

If you're living by default, there's a good chance that your thoughts and behaviors are out of sync with the results you want in your life. You can begin to understand the connection between your desires, your thoughts, and the actions you take by asking yourself three very basic questions:

- How am I treating myself?

- What kind of messages am I sending to myself?

- What kind of relationships am I creating in my life?

When you start asking yourself these questions, you're apt to find that your thoughts and behaviors are at cross-purposes with your desires. Here are a few examples that often emerge with my clients:

- *How am I treating myself?* Let's say you want to have an active social life, with a lot of intelligent, uplifting people around you. You want a high level of meaningful interaction and positive energy in your life. You're the person who's responsible for what happens in your life, and it takes energy to live that way. But if you're tired, if you're in a depleting job, if you're not taking good care of yourself, it's going to get in the way of your ability to live the life you seek. To have a healthy social life, you have to feel good about yourself; you have to possess and project a sense of well-being. So where do you begin? You begin with yourself. You have to think about how you're treating your body and what you need to do to have the energy you need to live the life you want. This means making healthy choices about what you eat and drink—and what you're not going to eat and drink—as well as healthy choices about exercise and sleep. By living deliberately, you can begin to change the way you treat yourself.

• *What kinds of messages am I sending to myself?* It may be that you want to feel good about yourself, but you're constantly telling yourself that you're lazy. That means you're undermining yourself. You're defeating your purpose by sending a message to yourself that lowers your self-esteem. Imagine that you want to find a better job. Instead of telling yourself how lazy you are, you should be sending yourself messages of love and compassion. Living deliberately means looking deeper into the patterns that are causing you to feel unmotivated, but at the same time sending yourself positive, loving messages.

Yet another example might be that you're thinking about starting your own business, but you're constantly undermining yourself by saying: *I'm not good enough.* Or: *No one will ever want my services.* If you're sending yourself negative messages, you'll never be able to get your business off the ground. You have to believe in yourself to be able to sell yourself to others. To be able to be successful in your own business, you have to send yourself positive messages—then you'll exude the confidence you need to attract customers.

Here are some of the self-defeating messages we send ourselves: *No one will ever love me. I'm lazy. I can't do anything right. I'm too old. I'm undisciplined. I'm stupid.* I had a client who—every time she made a mistake or misplaced her keys or dropped something—would whisper to herself, "You're pitiful." Imagine how you'd feel if someone told you how pitiful you were day after day. Ask yourself: *If I want to feel good about myself, what kinds of messages do I need to send to myself? What kinds of words do I need to be using?*

• *What kinds of relationships am I creating in my life?* Imagine that you want to have healthy, caring, supportive friendships with people, but you continually participate in friendships with people who make you feel bad—maybe your friends are not dependable; maybe they're critical and judgmental; maybe they don't show up on time or always cancel their plans with you at the last minute. Ultimately, they do things that make you feel bad about yourself. You have to make a conscious decision not to stay in those kinds of relationships or to address those issues as they arise.

I had one client who made a simple rule for herself when she began the process of living more deliberately. That was: I'm not going to hang around with anyone who makes me feel bad. That one decision dramatically changed the quality of her life and, of course, her relationships with others.

I'm working with a client right now who's struggling with whether or not to continue in a friendship with a woman she's known since she was 14 years old. Together, we made a list of all the pros and cons of the relationship. Her list of pros included only two items: that they had a history together and they both like to shop. Her list of cons was a long one, and included: my friend is condescending; she talks about me behind my back; she breaks commitments; she reveals my confidences to others. The bottom line: my client didn't like or trust her friend. She felt awful every time she was around her. In order to change her life and feel better about herself, she recognized that she needed to stop seeing this friend. She then began to change her relationships with the other people in her life as well.

I had an identical experience at one point in my own life. As I began my personal-development work, I began to notice that many of my women friends were critical and judgmental. I realized that I was replicating the relationship I'd had with my mother, who would say things to me like: "Your hair is so frizzy. Can't you do something about it?" Or: "Can't you put on a nice dress instead of those pants?" Once I recognized the problem, I learned to set healthy boundaries with my friends—to address issues as they arose, to set boundaries around how I did and didn't want to be treated, and to let go of relationships that were not supportive and healthy.

Mastering the art of aloneness involves changing the way you treat yourself and others. To change those patterns, you have to begin to live more deliberately. The first step toward living deliberately involves recognizing the relationship between cause and effect in your life. The rest of this chapter is devoted to the other four steps that will help you get there:

- Developing your Inner Nurturing Parent

- Becoming the master of your emotions

- Enlisting the power of thought

- Honoring your intuition

Developing Your Inner Nurturing Parent

We are, each of us, a mix of contradictory feelings and thoughts. There may be a part of you that says, "I want to master the art of aloneness. I want to become more complete on my own." Yet, at the same time, another part of you still longs for Prince or Princess

Charming to come along and rescue you so that, poof, all your troubles will go away. Following the same line of thought, part of you may believe that you're unworthy of love, while another part of you believes precisely the opposite: that you are a loveable and wonderful person. These conflicting thoughts and feelings don't mean that you're crazy—they are just part of the human conditions that affect us all.

I was trained in a phenomenal technique called voice dialogue that was developed by psychologists Hal and Sidra Stone. It's a therapeutic modality I use to help clients break through their defense mechanisms and gain greater awareness of the patterns rooted in the unconscious self. I use voice dialoguing to allow the different parts of my clients to emerge, to help them reclaim their innate wholeness by becoming more aware of which parts of them are dominant and activated in their lives and which parts of them are underdeveloped or have been submerged. The process involves identifying the various contradictory "voices" that find their home in each of us.

For example, say I have a client named Jane. Here's how a pared-down version of a voice-dialoguing session might sound. Jane might be talking about the fact that she's feeling lonely; she wants to have a fuller life and become more independent. Then, suddenly, she might say, "I'm afraid I'm going to be alone forever. I'm afraid no one is ever going to want me." We explore this part of Jane: Who is it? "This is the part of me that's afraid I'll be alone for the rest of my life." Then I might ask: "How often do you show up in Jane's life?" "All the time. But Jane's uncomfortable with me. She doesn't like me, so she just pushes me away by distracting herself with work." "Close your eyes and remember the first time you

showed up in Jane's life." "I was at school. I felt separate from everyone else and left out." Try to remember
a specific incident: "I went home and cried and told
my mom. She told me to go do my homework. Just do
your work. That's what school's for, she told me." Then
another part of Jane might appear: "I know I can be
happy on my own. I can focus on my goals and be self-
sufficient." "What part of Jane are you?" "I'm the part
that's strong, that knows what she wants, that possesses
self-confidence. I want to start my own business." This
is not a case of a split personality or multiple personality disorder—in fact, voice dialogue would not be appropriate in either of these cases. Jane, like many of us, is
simply a multifaceted human being made up of many
different parts.

In the course of voice dialoguing with clients over
the years, I've noticed that there's one specific voice that
inevitably shows up: the *Inner Critical Parent*. It's the
part of you that criticizes, judges, or blames yourself.
It's the voice that just about everybody has inside that
says things like: "You should be ashamed of yourself" or
"You're not trying hard enough" or "You're too fat" or
"You're too loud."

The specific messages vary from person to person,
but the critical parent is typically in there somewhere.
Why? Because very few of us had truly nurturing parents
growing up. And that, of course, is because most of our
parents never had truly nurturing parents. Again, I want
to remind you that this process isn't about casting blame
on anyone. I hope you'll develop compassion for your
parents and yourself as you continue to move through
your inner work. Remember, most parents' operating
styles are a product of their own experiences growing

up—the patterns of their families of origin. In their own way, your parents have suffered just as you have.

So how do you break this self-defeating cycle and put an end to this painful legacy? By consciously developing what I call the *Inner Nurturing Parent* inside yourself. This technique is one of the cornerstones of mastering the art of aloneness, and it will significantly transform your life. With it comes the ability to love yourself, to nurture yourself, and to create ideal relationships—starting with your relationship with *yourself.*

If you step back and think about it, you may discover that you really don't treat yourself very well. Most of us break promises to ourselves. We eat poorly. We don't get enough sleep. We don't take good care of our bodies. We engage in relationships that are abusive, at worst, and unsupportive, at best. We settle for less at every turn. We allow ourselves to be undercompensated at work and undervalued in our relationships. It's no wonder that so many of us look to others for our self-validation. We're not very good at validating ourselves. In fact, if most people treated others the way they treat themselves, they wouldn't have too many friends.

To begin treating yourself better, you're going to develop your own Inner Nurturing Parent. How? Imagine you had a little child in your care. What would you do? You'd make every effort to keep him healthy and safe; to love and support and praise him; to be forgiving of his mistakes, his inevitable slips; and to let him know how special, how precious, how important he is. That's what a loving parent does. Only, in this case, you're going to be the parent *and* the child. Here, in the most practical terms, is what you do:

- *Send loving messages to yourself.* Tell yourself, "I love you and appreciate who you are." When you do something well, give yourself a pat on the back. Say: "Great job! I'm so proud of you." When you're struggling or feeling low, be supportive by saying: "I'm here for you. You're not alone."

- *Take good care of yourself.* A loving parent would make sure you eat right and get plenty of rest, sleep, fresh air, and exercise. Keep yourself healthy and fit. Practicing good self-care is an essential step in this process.

- *Do nice things for yourself.* Get into the habit of doing special things for yourself. Make yourself a cup of tea with the nurturing energy that you'd have when preparing tea for someone you love, and find a relaxing place to sit and enjoy it. Visit the sauna, get a massage, or draw yourself a bath filled with special salts or bubbles. Linger in it and relax. Make yourself a candlelight dinner—a delicious meal in a special setting. Coddle yourself. Treat yourself as a loving parent would treat you.

- *Set boundaries with other people.* Let people know what you want and don't want. Tell them what's okay for you and what's not. If you have a friend who's always late and you end up waiting for her and feeling annoyed, tell her how you feel. Let people know when something's bothering you. A nurturing parent wouldn't let someone treat you badly. A loving parent makes sure his or her child's needs are met.

- *Become your own advocate.* If someone is disrespectful or hurtful to you, speak up. Tell them you don't want to be spoken to that way. If someone was unkind, hostile, or verbally abusive to your child, you'd stand up for him. Protect yourself as a nurturing parent would protect you.

- *Believe in yourself.* A nurturing parent would highlight your uniqueness, tell you how special you are, encourage you to build on your strengths, and support you in a loving, nonjudgmental way. A nurturing parent says: "You can do it." "I believe in you." Become your strongest supporter, coach, and cheerleader.

- *Be compassionate.* Have compassion for your humanity and your flaws. You're human and you're going to make mistakes. Look at yourself through the eyes of a loving parent; don't punish or criticize yourself. Reassure yourself. Comfort yourself. Accept yourself unconditionally. And show that same compassion for your own parents and others, because, remember, they too are human.

Becoming the Master of Your Emotions

When you begin to live more deliberately, you'll find that your emotions will inevitably trip you up. You find yourself feeling sad and lonely on a Saturday night, and it drives you straight to the donut store—despite your intention to eat a healthier diet—because that's your default pattern. Or you're feeling good about yourself until someone's sneering comment about your ideas at a meeting derails your presentation by tapping into your insecurities. Again, you've been pushed into default mode. Or maybe your ex-spouse disrupts your day, triggering old feelings of anger and resentment, and you blow up unexpectedly. Then you're no longer treating yourself—or others—in a way that's aligned with the results you want to have. It's because your habitual behaviors—and the core limiting beliefs that underlie them—are driving your emotions. It takes a lot of work and energy to begin to internalize a new set of beliefs; until you do, you'll be at the mercy of your feelings and your habitual reactions to them. Those reactions can drive you off course.

A key element of this phase of mastering the art of aloneness involves managing your emotions. That takes a conscious effort. It means stepping back from yourself and looking at your emotions from a place of detachment, as if through the lens of the neutral observer, without ego attachment or judgment. It means deciding consciously how you want to respond, instead of simply reacting and letting your emotional impulses take over.

Different people have different levels of emotionality. Some are more feeling-oriented; they experience their emotions more intensely. For them, emotions can swell like a tidal wave, so they can easily find themselves completely at the mercy of their feelings and reactions. It might be their innate nature or it might be that they grew up in a family where people thrived on drama. Or it could be a combination of factors. If you're a person who can be ruled by or overwhelmed by your feelings, you may find managing them a bit more challenging. For other people, who are more analytical and thinking-oriented, emotions may feel like a ripple instead of a wave. Still others are so used to suppressing their feelings that they might not even recognize them when they arise. But recognizing your feelings is the first step toward managing them.

Daniel Goleman, in his landmark book *Emotional Intelligence,* made the case that a high level of emotional intelligence—which includes such fundamental characteristics as self-awareness, self-management, social awareness, and the ability to manage relationships[1]—is just as important to success in life as a high IQ, and that, ultimately, moral instincts spring from such "underlying emotional capacities" as impulse control and empathy.[2]

For our purposes, emotional intelligence involves impulse control and self-management. It means being able to exercise enough self-discipline when you're in the middle of an emotional reaction to make a conscious decision about what kind of behavior you want to exhibit or what action you want to take. Take the incident I described earlier when my car was keyed. At the time, I lacked self-awareness and impulse control. I wasn't thinking about anything except parking my car and running off to lunch, and I reacted to anger with anger. Today, I would decide that it's more emotionally intelligent to let the angry man have the space. I certainly understand now that when you greet anger with anger, it's like natural combustion: everything escalates. And I know more now about how to defuse such a situation.

To begin to develop greater emotional intelligence, ask yourself: *What kind of inner emotional state do I want to walk around in? Do I want to walk around with a junkyard inside of me—full of negative feelings such as anger, sadness, and resentment? Or do I want to walk around feeling loving, joyful, and compassionate? Wouldn't I rather walk around with a beautiful garden inside of me?*

Imagine you're at the grocery store, riffling through your wallet and you're taking too long. Somebody behind you snaps, "Can't you hurry up?" You have a choice. You can react emotionally and snap back in anger, or you can say, "I'm sorry I'm taking so long. I'll just be a minute." That will defuse the situation immediately. It's like when you're on the phone waiting for a customer service representative to come on the line, very nearly at your wit's end, and then this friendly, warm voice comes on and says, "I'm really sorry you're having a problem. How can I help you?" It naturally defuses your irritation. The key to emotional intelligence is to consistently and deliberately respond to situations in ways that say: I'm not interested in escalating this situation; I'm interested in letting my inner garden flourish, and I'm not going to let other people's emotions pollute my internal environment.

Often, when people react emotionally to a situation, it's their egos that have been triggered. The ego is saying something like: You can't push *me* around. You can't take *my* space. Who do you think you are? All too often, the short-term gratification of getting back at somebody becomes more important than the long-term gratification of living a peaceful, joyful, happy life.

Of course, anger and irritability are just two emotions that can derail your sense of well-being and relationships with others. Sadness, pain, hopelessness, frustration, disappointment—all are feelings that can derail you. For many people grappling with aloneness, depression can be a major stumbling block. Depression can be experienced in different ways, from a mild sense of the blues related to a specific situation to a full-blown clinical depression driven by biological factors. A biologically based depression typically can't be remedied by simply refocusing your thoughts, and in many cases it requires medication. But refocusing your thoughts can be a valuable way to handle a mild or situational depression. In *Emotional Intelligence,* Daniel Goleman notes that the worst way to deal with a case of the blues is rumination—giving in to your feelings and thinking and rethinking through what's bothering you. According to Goleman, the best response is to focus your attention on something else—get up and get out; be around other people; engage in some activity to get your mind off it and get out of yourself. That's a great example of living deliberately.

Enlisting the Power of Thought

"Every thought you have has an energy that will either strengthen or weaken you," writes Wayne Dyer in *The Power of Intention.*[3] Early in this book, I talked about the importance of changing the way you think about being alone and about the fact that "you are what you think." In this chapter, I've talked about some of the undermining messages we send to ourselves. What *we think* plays a significant role in transforming our lives.

It goes beyond having a positive attitude; it extends to directing your thinking toward your purpose.

Remember the woman I mentioned earlier who made a simple rule: she wasn't going to spend time with anyone who made her feel bad. Once she started living more deliberately, she found herself drawn to people who exuded what she called "positive energy," because they made her feel good. She made a study of them. Who were these people? What did they have in common? She found that either they'd been brought up in loving, nurturing families—meaning that they had close, supportive relationships with their parents and siblings, believed in themselves, and were comfortable being supportive of others—or, more often, they had done intensive personal-development work through therapy, support groups, coaching, or some spiritual practice. Some were practitioners of yoga and meditation; they were people who made a conscious effort to stay centered, to live a healthy life, to be loving and compassionate. Others were deeply spiritual; they were connected to a higher power; they looked for the good in others; they were deliberate in their desire to be loving and compassionate, and they were neither judgmental nor self-righteous nor critical. Their positive energy infused everything they did.

Countless books have been written about the power of positive energy and of directing your thinking toward your goals, often called the power of attraction. These range from Norman Vincent Peale's *The Power of Positive Thinking,* first published in 1952 and read by millions of people, to Wayne Dyer's *The Power of Intention,* to the many books of Deepak Chopra and of Tony Robbins. Each offers a unique philosophy and approach for tapping into positive energy and directing it toward the achievement of a central purpose. Like my fellow writers, I, too, believe that positive thinking—and harnessing the power of positive energy—is an essential piece of the work that's necessary for aligning your actions with your purpose. But I *do* believe that it's work. While deliberately focusing your thinking on the results you want to create is essential to personal transformation, the work doesn't stop there. You must *take action* to produce the results you want; you can't *rely solely* on meditation, harnessing the energy of the universe, thinking positively, or aligning your thoughts with your purpose. Even so, I believe that your thoughts are a powerful tool that support and help facilitate your actions. I also believe that people emit positive and negative energy through their thoughts, and that by directing your thoughts toward the results you desire, you are far more likely to move in that direction.

There is a growing body of scientific evidence that the mind is a far more powerful force than ever imagined. For almost three decades, Bernie Siegel, M.D., has been working in the area of mind-body healing. His credentials are impressive: a medical doctorate from Cornell Medical College and surgical training at Yale. Siegel has been the proponent of such techniques as visualization, imagery, and positive thinking to help patients heal and to increase the effectiveness of standard medical and surgical treatments. Research has shown that, by using visual imagery, people are able to control body functions such as heart rate and bleeding, and Siegel maintains that he has seen patients cure themselves of cancer using visualization and positive thinking.

In fact, evidence of a mind-body connection abounds in the field of medical science. Once found almost

exclusively in New Age books about energy and healing, evidence of the power of positive thinking can now
be found in an increasing number of clinical studies. In
a testament to the legitimacy of the field, the National
Institutes of Health (NIH) dedicated an estimated
$153 million in 2005 to research related to the mind-
body connection and continues to fund such studies.
Research has demonstrated links between higher levels
of well-being and lower cardiovascular risk, lower levels
of stress hormones and lower levels of inflammation.[4]
Other studies clearly demonstrate that chronic stress can
compromise the healing of wounds and may impair the
effectiveness of vaccines.[5] A host of studies of the so-
called placebo effect suggests that *believing* you are getting medication can actually trigger the body's natural
curative powers. In one study, brain scans showed that
subjects who believed they were receiving painkillers
released endorphins—a natural pain reliever—and felt
better despite the fact that they weren't given any real
medicine.[6] When patients in an Italian study of Parkin-
son's disease were given a placebo, their bodies began
firing the neurons responsible for their muscle rigid-
ity and they were able to move more easily.[7] Similarly,
new research suggests that once Alzheimer's disease robs
someone of the ability to expect that a proven painkiller
will help him or her, it doesn't work nearly as well.[8]

The entire field of psychoimmunology is based on
the premise of a mind-body connection, springing from
the fact that a clear relationship has been documented
between the human brain and the immune system.
Studies have amply demonstrated that stress affects the
body's ability to resist disease, and psychological factors
have been shown to have an effect on many illnesses,

including rheumatoid arthritis, diabetes, hypertension, heart disease, and inflammatory bowel disease.

Just as compelling is the body of evidence being amassed to support the validity of the field of parapsychology—the study of extrasensory perception (ESP), telekinesis (moving physical objects with the mind), and mental telepathy. You've probably had the experience of thinking about someone you haven't heard from in years, then getting a call from that person the next day—or even in the next moment. How often do you call someone who says, "I was just thinking about you?" People in close relationships sometimes report that they raise a subject only to find that their mother or husband or sister was thinking the same thing at the same time. We usually chalk it up to coincidence, but studies of the paranormal demonstrate that there may be something else at work.

The field of parapsychology is gaining credibility, thanks in part to Dean Radin, Ph.D. In his book, *The Conscious Universe: The Scientific Truth of Psychic Phenomena,* he reviews almost a century of increasingly rigorous scientific experiments that demonstrate the existence of paranormal phenomena. Minds have been shown to move objects. Subjects in these studies have demonstrated the capacity for telepathic communication. And, in some studies, the subjects have picked up information from photographs, actual scenes, and events about which they knew nothing, apparently through extrasensory perception. Radin calls the entire body of research "evidence of our deep interconnectedness." At the very least, it suggests that there are paths of communication or energy fields that remain untapped.

As we move through the process of mastering the art of aloneness, you'll be using techniques such as visualization; you'll be directing your thoughts toward your aspirations; and you'll be fine-tuning your ability to think deliberately and harness your own positive energy.

Honoring Your Intuition

I had a woman call me several years ago seeking coaching services; she said her life was falling apart. She had just gotten out of a relationship and was terrified of being alone. She had broken up with her boyfriend because, she said, the relationship "just didn't feel right"—although she couldn't really put her finger on why. She came to me because she was terrified of ending up alone. After six months of intensive personal-development work, she decided to try to reconstruct that relationship. She felt that she was different and better prepared to be in the relationship. Because she had dropped him so abruptly six months before, the man insisted that they marry; he wanted to avoid another abrupt ending, another broken heart; and they did so, very quickly. But she had under-estimated how much she'd changed; the old relationship dynamic just didn't work anymore and they ended up dissolving the marriage. The lesson: her intuition was correct. It wasn't the right relationship for her or for him. But she ignored those very clear signals and went through the painful experience of breaking up yet again. Several months after her divorce, she resumed her personal-development path. Within a year, she had achieved the ideal life she'd visualized at the beginning of her coaching work. Now she's built the house of her dreams in Spain, where she's taking Spanish and salsa lessons. She has an extensive network of supportive friends and is about to start taking painting classes. She's happier alone than she ever could have been in the marriage she imagined would deliver her from her own fears and unhappiness.

Usually, when I'm working with a group, I ask everyone if they've ever had a gut feeling about something—a sense of whether something's right or wrong for them. Everybody knows that feeling. That gut feeling—your intuition—is a valuable tool. When you're able to cut through the layers of the conditioned self, at your core you often have a sense of what's right for you and what is not. As we go through the process of mastering the art of aloneness, you'll begin to peel away those layers and recover what I call your *authentic self*. At that point, your actions will begin to align with your life vision. Your intuition—your instinctive knowing—will become a valuable tool for living in alignment with your purpose, what I call *living on course*.

To develop your intuition, you have to start paying attention to it. It's the final key step in living more deliberately. As situations arise in your life in which you have to make a decision, start asking yourself: *How does this feel for me? Is this what I should be doing? How does this sit with me?* Before making a decision, ask yourself: *Is this an emotional reaction? Or is this something that's going to stick?* Ask for insight from your intuition.

When you're looking at a relationship, ask your intuition: *How does this person sit with me? What's my gut feeling?* Use it in the work you do. Use it in your everyday life. Remember my car-keying incident? I "had a feeling" that this guy was going to do something to my car, but I completely ignored it. I didn't trust my intuition. People tap into their intuition in a variety of ways. They ask themselves: *Deep down, how do I feel about this?* People who believe in a higher power often turn to prayer for answers. Others use meditation to invoke the intuitive part of themselves. Others just ask the universe for a sign. The key is to begin trusting that your intuition is trustworthy and able to guide you.

Over time, the more you trust your intuition and allow it to set your direction—the more often you find it doesn't let you down—the more you build that trust. The core issue, from a perspective of living deliberately and finding your life focus, is beginning to ask yourself the question: *Does this feel right?* If you stay connected to your intuition as you go through the process of mastering aloneness, it will become an important guide for retrieving your authentic self. And, ultimately, it will become your barometer for determining whether you're on course or off course in your life.

Exercise: Developing Your Intuition

Part 1: Find an Example of a Negative Outcome
In your journal, write down a real-life example of a time when you had a "gut feeling" about a person, situation, or action that you discounted or ignored, and, by ignoring your intuition, produced a negative outcome:

- Describe the specific person, situation, or action about which you had a "gut feeling."

- Describe the "gut feeling" that you had at the time. For example, it may have been a physical sensation like butterflies in your stomach, breaking out in a sweat, or constriction in your chest; a feeling of dread, fear, or uncertainty; a sense of caution, reluctance, or resistance; or just a strong sense about something you should or shouldn't do.

- Describe the negative outcome(s) you experienced by not following your intuitive messages and signals.

Part 2: Find an Example of a Positive Outcome

Now, write down a real-life example of a time when you had a "gut feeling" about a person, situation, or action *that you acted upon,* and, by acting on your intuition, produced a positive outcome:

- Describe the specific person, situation, or action about which you had a "gut feeling."

- Describe the "gut feeling" that you had at the time. For example, it may have been a physical sensation like butterflies in your stomach, breaking out in a sweat, or constriction in your chest; a feeling of dread, fear, or uncertainty; a sense of caution, reluctance, or resistance; or a just a strong sense of something you should or shouldn't do.

- Describe the positive outcome(s) you experienced by following your intuitive messages and signals.

PART II

LIBERATING YOUR AUTHENTIC SELF

CHAPTER 6

Reclaiming Your Innate Wholeness

The movie *Becoming Jane* is a love story, a fictionalized account of a relationship between Jane Austen and Tom Lefroy. Lefroy is believed by some to be the inspiration for Mr. Darcy, a central character in Austen's novel *Pride and Prejudice.* Jane Austen is played as a spirited, independent-minded young woman with a knack for irony, living in the British countryside with her loving family at the end of the 18th century. Encouraged by her family, she writes constantly; writing is, the audience begins to see, her life's purpose. As the story unfolds, Jane falls in love with the charming and roguish Lefroy, and they plan to marry, but, naturally, 18th-century Britain being what it is, social conventions pose a problem. Lefroy's rich uncle opposes the union. And, for reasons not at first clear, the young man is hesitant to defy his uncle. But ultimately his passion for Jane wins out and the two conspire to elope.

Of course, the real Jane Austen never married, so, the audience wonders, how is this going to end? Here's how: As the horse-drawn carriage departs, carrying them off into happily-ever-after, it gets stuck in the mud; as Lefroy struggles to free the wheels, Jane ends up holding his jacket. A letter falls out, revealing that his parents rely on him for support and that by defying his rich uncle, Lefroy will leave his entire family destitute. Jane Austen turns and walks away from the love of her life, and there's not a dry eye in the house.

It's a wonderful romance. But, after the tears, you realize that the beauty of the story is this: This Jane, this character, is profoundly consistent. She knows her true self. With Lefroy, she'd explored the question of whether she'd be able to pursue her writing as a married woman, something she knew she wasn't willing to sacrifice. She was also willing to buck the system and marry Lefroy in defiance of social mores. What she *wasn't* willing to do was to watch their love destroy his family. She knew, we assume, in the instant she read that letter, that they couldn't be happy at his family's expense. She possessed the inner strength to trust her intuition, to honor her truth, and walk away. She was making the decision, not through the haze of romance but from a position of the authentic self. It seems a fitting depiction, given that the real Jane Austen more than fulfilled her potential. She went on to become one of English literature's most celebrated authors. She must surely have been living from her authentic self.

In reality, most people are unable to gain access to or honor their true selves with the ease of the Jane character in this movie. In fact, I'd wager that very few people go through life living from their authentic selves. When I refer to the authentic self, I mean who you really are beneath all the layers of your conditioning. Remember those core limiting beliefs? When you're living from your authentic self, you've moved beyond them. Trance states? You're making a conscious effort to identify and override them. The more authentic you are, the more you're connected to your innate nature, strengths, values, and needs and to your inherent ability to feel and express the full range of human emotions.

No one is exempt from familial, societal, and cultural conditioning. It's an inevitable part of being human. In earlier chapters, I've talked at length about core limiting beliefs. Our cumulative life experiences—the family, culture, circumstances, and environment in which we were raised—have a powerful influence on the way we think, behave, and live. The challenge is to emerge from the conditioning process with as much of our authentic self intact as possible. When clients first come to me for coaching, it's usually because they are living *out of alignment* with their authentic selves. However, most are not aware that this is the root cause of their difficulty in creating the lives, careers, relationships, or success they want. They attribute their difficulty to the *symptoms* of living out of sync with their authentic selves, such as a dead-end or dissatisfying job, conflict-ridden relationships with others, or loneliness stemming from not having a partner or spouse. Retrieving the authentic self is a core component of all of my coaching programs and the point at which I begin with every client; it is the foundation for mastering the art of aloneness and for becoming the person you were born to be.

Mastering the art of aloneness is about reclaiming your innate wholeness so you can live a full and happy life, whether you're alone or in a relationship. So a crucial step involves identifying and retrieving the parts of you that were lost as a result of your own life conditioning process. That's the work we'll be doing in this chapter.

The Components of the Authentic Self

Carl Jung, a young colleague of Sigmund Freud and the founder of analytical psychology, first introduced the concept of psychological type in the 1920s with the idea that there are two basic attitude types—*extroverts* and *introverts*—and what he called the four functions of consciousness: thinking, feeling, sensing, and intuiting. Jung was the first to fully develop the idea that different people have different ways of perceiving and approaching the world and that these differences are innate. For example, "one person may favor thought as a guide to judgment, another will follow feeling; and whereas one will tend to experience both the world and his friends through impressions made directly on his senses, another will be given, rather, to intuiting potentialities, hidden relationships, intentions, and possible sources."[1] By identifying these psychological types, he laid the foundation for our modern-day understanding of personality.

Like Jung, I believe that we all have innate personality traits and temperaments. Most parents will tell you that they can identify traits in their own children from birth—distinct temperaments and predispositions. Some toddlers, for example, are quiet and still, hanging back, observing everything around them. Others jump into the fray feet first, full of energy and enthusiasm. However, research on twins reared apart, conducted over the past 30 years at the Minnesota Center for Twin and

Family Research (University of Minnesota) by professor Thomas J. Bouchard, Jr., and his team, provides perhaps the most powerful evidence of innate personalities. In research originally published in the *Journal of Personality and Social Psychology* in 1988 and discussed at length in a *New Yorker* piece published in 1995, the Minnesota team assessed twin pairs for personality characteristics such as a "sense of well-being, social dominance, alienation, aggression, and achievement . . . They concluded that identical twins reared apart were as much alike as identicals reared together."[2] The Minnesota twin studies, combined with a slew of other studies conducted over the past two decades, provide ample evidence that we are born with certain personality characteristics.[3]

Part of retrieving your authentic self involves identifying *your innate personality traits,* the characteristics you were born with that may have been suppressed through the conditioning process. For example, you may be more innately extroverted—more outwardly than inwardly directed. But say you grew up with a father who was an alcoholic and he'd fly into rages when he was drinking. Your coping mechanism may have involved staying below the radar screen and not making a peep. You withdrew from the world, a characteristic that's in conflict with your true nature. In my work, as part of the process of identifying innate personality characteristics, I use the Myers-Briggs Type Indicator (MBTI), a popular personality test developed by Katharine Cook Briggs and Isabel Briggs Myers in the 1940s based on Carl Jung's theories. Since its inception, millions of people have taken the MBTI assessment, and it's been updated and refined through ongoing research. The results are remarkably comprehensive and illuminating. At the end of this chapter, you'll be given information about how to take the MBTI assessment. If you do, recognize that the MBTI tool is valuable for helping people understand their innate natures, but it is only one piece of the puzzle of discovering the authentic self.

Retrieving your authentic self also involves identifying *your true passions*. As you work through this process, you'll be identifying your innate strengths, as well as your interests and that which inspires you. What do you care about? What captures your interest? What motivates you? What do you like and dislike? At the close of this chapter, you'll do a series of exercises designed to help you begin to uncover your authentic self. But the process of retrieving your authentic self also involves a good bit of detective work. Each of us is unique, and the formula for finding that uniqueness is as individual as we are.

Ultimately, as you move toward wholeness, you'll identify *your life purpose*. Like Carl Jung, I believe that we all have an inborn purpose, and fulfilling that purpose is critical to the quality of our lives and our sense of well-being. I also believe we all have a soul or spirit. It's a nonphysical part of us, which explains why there is no scientific means for proving its existence. Merriam-Webster defines the soul as "the immaterial essence, animating principle, or actuating cause of an individual life." I think of the soul as some sort of energy that connects us to the nonphysical realm. I believe our soul carries the blueprint for our lives, and that's where our purpose resides. Of course, just as a builder can either adhere to a construction blueprint or build some variation of the original design, you have the capacity to veer off course from your life purpose. That's where your free will and your conditioning come in. Mastering aloneness means knowing and activating your innate personality, your true passions, and your life purpose—that which gives your life meaning. Achieving that understanding can be transformational. As D. H. Lawrence wrote, "You've got to know yourself so that you can at last be yourself." That's what retrieving the authentic self is really about.

The Benefits of Living from Authentic Self

Every now and then, when we embark on the process of retrieving the authentic self, a client will ask, with a note of impatience, "How much energy does this whole thing take, anyway?" My answer is always the same. "Take?" I respond. "It doesn't *take* energy. The more you immerse yourself in the process, the more energy you have." Even though living from the conditioned self—from your default operating system—seems like the path of least resistance, it requires tremendous energy to live out of alignment with your authentic self. The greater the disparity between the way you're living and your authentic self, the more conflict there will be within you, in your relationships, and at work. Living by default creates resistance, dissent, problems, and barriers in our lives. Maybe you find your work draining and unsatisfying because it's out of alignment with your innate strengths. Over time, this affects your level of motivation and, ultimately, your job performance. Or you consistently find yourself in relationships plagued by conflict because you're replicating the dysfunctional dynamics of your family of origin. Maybe you're not getting your emotional needs met because you can't express them or you have a pattern of putting other people's needs first. When the way you live conflicts with your innate nature, strengths, passions, and values, it's as if you're living in a continuous state of resistance. And that takes energy. As you move toward living in alignment with your authentic self, you'll see a lot of changes in your life, including a greater sense of peace, energy, and overall well-being.

Rana's Story

When Rana came to me in the spring of 2007, she was lethargic and depressed. Raised in a close-knit, traditional Middle Eastern family, she was a successful orthopedic surgeon, and, at 37, she'd been married for nine years. Her husband had just finished his law degree and was looking for a job with a big firm. The two of them were living with her parents in a Boston suburb, and every evening after work, Rana had gotten into the habit of withdrawing to the family's finished basement where she'd watch television. She wasn't taking phone calls from her friends, she wasn't socializing, and she wasn't going to the gym much after work, though that had always been important to her. "Something's wrong," her mother kept insisting. Everyone else in her family was worried about her as well. Growing up, Rana had been an outgoing teenager with lots of friends and energy. She didn't seem like her old self, her family told her; she seemed angry and upset. In truth, she felt like no one understood her. Just recently, her father and brother had started talking about opening an office with her. She would be performing the surgery—what she refers to as "the manual work"—and they would be her business partners. She would, in effect, be supporting her entire family, although that wasn't how she expressed it at the time. Spurred on by her family's concern and her own lack of interest in starting up this new office, she came to see me. She wasn't happy in her work, she said. She wanted to explore some other career options.

We had 18 coaching sessions, beginning with the assessment process focused on identifying the conditioned self and the authentic self, then moving forward with a series of exercises designed to identify her life purpose and new career options through which she could fulfill it. As our work continued to unfold, it became clear how intensely Rana's family and cultural conditioning had been dictating her life. She'd spent her entire adult life doing exactly what her family wanted her to do. She'd gotten married because it was expected, and she'd pursued a successful career as a physician because it was expected. Now that she found herself wanting to make a change, she was terrified of rocking the boat, of how her family would react. She'd grown up in a culture full of rules, rules that she'd followed without questioning them. Rana was an extreme example of someone living against her nature, to the point where it was making her depressed and beginning to cause health problems. When she first came to see me, she was having chronic migraines. Living in a state of constant stress was beginning to take a toll on her physical health. When you're living your life based on what everyone else wants you to do, versus what *you* want to do, it's a setup for anger, resentment, depression, and—as in Rana's case—even illness.

When we first began our work together, Rana believed that her unhappiness was *her* problem. She thought that if she could just try harder, if she could just be a better wife and daughter, then she could make her life work. That was her habitual pattern—doing what everyone else wanted her to do, taking care everyone's needs but her own. In the initial phase of her coaching program, she remained in that pattern, determined to fix things. Then one day she had a breakthrough. During one of our voice dialoguing sessions, we focused on her ideal life. What would it be like? What would she be doing? Whom would she be living with? "Alone," she responded. The answer stunned her. For the first time, she'd acknowledged out loud that she was unhappy in her marriage. It was frightening for her to admit that the marriage was in trouble, because, in her culture, divorce was out of the question.

Two pivotal changes occurred that enabled her to look at life differently. First, through our work and the books I asked her to read, she had an epiphany: it became very clear to her that *she* was responsible for her own life—that *she*, not her family, was responsible for the choices she was making. Second, she uncovered her passion: health and wellness, and, in particular, physical fitness. Once she recognized this, she fully embraced and honored it, and the more she followed her passion, the more her authentic self began to take hold.

The turning point came when she made going to the gym a top priority. She joined one of the best health clubs in the city, one with beautiful, state-of-the-art facilities and equipment. She started going to this new gym every day, and when she was there, she made a deliberate effort to reconnect with her old, happy, high-energy self. She took the initiative to introduce herself to people, make new friends, and be a source of encouragement to others at the gym. She was feeding her passion for fitness by exercising regularly. Her innate personality—outgoing, upbeat, and people-oriented—resurfaced. She'd found a place where she could be herself. "It's become my playground," she told me one day. "It's a place where I can allow myself to be me. I just love being there." Her workouts were giving her more energy, and she began to see changes in her body. The physical transformation helped change her perspective. She realized that if she had the power to change her body and her attitude, she had the power to change her life. The experience gave her a tremendous sense of strength and freedom—including freedom from meeting other people's expectations.

Rana's personal-development work was also changing her perspective on her marriage. Over a period of months, she addressed these issues with her husband, but he seemed to express no interest in pursuing a healthier relationship. As it became increasingly clear that her husband's values dramatically differed from hers, she began to explore the possibility of leaving the marriage. She was beginning to recognize that she had based her life on her husband's dream and her parents' dream—but not on her own dream.

Interestingly, although Rana first came to me about work-related issues, she ended up leaving her marriage, and now that she's retrieved her authentic self, she's happier in her career as a surgeon. She's rethinking her original idea of leaving medicine and may not end up changing careers at all. She explained it to me this way: "The other day, I had a new patient. She's a teenage girl and she was really afraid of the surgery. I ended up singing to her. It relaxed her. I never would have done anything like that before. I'm approaching life from a place of love, compassion, and freedom instead of feeling trapped in a life I didn't enjoy. And, as a result, I'm enjoying my work more."

As Rana went through this process, a vivacious, passionate, excited person began to emerge. She was transformed. For the first time, she was living fully in alignment with her authentic self.

Wake-Up Calls: Signs from the Universe

Initially, Rana came to see me because her family had recognized that something was wrong. Rana herself identified the problem as unhappiness that centered on her work and thought she needed career coaching. The truth is, Rana was getting plenty of signals that there was a problem—migraines, depression, withdrawing to the basement every evening, and a lack of marital connection and affection. But her habitual patterns were so deeply ingrained that she wasn't paying any attention to the signals. In his book *Wake-Up Calls: You Don't Have to Sleepwalk Through Your Life, Love, or Career!*, Eric Allenbaugh, Ph.D., explains that that's something we all do. Most of us are sleepwalking through life, trapped in the habitual patterns of our conditioned selves. Often, it takes a life-changing event to snap us out of it by interrupting the normal flow of our lives. Allenbaugh calls these events wake-up calls. I think of them as our soul's attempt to get our attention and let us know that we've moved off course in our lives and away from our life purpose. If you're not living authentically, at some point you'll begin to get signs. Perhaps your wife suddenly announces—seemingly out of the blue—that she wants a divorce, and you didn't have a clue she was unhappy. When a relationship isn't working, there are always signs. But if you're not paying attention, if you're stuck in habitual patterns, if you're sleepwalking, you don't see them. Divorce tops Allenbaugh's list of personal wake-up calls, which runs the gamut from losing an important friendship to experiencing a serious injury or illness, losing your job, or falling into financial difficulties. If we don't consciously choose to become more aware and deliberate in our lives, often it takes a wake-up call to snap us to attention and motivate us to address whatever's not working in our lives.

When I left my marriage, I hit bottom emotionally and financially. It was my wake-up call—the signal that I was off course in my life. As painful as this was, it was an opportunity for self-discovery, for learning, and for getting my life aligned with who I really am. Wake-up calls can lead to major shifts in awareness. "And those awareness shifts can lead to transformation," Allenbaugh writes, noting that disruptive events are often viewed as "bad" but in fact can serve as springboards for greater learning. They can be the catalysts for transformation.

We've talked about living by default—when your *modus operandi* is driven by core limiting beliefs that aren't based on your present reality—and trance states, in which you're unconsciously reacting to current events based on the past. Oftentimes, those habitual patterns can cause accidents or health problems that serve as wake-up calls. When you live in conflict with your authentic self over an extended period of time, the symptoms tend to reveal themselves gradually. First, you might experience a sense of dissatisfaction. If you don't pay attention and address your dissatisfaction, it can intensify into a depression. Then, if you still aren't listening, the underlying conflict may manifest itself in physical symptoms such as headaches, gastrointestinal issues, and back problems. If you continue to ignore the messages that your system is sending you, the problem can escalate to the point where the stress of living out of alignment with your authentic self begins to compromise and weaken your immune system. When that happens, if you have any predispositions to certain diseases and life-threatening illnesses, you can become vulnerable to serious health problems.

Often, when I'm working with a client who I can tell is living out of alignment with his or her authentic self, I'll ask: "Do you have any physical ailments such as migraines, stomachaches, back pain, or any other health problems?" A great deal of the time, the answer comes back yes. In the early '90s I ran a series of workshops for cancer patients called *Cancer as a Chance to Live,* which addressed the impact of thoughts and emotions on health and illness. In nearly every case, the workshop participants—all of whom were battling cancer—had been in a relationship, job, or other life situation for an extended period of time that was a source of chronic stress or unhappiness. Almost all of them had experienced a period of unrelieved stress that preceded their illness. Of course, that doesn't mean that their life circumstances caused their illness. Cancer can be the result of many factors, including a genetic predisposition, environmental exposure, and lifestyle choices such as smoking. Whatever the root cause, long-term, chronic stress may have been a contributing factor—the tipping point that weakened their immune systems, leaving them more vulnerable to illness.

When you're unhappy and dissatisfied, or grappling with a major life change, it can affect your focus and concentration. That means you may be more prone to accidents. Not long after my husband and I separated, I absentmindedly ran my car right into the back of someone's truck. In fact, according to the American Automobile Association, traffic accidents are often caused by people who have recently suffered an emotional or professional setback, such as a job loss or a divorce.[4] Why? Because they're under stress. They're distracted. They may even be stuck in trance states much of the time. Maybe they're experiencing depression or caught up in ruminating on the crisis in their lives. Their minds are somewhere else.

So, at this point, it may be valuable to check in with yourself. How are you feeling? How's your health? Are you able to maintain your focus or are you distracted a lot of the time? These can be clues to whether or not you're living in alignment with your authentic self:

- *Your feelings.* Emotional and mental distress can be a symptom that something is out of whack in your life. These feelings can range from a general sadness, dissatisfaction, or frustration to a full-blown depression. Lack of motivation, boredom, or a sense of hopelessness, ranging from mild to severe, can be signs that you're living out of alignment with your authentic self.

- *Your health.* Physical ailments or illnesses are common among people whose lives are out of alignment with their authentic selves, particularly those illnesses that can be exacerbated by stress. If your immune system becomes compromised because you're under constant stress, you're more vulnerable to health problems.

- *Your ability to focus.* Distraction and lack of focus; being accident-prone, dropping things—these can all be signs that you're off course in your life. You're using a lot of mental and emotional energy just to keep the old mechanisms in place that override your innate nature and authentic self. Trance states are the ultimate distraction. When your mind is preoccupied with memories of and feelings from the past, it impedes your ability to maintain your focus in the here and now, and you have less emotional energy to fully activate your potential.

Midlife and the Authentic Self

For many people, midlife is the ultimate wake-up call. The midlife transition can begin as early as the age of 30 and as late as 60. Midlife is a time when many people find themselves stepping back and evaluating how they want to live for the rest of their lives. They've had the chance to build a life and reap the rewards of their endeavors. As they look toward the second half of their lives, they may find themselves asking: *Who am I? What's the meaning of my life? What do I really want?* Women approaching midlife are confronting many of the same life changes that adolescents experience: Their bodies are changing, and, for those who have raised children, their life purpose may be shifting. They're embarking on a new phase of life that leaves them asking: *What am I going to do now? Who am I?* The physical changes they're experiencing may add an edge to those questions. As Christiane Northrup, M.D., author of *The Wisdom of Menopause: Creating Physical and Emotional Health and Healing During the Change,* reminded viewers on a recent PBS special: if you have unresolved issues in your life that you haven't dealt with by the time you get into menopause, they'll come up and hit you right between the eyes. Of course, in midlife, men and women face many of the same questions—about mortality, what they've achieved, their life's purpose, and whether or not they've fulfilled their life dreams.

This kind of intense reappraisal often lends itself to feelings of turmoil, insecurity, or even despair. In response, some people do a lot of acting out—they buy that wild sports car, have an affair, leave their life partners, or resort to addictive behavior involving alcohol, relationships, sex, or work. In his book *The Seasons of a Man's Life,* Daniel J. Levinson writes: "Every genuine appraisal must be agonizing, because it challenges the illusions and vested interests on which the existing structure is based."[5] In other words, it's threatening—even frightening—to examine your life, particularly if you've reached a point where you recognize that your life might be based primarily on illusions.

This reappraisal process can lead to the dismantling of what Levinson calls The Dream. The Dream, according to Levinson, can be "modest or heroic, vaguely defined or crystal clear, a burning passion or a quiet guiding force," but it's the thing that's kept you going—the thing you wanted to achieve, the focus of your life, or even the thing that you couldn't really find. The Dream can be a reflection of your authentic self—your purpose—but for many people The Dream is based on the conditioned self, the layers that have overridden the authentic self. The Dream is whatever you've imagined you need that will make you happy, whether it's the perfect relationship, a successful career, your dream home, successful kids, or a trendy lifestyle. The truth is, when you reach midlife, you know whether or not you've achieved your dreams. That knowledge can be a double-edged sword. If you didn't achieve your dreams, you may feel like a failure. But what if you succeeded in realizing your dreams but you still didn't achieve the sense of happiness and fulfillment you'd imagined? When that happens, you feel a tremendous sense of despair. Midlife is the time when you start to see the cracks and holes in The Dream. Then, when the wake-up call comes—in the form of a divorce, a life-threatening illness, the death of a parent—it can turn into a full-blown midlife crisis. Your dream is falling apart; your life is losing its meaning. That can trigger a profound transformation. What feels like a breakdown can be a pathway to breaking open.

When I work with clients who are going through this experience, I encourage them to listen to what I call their inner voices. Often, these are the parts of them that became submerged when they were younger—the parts that typically start to reemerge during our voice dialoguing sessions. We all have lost parts. These lost parts are components of the authentic self. By listening to your inner voices and allowing those lost parts of you to resurface, you're taking an important step toward reclaiming your innate wholeness. Maybe it's your creative part, the voice of your sensitivity. It may be the part that longs for independence or the one that loves adventure. Perhaps it's the assertive, strong part or the playful, spontaneous one. In order to become aware of what parts of yourself may have gone underground as the result of your conditioning—and that long to reemerge and find expression in your life—it's important to begin to listen to and embrace what they are communicating to you.

Uncovering the Clues to Your Authentic Self

Retrieving your authentic self is like putting together the pieces of a puzzle. For Rana, the path to uncovering her authentic self involved acknowledging, embracing, and acting on her passion for exercise and wellness and addressing the root causes of her unhappy marriage. When I began my own personal-development work, I started to uncover the independent, fearless, and creative person I was before I got married. The work involved peeling back those layers of the conditioned self and being able to differentiate between what was mine, what was true, what was in alignment with my authentic self, and what came from someone else's belief system that I had adopted as my own. Making those distinctions—between the parts of your true self and your conditioned self—is a critical step toward uncovering your authentic self.

You've already begun the process of retrieving your authentic self by beginning to understand your family of origin, the role you took on within your family, your fears, and your core limiting beliefs. Now, you have to become the interpreter of your own life. You're going to be asking questions such as: *What are my needs and*

aspirations? What do I like and dislike? What are my pas-
sions? And, ultimately, what is my life purpose?

Here's some guidance on how to move forward with
this process:

- *Take a holistic approach.* Don't rely solely on
  the results of your MBTI assessment or what
  you learn from the exercises that appear at
  the end of this chapter. Use all the exercises
  to gain valuable information about yourself,
  but then dig deeper. We're all more complex
  than tests can reveal. By using a variety of
  different approaches, you'll start to see patterns and the pieces of your puzzle will begin
  to come together. You should have an understanding of some of your life conditioning from the preceding chapters. Let those
  insights help guide you through the process.

- *Look for clues in your responses to situations
  and people.* Operate from a place of awareness and check your reactions against the
  new information you have about your family
  of origin, core beliefs, family role, and fears.
  When you have a reaction to a situation, ask
  yourself: *Is this coming from the conditioned self
  or my authentic self?* If you experience fear or
  anxiety, you'll want to check it out. But—and
  this is important—don't assume that every
  emotional or behavioral reaction you have is
  based on your conditioned self. You have to
  do the investigative work and examine yourself and situations as they occur. For example,

if you walk into a crowded room full of strangers and you experience fear or anxiety, you'll want to check that out. You want to ask yourself: *Where is this anxiety coming from? Is it a fear of being judged or rejected? Or is it an innate discomfort from being in an environment that's very loud, where there's too much going on, and that feels overwhelming? Does that kind of environment conflict with my innate nature? Do I generally prefer quiet environments and small groups of people?* When you reach a conclusion, double-check it with your intuition. See how it compares with what you've already learned about your fears and innate nature.

• *Use your journal as your workbook.* Your journal is a valuable tool to help you track your feelings and reactions and how they compare to your core beliefs. Don't censor your feelings and reactions. This is the place where you ask yourself: *What's truly mine and what have I adopted from someone else?*

• *Be discerning in your friendships.* As you begin to live more deliberately and become more aware of your life conditioning, you'll start to see patterns in your relationships. Explore the characteristics of those relationships. Ask yourself questions such as: *Am I habitually drawn to people who are critical? Am I replicating the dynamics I had with my parents in my relationships with others? Am I always comparing myself to others and feeling bad about*

myself? Check the dynamics of your relationships against your core beliefs and habitual
behaviors. Perhaps you notice a pattern with
others in which you always feel like you're
giving and never receiving, based on the
core belief that *others' needs are more important than my own.* To consciously change
this old pattern, you'll have to start communicating your needs to others. And, by
starting to communicate your needs to others, you'll gain valuable information about
those relationships by how the other person
responds. Then, you're in a good position
to ask yourself: *Is this someone who respects
who I am—my needs, dreams, and boundaries?
Is this a relationship based on the beliefs and
habitual behaviors of my conditioned self? Or is
this someone who is compatible with my innate
nature?*

- *Use your intuition.* I believe our souls communicate to us—about ourselves, about others,
and about our lives—through intuition. That
makes your intuition a good barometer for
checking in with your authentic self as you
go through the process of assessing whether
something is right for you. Recognize that
emotions are often unreliable; they fluctuate
easily, changing from one day to the next
based on immediate circumstances. Consider
this example: I had a friend in high school
who had begged her parents to let her withdraw from her Catholic school and attend

164

public school, where she thought she'd feel more comfortable. She had a dozen reasons to make the move, and she made a strong case for it over a two-month period. Her parents finally agreed, and she planned to switch schools mid-year. Two days before the switch was to occur, the football captain at the Catholic school asked her out on a date. She was elated and abandoned her plans to change schools. She let her emotions drive a decision that was based on months of soul-searching—and within days, she regretted it. You don't want to make decisions driven by the changeability of your emotions. Give it time to see how something sits with you. As you work to retrieve the authentic self, your intuition is a valuable ally.

- *Practice effective communication.* A big part of living from your authentic self is being able to communicate your feelings, opinions, needs, and boundaries to other people. If you're afraid to share who you really are and express your true feelings—because of how other people will react or what they will think—you're living from your conditioned self. I've devoted a big piece of this chapter to effective communication. It's an important tool to help you honor your authentic self as you go through your everyday life.

Potholes along the Way

For people with certain habitual patterns and behaviors, the process of retrieving the authentic self can be particularly challenging. High achievers often have a difficult time. Let's say, you're a classic Type A—success-oriented and driven—and you're approaching midlife. You've probably been on track all your life, successfully negotiating all the earlier phases of human development: building a foundation for your personal and professional life, perhaps settling down, having kids, climbing the corporate ladder, or establishing yourself in your field. That's the American paradigm. Then the kids leave and you feel like you've accomplished your life goals, but you don't have a roadmap for the rest of your life. Often, the person who as a child took on the family role of the Hero experiences the greatest angst in midlife. If you're a Hero, you're all about success and recognition. But to successfully negotiate a midlife transition often involves surrendering the ego. The ego is often attached to outward symbols of success such as titles, status, money, and prestige. If you discover that you need to make a major life change in order to be happy and fulfilled, and it involves letting go of your title and prestige, you may find that your ego presents an obstacle. I had a friend who came from a family characterized by poverty and physical and emotional abuse. He had five siblings, and both his mother and stepfather had difficulty holding down jobs. He rebelled against his family patterns and made a decision early in life that he wasn't going to be like them. He took on the role of the Hero. His core belief was: *To survive, I have to be educated, successful, and independent.* Not only was he the only member of his family to go to college, he was the only one who ever graduated from high school.

My friend became a successful corporate executive with a six-figure income. But he hit the skids when he approached midlife, feeling the conflict between his authentic self—which craved a more contemplative existence—and the high-powered, relentlessly driven conditioned self. After a lot of soul-searching, he left his job and announced an elaborate plan to travel, read, meditate, and spend more time in nature. He was try-ing to recover his authentic self, and he and I shared many conversations on the subject. But for him, retriev-ing the authentic self promised to be a lengthy and complex process, because those lost parts of him hadn't been expressed for many years. Ultimately, he got scared and his ego-driven, conditioned self kicked back in. Out of the blue, he was offered a position with a big com-pany that gave him a higher salary, a more impressive title, and even more prestige than he'd had before. He accepted the offer, and I lost touch with him for several years. The last time I saw him, he'd retreated back into the corporate world—his comfort zone—but he was still conflicted and uncertain about his decision.

I don't mean to imply that everyone who's moti-vated to succeed is operating from the conditioned self—indeed, that drive is often the authentic self seek-ing expression. But if your drive for success is based on old childhood wounds or an attempt to compensate for feelings of unworthiness—as was the case with my friend—if left to its own devices, that drive will often pose problems.

People who are habitual people-pleasers also tend to have a hard time retrieving their authentic selves because so many of their habitual patterns are built around meeting the needs of others. If you've spent your life focusing on other people's needs instead of your own, you really haven't had the chance to know yourself well. It may be hard to determine what you like, what you don't like, what's okay for you, and what's not okay. I had an example recently in my practice—a client who grew up outside the United States where the cultural conditioning was very strong. It was all about getting a good education and a good job, and about the children, ultimately, being able to provide for their parents. This woman recognized early in life that she was interested in art. She loved to draw, but she never let her family know, because it was so against their beliefs and expectations. When she graduated from high school, she came to the United States to attend Harvard and then went into the field of finance. She was tremendously successful professionally and made a great deal of money. But when she came to me in her early 30s, she was an isolated, sad, and very insecure person. She felt like she was living a life that wasn't her own. She'd spent her entire life trying to meet her parents' high expectations of professional success. Her authentic self was so deeply buried and her life experience had been so limited that she had no idea how she wanted to live. She didn't have enough information about who she was, and about her own values, needs, and life preferences, to start living from her authentic self. So we devised an action plan: she was going to use some of her savings to learn about herself and what she wanted in her life. She went to South America and taught English, spent a month in India, and traveled to Thailand to scuba dive. She unleashed the sense of adventure that was part of her innate nature.

She was seeking information about *who she really was*. Of course, not everyone can afford the luxury of going around the world to find their authentic selves. The key is this: if you don't know what you like, what's important to you, or what you feel passionate about, you have to make a conscious effort to experience new things. In my coaching work, I use an assessment tool that identifies habitual behaviors. People-pleasers tend to score high on approval-seeking behavior, on dependency, and on the conforming, risk-adverse behavioral styles that relate to being cautious and staying safe. As a result, it's often harder for people with those patterns of behavior to explore the unknown than it would be for someone like me, whose habitual behavioral style was to rebel against the prescribed norms of my family. People-pleasers tend to be people who have had heavy expectations laid on them by others when they were growing up. That's a challenging pattern to break. Like my client who went scuba diving in Thailand, when people-pleasers try to uncover information about who they really are, they often can't gain access to it. If you can't answer certain fundamental questions—*What do I like? What's important to me? What do I dislike? What are my values? What do I want in my life?*—then it may be time to start jumping into life and testing the waters. Test *lots* of waters. And then, each step of the way, check in with your intuition. Over time, as you begin to move out of your comfort zone, take new risks, experience new people, and try new things—continually using your intuition as a barometer for how all this sits with you—your authentic self will begin to reveal itself to you.

Communicating Effectively

Effective communication is a powerful and crucial tool for living from the authentic self. If you follow the basic approach outlined here, it will help you
identify your feelings, improve and enhance your relationships, and develop your emotional intelligence. It
will also help you move out of trance states and into
the here and now. How? By incorporating reality checks
into your communications. Often, when conflicts arise
in relationships, it's because people are assuming they
know what the other person is thinking, and they're basing what they say on those assumptions. Effective communication involves dropping your assumptions about
what other people are thinking or feeling, and checking
in with reality to find out what's really going on. Effective communication involves checking in *with your feelings and intuition* before you respond. As such, it isn't just
a new pattern of behavior; it's a way to stay connected to
and in alignment with your authentic self.

Let me give you an example of what I mean. I have
a client in her mid-50s who has been divorced for more
than a decade and lives alone. Janet has a history of conflicts in her relationships. She grew up in a family in
which, to survive emotionally, she had to keep her head
down and avoid challenging authority. In addition, her
parents were highly critical, so Janet had a pattern of
either reacting defensively or avoiding conflict altogether
by not saying anything. She would let her feelings build
up over time and then let them rip—either overflowing
in a defensive rage or cutting herself off from the other
person. Because she rarely addressed conflict with her
friends and family when it arose, she didn't give other

people the option of responding to her concerns or feelings. She also had an aggressive communication style, one that tended to evoke a defensive reaction in others. Often, her feelings of anger and resentment were based on imagined slights. As a result of her poor communication skills, she alienated people and missed out on a lot of opportunities for relationships.

Here's an example of how Janet's communication style plays out. She has a friend, Margaret, who tends to be very critical and insensitive, and Janet has been unable to address the issue directly with her. One day, Margaret made a comment about a mutual acquaintance who was considering a divorce: "Doesn't she know that if she leaves her husband at this stage in her life, she's going to end up spending the rest of her life alone?" Janet felt angry and hurt by what she perceived as an insult. She said nothing, but after they parted, she vowed never to speak to Margaret again. Then, after fuming for a few hours, she called Margaret, angry and edgy, said, "I can't believe you said that to me." Margaret didn't even know what she was talking about. "You said that that woman was going to end up spending the rest of her life alone, as if that's the worst thing that could happen. In case you haven't noticed, I'm alone. That was a horrible thing to say. You *insulted* me." Margaret immediately got her back up: "You know, you say things like that to me all the time, but you don't see *me* blowing up." The conversation went downhill from there.

Effective communication is all about the intention and energy behind your words. It's not just what you say. It's also how you say it. Janet was engaging in a very emotionally charged communication. Communicating effectively involves learning to communicate in a way that will defuse conflict—not escalate it by invoking defensive behaviors in the listener.

When I reviewed this conversation with Janet, I first encouraged her to consider what she might have done to create, promote, or allow Margaret's response. Upon reflection, she realized that her message and tone of voice were hostile and critical. She also assumed that Margaret meant to insult her, when that may not have been Margaret's intention at all. She recognized, too, that she'd failed to address Margaret's hurtful comment the moment it came up. Instead, she'd fumed and fed her anger for two hours, then called Margaret on the phone, furious and upset.

Ideally, when a person says something that hurts your feelings or makes you feel angry, the best time to respond is immediately, and the best way to address it is in person, because you can communicate through tone of voice, eye contact, and body language. You also have to know yourself and express your feelings honestly and straightforwardly. A better way to handle Margaret's comment would have been to say something like: "I'm noticing that I'm having a really strong reaction to what you just said. I'm feeling hurt. It may not have been your intention to be hurtful, but those are the feelings I'm experiencing." That opens the door for Margaret to respond more compassionately, without feeling unjustly accused or feeling the need to defend herself. She might say, "Oh my gosh, I didn't even think of it that way. I'm really sorry." Addressing the implicit criticism of her single lifestyle, my client could have said: "I'd like it if you could please be more sensitive to the fact that I'm single; I'm alone by choice. I'm actually happy. I'd really like you to be supportive of my choice and my single lifestyle. If you feel critical about it, I'd appreciate it if you'd refrain from sharing those feelings going forward. I'd rather you didn't say anything about it." That's what I call communicating from the adult, emotionally intelligent ego state. The key to communicating from the adult ego state is to focus on *your* feelings, *your* reactions, and *your* concerns. You can't assume you know what another person is thinking or feeling, or even that your reactions reflect what's really going on.

This approach to communication is based on the transactional analysis model, which emanates from the work of psychiatrist Eric Berne, who first postulated the ego states of "parent," "child," and "adult" as the key individual systems of thoughts, feelings, and behaviors from which we interact with others. The basic premise of this line of thinking is that, at any given time, we're communicating from one of those three ego states. I've expanded this model to include what I view as the six most common communication styles, in addition to the "adult state," which is the most effective way to communicate in most instances. As you read through the following descriptions of these communication styles, notice which ego state feels the most familiar to you.

Parent Ego States

The Critical Parent

The Critical Parent is the voice that's laced with reprimands and criticism, and loaded with self-righteousness and judgment. This is where you hear a lot of "shoulds." When the word *should* enters into a conversation, as in "you should," I call it "should-ing" on people. That's a tip-off that whoever's on the receiving end of your "shoulds" is going to shut down and go into a defensive mode. Here's an example of the Critical Parent making a service call. Let's say her Internet service is down: "My service is out once again and you people can't seem to get anything right. I don't know what you think you're doing over there, but you're obviously not doing your jobs. You people should be ashamed of how you treat your customers. Now I expect you to get someone over here today and fix it."

The Enabling Parent

Partners of active alcoholics are often referred to as "enablers." It's because they have a habitual pattern of allowing, or enabling, dysfunctional behavior. An Enabling Parent is someone who routinely excuses bad behavior, thereby letting others abdicate responsibility. Enablers don't want to deal with conflict, so they avoid confrontation altogether. The enabler is the one who says, after the 30th time it happens: "Oh, don't worry about being an hour late again. I know how bad the traffic is." Here's how an Enabling Parent might communicate to that same service representative: "I know you have lots and lots of customers, and I'm sure you're really busy, which is probably why no one's called me back this week. But my Internet service has been down for ten days, and I wondered if you could possibly send someone over. I don't want to cause you extra trouble, but if you could possibly send someone over to fix it, I'd really appreciate it." The service rep says: "The first appointment I can give you is three weeks from today." The Enabling Parent responds: "That's no problem. I understand. I know you have a lot of customers to take care of."

The Nurturing Parent

This is a communication style you see less often. It's most common among people-pleasers as their habitual ego state for communicating with others. Of course, when you're hugging a loved one or sharing time with someone you care about, communicating from the Nurturing Parent can be very appropriate and feels great, but generally it's not appropriate for adult communication in times of conflict. Here's how a Nurturing Parent might talk to the service rep on the receiving end of the line: "Hi! You sound like a cheerful person. Where are you based? Minnesota? Well, how's the weather out there in Minnesota? Well, I have a little problem, and I wondered if you could help me out with it." Then, as the conversation progresses, she might say: "You are so patient and understanding. And I really appreciate it."

Child Ego States

The Entitled Tyrant

This ego state, as the name suggests, is demanding and laced with anger. It's full of blame and comes from a place of outrage and entitlement. The Entitled Tyrant says things like: "Why do I have to do everything myself?" "I want you to do this!" "It's not fair!" This is also a voice that can be verbally abusive, full of cutting insults, and overflowing with foul language. Here's how the Entitled Tyrant might handle a call to the customer rep: "I'm getting really tired of this @& bull#&@! My Internet connection's been down for two hours. I've been on hold for five minutes, and I can't even get anybody on the #@*ing phone!"

The Helpless Victim

This communication style reflects not only a sense of helplessness but also an unwillingness to accept responsibility. The Helpless Victim says things like: "It's not my fault," "I can't help it if I was late; there was a lot of traffic," "No one ever told me; I don't think I got the e-mail." To a customer service rep, the Helpless Victim might meekly say: "My Internet's down. I don't know what to do. Can you please fix it?" "What seems to be the problem?" "I don't know. It's just not working. Can you send someone over here to help me?" "Did you shut everything down and reboot your computer?" "I'm sorry, I don't know how to do that."

The Passive-Aggressive Child

This is the style often used by people who have difficulty addressing issues directly. When they're angry and annoyed, they might not say anything at all. Instead, they file it away and retaliate later. For example, if you don't return a phone call, instead of asking you where you've been or expressing the fact that they'd appreciate your returning calls, they don't return *your* phone calls, or they just write you off altogether. Because they don't address issues as they arise, Passive-Aggressives often hang on to old resentments, which they then express through demeaning comments or jokes like this one: "You mean, you actually *paid* for that haircut? Hey, I was just kidding—don't be so *sensitive*." With a customer service rep, instead of directly addressing the problem at hand, someone in the Passive-Aggressive ego state would be sarcastic and indirect: "Nice of you to pick up the phone. I've only been on hold for about 20 minutes. But it's no big deal. I mean, what's my time worth anyway?"

These are all ineffective communication styles if you want to get your needs met and maintain good relationships. They don't accomplish your objectives and, in times of conflict, they typically make matters worse. They're laced with words, tones, and emotions that spring from the conditioned self, and, as a result, they tend to tap into the listener's conditioned self. For example, speaking from the role of the Critical Parent is almost guaranteed to invoke a defensive response from the Child ego state. In contrast, the Adult ego state is the one that's the most emotionally intelligent—and the one that usually gets the best results.

The Adult Ego State

Let's start with how to handle the same service call from the *Adult ego state*. First of all, the tone is respectful and polite; it doesn't assault the dignity of the person on the other end of the line. When you're in the Adult ego state, you directly address the problem at hand, sharing your perspective, adult-to-adult. For example: "Good morning. I'm having a problem with my Internet service. This is the third time it's gone down this week, and I'm unhappy about the situation. At this point, I'm feeling pretty frustrated. I'd really like to get it fixed." The response to this might be: "I'm sorry you're having a problem. Let's see if I can fix it." Of course, you're talking to a customer service rep. They're trained to deal with Critical Parents and Entitled Tyrants. But out in the real world of adults, operating from the Adult ego state is more likely to elicit an adult response from others—particularly when you're engaged in a potentially conflict-ridden interaction. You're communicating in an honest and clear manner, without attacking or blaming the other person—"At this point, I'm feeling pretty frustrated, and I would really like to get the Internet up and running." Speaking from the Adult ego state in an emotionally intelligent manner is a far more effective way to communicate your needs, and it increases the likelihood of getting them met.

Let's revisit some alternatives for how to communicate from the Adult ego state, with some of the reasons why it's effective:

- *"I'm feeling hurt."* By starting your sentences with "I" instead of "you," you clarify the fact that these are *your* feelings and experiences, without accusing, attacking, or blaming the other person or making him or her responsible for your feelings.

- *"It may not have been your intention to be hurtful, but that's how I experienced it."* This is how you defuse conflict instead of escalating it. It's important to acknowledge that your perceptions are not necessarily accurate and that your feelings are not always appropriate to the situation. Imposing your reality on others or making assumptions about what others are thinking or feeling—and that your perceptions are the "right" ones—usually leads to conflict or miscommunication. You don't want to communicate with words such as: "You don't care at all about me or my feelings." Or "You're selfish and insensitive."

By saying, "This may not have been your intention," you make it far less likely that others will react defensively and give them the opportunity to share their own reality and feelings. When you speak from the heart and share your feelings in a direct and non-accusatory manner, you'll find that people are more likely to respond more positively. "Oh my gosh, I'm so sorry. I spoke without thinking. I didn't realize how judgmental that sounded."

- *"I'm noticing that I'm having a really strong reaction to what you've just said."* By addressing the issue immediately, you're staying in touch with your emotions and responding from your authentic self. You're also being totally honest. That puts you in a vulnerable spot. But that means you're being true to yourself and you're putting the truth out there. That's a critical piece of living from the authentic self. That's how you build deeper relationships, deeper friendships, and a deeper understanding of yourself and others. And once it becomes your new, habitual way of relating to others, it's also much easier. You're not always worrying about saying the wrong thing or how the other person will react. You're not avoiding conflict. You're not spilling over with anger or criticism. Your goal is straightforward: to tell the other person what you're experiencing. When you focus on that goal, you're less likely to provoke a confrontation and more likely to successfully resolve the conflict and get your needs met.

- *"I'd like it if you'd be more sensitive to the fact that I'm single; I'm alone by choice. I'd really like you to be supportive of my choice and my single lifestyle. If you feel critical, I'd prefer that you not share those opinions when we're together."* By addressing an issue head-on—the source of your reaction—you're setting clear boundaries, with the intention of getting your needs and wishes met. You're saying: "This is the way I want to be treated by my friends. I want you to be supportive. I don't want you to communicate to me in critical and judgmental way." That also gives you a way to find out more information about your friend. Is she able to respect the boundaries? Is she able to respond from the Adult ego state? Ultimately, you may find that a friend can't rise to the occasion, but this approach will be the most effective way to help you accurately assess the situation.

When you have to address a thorny issue—at work, in your family, with your friends—here's the basic framework for effective communication:

- Describe the situation as neutrally as possible. Say: "When you made that comment about being single, I had a very strong reaction." Don't say: "You always make me feel bad and don't care about my feelings. You're such an insensitive, uncaring person."

- Describe how you perceived the situation, your feelings, and your reactions, using "I" words. "I don't know if that was your intention, but your comment sounded judgmental to me, and I reacted by feeling hurt and angry."

- Next, describe what you'd like to have happen. Set your boundaries. Define your needs. "I'd really like you to be more supportive of my choice and my single lifestyle. And if you feel critical, I'd appreciate your not sharing those opinions when we're together."

Communicating from the Adult ego state is an art. As such, you have to practice it to master it. But it can be life-transforming. You're sharing your truth in a resourceful and effective way, and you're speaking deliberately from the authentic self instead of reacting from the conditioned self. It builds your self-respect and fosters healthy, constructive relationships with others.

A few caveats: First, like all the other components of mastering aloneness, learning to communicate effectively takes time and practice. We all fall into the Parent and Child ego states. When you find yourself falling into old, limiting patterns, make an effort to clear them up. Talk to the person: "I'm sorry I overreacted today. I was upset, but instead of talking with you right away, I didn't say anything. Then my anger built up, and when I finally said something, I lost my temper and screamed at you."

Second, realize that, regardless of how effectively you communicate with someone, you won't always get your desired response. There are situations where you're exercising emotional intelligence and communicating from the Adult ego state, but you still get a defensive reaction, because of the other person's patterns. If Margaret, for example, continued to be critical and insensitive to my client Jane after she had expressed her needs and wishes, it would be important for Jane to examine the relationship more closely: *Is this a person who can support who I really am? Is this a person with whom I can share a healthy relationship?*

Being True to Yourself

Being true to yourself lies at the heart of living in alignment with your authentic self. No matter what situation arises, you know yourself so well that you're able to identify, communicate, and act upon what you know is right or true for you. Like Jane Austen in *Becoming Jane:* Faced with a choice between sacrificing love or contributing to the financial ruin of Lefroy's family, she didn't hesitate. She knew in an instant. Imagine knowing what's right for you, and honoring it, at any given moment—in every moment. It means making your truth more important than other people's opinions, judgments, or disapproval. That's not always easy. Sometimes, being true to yourself has fallout. If you're in a relationship with someone who is unable to meet your needs or communicate with you from the Adult ego state, it's important to address the issue. If you're in a situation that's in conflict with your authentic self or out of alignment with your values—like the fictional situation Jane Austen faced—you have to make a decision. Being true to yourself means being 100 percent committed to your true self and being able to act in alignment with that truth at any given moment. That takes a great deal of self-awareness, self-respect, and, often, courage. Consider the example of Rana, who came from a culture with strict prohibitions against divorce. It took tremendous courage for her to recognize and address the issues in her relationship with her husband. And, when she couldn't resolve those issues, it took tremendous courage for her to defy the norms of her culture and leave her marriage.

Learning to live authentically is a lot like learning to walk. It takes practice. You'll stumble at times, and at first you won't get very far. But, with perseverance, it will become your new way of living, something you do automatically. You may fall down a hundred times—or even a thousand times. But, in the end, you'll experience greater freedom than you've ever imagined.

Exercises for Retrieving the Authentic Self

As you complete the exercises designed to help you uncover your authentic self, be aware of your thoughts, feelings, and reactions. Some people find it easy to identify their nature, strengths, and passions, while others find it challenging because of old limiting beliefs ("I'm not good enough," "It's not okay to boast about myself," "I'm unworthy," "I'm a failure," "I'm undeserving"). Complete these exercises to the best of your ability.

Exercise: Taking the Myers-Briggs Type Indicator

Earlier in this chapter I talked about the Myers-Briggs Type Indicator (MBTI), a personality assessment originated by Katharine Cook Briggs, along with her daughter, Isabel Briggs Myers. Students of the Swiss psychiatrist Carl Jung, Briggs and Myers based the development of and research for the assessment upon Jung's premise that each of us is born with a specific set of innate personality traits and preferences, part of the hardwiring of who we are as human beings. While there are a variety of different personality assessments out there, I use the MBTI assessment in my practice because it's based on substantial research; it's been around for many years; and it does a particularly good job of assessing one's innate personality traits.

You may want to take the Myers-Briggs Type Indicator (MBTI) yourself. You can accomplish this in one of two ways:

- You can take the MBTI in person by visiting a certified administrator or facilitator. That would include coaches, career counselors, and psychotherapists who've been trained and certified in the MBTI assessment and are properly trained to interpret the results.

- You can take the Myers-Briggs Type Indicator (MBTI) online through the publisher, CPP, Inc., at www.mbticomplete.com. After you've taken the assessment, you'll receive interactive feedback online. One caution: You'll find a variety of other, unauthorized MBTI tests on the Internet. I don't recommend that you take these tests, as their reliability may vary.

The best way to take the MBTI assessment is in person with a certified facilitator or at the authorized Website. The findings will be valuable in retrieving your authentic self by helping you identify your innate personality traits.

Exercise: Identifying Your Personal Qualities

Take out your journal and write "My Personal Qualities" at the top of the page. Using the examples provided below as a guide, make a list of the personal qualities *you currently possess*. Write down any you feel are important to you.

Compassionate	Resourceful
Loving	Strong
Creative	Intelligent
Fearless	Adventurous
Flexible	Supportive
Powerful	Inspiring
Authentic	Intuitive
Self-confident	Peaceful
Charismatic	Gentle
Caring	Self-sufficient
Accepting	Radiant
Passionate	Physically fit
Self-disciplined	Healthy
Playful	Balanced
Joyful	Energetic
Spontaneous	Nurturing
Generous	Engaging

Exercise: Identifying Your Interests and Passions

Now, turn to the next page in your journal and write "My Interests and Passions" at the top of the page. Below that heading, make a list of all the activities and ideas that capture your interest, or engage or motivate you, using the examples below as a guide.

Community service	History
Personal development	Science
Nature	Spirituality
Environmental issues	Children's issues
Gardening	Women's issues
Cooking	Men's issues
Art	Politics
Physical fitness	Animals
Health and wellness	Comedy
Professional development	Travel
Writing	Skiing
Dance	Education
Theater	Biking
Music	Literature
Sports	Crafts
Hiking	Antiques
Sailing	Carpentry
Rock climbing	Technology
Architecture	Fashion

Exercise: Identifying Your Contribution

Now, think about the kind of imprint you'd like to make in the world. In your journal, write "My Contribution," and then write down any contribution or contributions you'd like to make, using the examples below as a guide.

Foster greater joy or fulfillment in people's lives	Raise my children to be healthy, joyful, self-sufficient, and responsible individuals
Help people to improve their health and wellness	Promote greater peace and harmony in the world
Improve people's quality of life	Help people become better educated or informed
Foster greater environmental awareness and responsibility	Foster others' personal growth and development
Promote social justice and equality	Foster others' professional growth and development
Help people to enjoy more pleasure in their lives	Foster others' creativity or innovation
Help people to create more beauty in their lives	Help people have more fun
Help people to heal physically	Help people unleash their greatest potential
Help people to heal emotionally and mentally	Help others create greater abundance or prosperity
Promote a greater sense of community	Inspire others to induce positive change in their lives or in the world

CHAPTER 7

BECOMING THE PARTNER YOU SEEK

See if this experience sounds familiar. You've been invited to a party, and the host mentions that there will be half a dozen single people there whom you've never met before. Immediately you begin thinking that maybe this will be the big night, the night you'll meet that special someone, your soul mate, the person who will transform your life forever.

The evening of the party, you take extra care getting dressed and you arrive on time. After greeting your host, you begin scanning the room for the new faces, ignoring old friends and acquaintances you haven't seen in months because of your busy schedule. You introduce yourself to the first new, attractive person you see but then notice that someone else across the room looks even more promising. Although you've barely begun talking with the first person and have learned little about him or her, you end the conversation abruptly. Then you wander over to the buffet table where the second person is standing, introduce yourself, and start up another conversation—but still your eyes are roving about the room, trying to figure out if this person is the best prospect or whether there might be someone else even more appealing.

When the party ends, you still haven't met that special someone, and after you return home, you feel sad and empty. You realize that you didn't make a connection with anyone. By focusing your energy on finding that one person who might rescue you from your unhappy life alone, you were unable to enjoy just being at the party, and you barely spoke to any of your friends. In other words, you were never really present at the party; instead, you were living your life in the future, where you pictured yourself in bliss with your ideal mate.

What if you could do that evening over again? Imagine if you went to the party to meet people just for the sake of meeting people, rather than determined to find a potential partner. You'd have the opportunity to engage with all kinds of men and women who might enhance your life. You'd be putting yourself in a better position to enjoy the event.

In order for that to happen, you have to begin to change the way you approach your life. Instead of imagining that someone else is going to transform your life, you have to start transforming it yourself. And rather than single-mindedly focusing on finding your soul mate—that special person who will make you whole—you have to focus on making yourself whole. The question you should be asking yourself isn't: *How do I find my soul mate so I can have the life I want?* The question you should be asking yourself is: *What do I need to do to create the life that I want for myself?* Then you'll start taking the steps that will move you in the direction you desire.

Put another way, instead of *pursuing* your ideal partner, you're going to *become* the ideal partner you seek.

Becoming Your Own Ideal Partner

Liberating the authentic self is the key to personal transformation and to creating a fuller, richer, and more joyful life. It's only when you're connected to, expressing, and meeting the needs of your true self that you're able to realize your greatest potential. You're no longer expending energy on finding someone else to make you happy. Instead, your energy goes toward creating the life you want and to enjoying that life. By living authentically, you're building a sense of self-worth from the inside out. You'll be taking responsibility for your own life, building your own financial security, creating the life experiences you seek, and creating a sense of love and fulfillment from within. Then, if and when you do meet someone with whom to share a partnership or marriage, the relationship will be the icing on the cake instead of the source of your self-esteem, your happiness, or your life sustenance.

The world is full of fascinating and caring people who can enrich your life: friends, neighbors, and colleagues who may share your interests; men and women who can offer emotional support and intellectual stimulation; people who can teach you new things, inspire you, and make you laugh. But when you perceive new people exclusively through the limited lens of whether or not they are potential life partners, you close the door on a wealth of opportunities. Many people spend so much time looking for—or waiting for—their soul mates that life passes them by, leaving them feeling empty, alone, and dissatisfied, like the person who attended the hypothetical party at the opening of this chapter.

In mastering the art of aloneness, you're moving your life in a new direction by:

- Creating the kinds of experiences that you want to have

- Generating the financial security to which you aspire

- Building support systems that develop your inner and outer resources

- Expanding your social life to include exciting activities that aren't necessarily planned around trying to find a partner

- Developing self-esteem from within, and, as a result, experiencing and exuding greater self-confidence

In short, you're going to create a very rich and full life by yourself and for yourself, which will jump-start a remarkable change. As you build confidence and self-esteem, you'll develop a greater appreciation of the person you are. As a result, you'll take better care of yourself and do nice things for yourself. You'll be engaged in actively loving and valuing yourself, thereby facilitating a self-fulfilling prophecy.

Overcoming the Fear of Being Alone

For many people—men and women alike—it's fear that fuels their intense drive to find a mate: the fear of being unloved, the fear of being financially insolvent, the fear of being alone. For women, the fear of being alone often centers on an underlying belief that they can't take care of themselves—either emotionally or financially. For both men and women, the fear of aloneness can revolve around the issue of emotional dependency. Many people are simply afraid that they can't be happy without a mate. These fears are grounded in our limiting beliefs, not in reality. I had a client who was a multimillionaire as a result of her own business success. She had achieved complete financial independence and was perfectly capable of taking care of herself. Nonetheless, she married a man she knew was wrong for her out of a deep-seated fear of being alone for the rest of her life. Ironically, she married someone who couldn't make her happy, because she was afraid if she didn't get married, she'd end up unhappy. She married him in a panic, and her marriage ended in divorce within six months. Her core limiting belief: *I need a man to take care of me.*

In her landmark book *The Cinderella Complex: Women's Hidden Fear of Independence,* Colette Dowling makes a compelling argument that "personal, psychological dependency—the deep wish to be taken care of by others—is the chief force holding women down today."[1] In Dowling's view, many women are unable to realize their full potential because they believe someone else will take care of them. In fact, they believe someone else *should* take care of them. With *The Cinderella Complex*, she put a name to the internal conflict many women experience between their desire for independence and their wish to be taken care of by men. Dowling wrote her book in 1981, after the cultural changes inspired by the women's movement, but the stories she shares could just as easily have surfaced today—stories of women so afraid of losing the security of a relationship that they sabotaged their own careers; women who retreated into unsatisfying marriages because of the deeply held belief that they needed a man's support; women who were "utterly paralyzed at the prospect of being on their own"[2] or who stayed in troubled relationships out of a fear of being alone; and women who, like Cinderella, were trapped in time waiting to be rescued, longing for a man to come along and save them, "waiting for something external to transform their lives."[3] I've observed these patterns in my clients, and I've recognized them in myself. I not only experienced the desire to be rescued by a man but was also convinced that I'd be destitute without one.

The problem with waiting for Prince or Princess Charming is, all too often, you're sabotaging your own life by living in a kind of limbo. I've had clients who put nearly every aspect of their lives on hold, who behave as if their real life hasn't yet begun, because they're expecting a man or woman to come along—so their dream of having a mate, a family, and children can come true. They might hold off on buying a house, delay plans for an advanced degree, and turn down job promotions. Just as importantly, they spend much of their leisure time in limbo—watching television, hiding out at home, staying in their comfort zone—instead of actively developing their interests, pursuing their passions, and fully engaging in life. They're waiting for a man or woman to complete their life picture. This is particularly common among women whose biological clocks are ticking or those who, since early childhood, have imagined a life that includes a husband and provider. But I've also seen it with divorced women and older women, as well as with men of all ages who aren't engaged in a relationship.

Despite the societal changes of the past 30 years that have increased gender equity and promoted greater self-awareness, many men and women continue to look for a partner to provide the happiness, love, and security they crave. They're afraid of going through life alone. It's a fear they share with many people who are *in* relationships. The fear of being alone is the glue that holds many bad marriages together. It's the reason why many women give up their careers to care for their families, a choice that can have significant negative financial consequences in the long run. And it's often why people are drawn into and remain in relationships that aren't working.

Among people who are alone, this fear reflects a variety of beliefs. Here are a few of the most common:

- No one will ever love me, and I'll be alone forever.

- If I get sick, there won't be anyone to take care of me.

- I'll be poor and destitute.

- I'll never get married.

- I'll never have children.

- I'll die alone.

If you share some of these fears, you're deep in the grip of FEAR—Fantasizing Events As Real. To uncover where the fear is coming from, you'll want to move through the Five Steps to Managing Fear that I talked about earlier. Ask yourself: *What am I really afraid of? What's the movie I'm running in my mind?* Do a reality check and dig deeper to uncover the core limiting belief that's driving your fears. For example, fear of never having children is a major issue among both men and women who are single and in their 30s and 40s. If that's your fear, ask yourself: *Is this fear stemming from cultural expectations or pressure from my family? Am I afraid that people will think less of me because I don't have children? Is this about something that's expected of me? Is it the biological imperative that is driving this fear? Or is it something that I truly want for myself?* As you begin to uncover and free yourself from the drivers of your fear, you can begin to evaluate different options: Single people do give birth and adopt. There are also plenty of other opportunities for nurturing others—as a loving aunt or uncle, as a volunteer, and in the education and child-care arenas.

When the fear of being alone rears its disconcerting head, here are some other things to keep in mind and to include in your reality check:

- Remember that being alone is a *choice*. If you wanted to be in a relationship, there are plenty of single people out there. For whatever reason, you're choosing aloneness over having a relationship. Dig deeper into what those reasons may be and you'll make a major move forward.

- At its root, imagining that you will get old or die alone isn't usually about having a life partner; rather, it's about wanting to have loving and supportive relationships in your life. When you focus your energy on building those relationships, you can begin to alleviate those fears.

- The next time you look around and feel as if all you can see are happy couples, remember that many of those relationships are riddled with conflict; many are built on people's default patterns and core limiting beliefs. That's a subject I'll be addressing further in this chapter.

- If you're a woman, don't fall into the trap of imagining that you'd be better off with a mate to support you financially—a limiting belief that many women still hold. In truth, 90 percent of all American women will be in charge of their own finances at some point in their lives.[4] As Leslie Bennetts points out in *The Feminine Mistake:* "In striving to become a fully mature, fully realized human being, there is no substitute for taking complete responsibility for your own life."[5]

- Many people tend to glorify the idea of approaching old age with a longtime mate. But, for women in particular, that's a dangerous fantasy. Women tend to outlive men, and, as a result, many women end up approaching old age alone. In fact, among people aged 65 or older, 43 percent of women are widowed, compared to only 14 percent of men.[6] And, because women on average have lower earnings than men and many have relied on their husbands for support, they often end up with lower social-security payments, lower pensions, and meager 401(k)s.[7] Women are twice as likely as men to slide below the poverty line in their later years,[8] and four out of five widows living below the poverty line had not been poor before their husbands died.[9] Writes Leslie Bennetts: "It's simply too risky to count on anyone else to support you over the long haul."[10]

- Relationships do end. The high divorce rate confirms that fact. And when your sense of self-worth, personal fulfillment, or financial security is dependent upon another person, if that person disappears from your life, so does your self-esteem, happiness, and quality of life.

- Most people never do the work that takes them to the point where they feel truly fulfilled and whole on their own. You're doing it now. That puts you ahead of the game and prepares you for healthier relationships with others.

- Feeling unlovable is a state of mind that springs from your core limiting beliefs. As I've said before, feeling lovable starts with loving yourself. When you begin to live more deliberately and master aloneness, you begin to treat yourself better and feel more loving toward yourself. As a result, your sense of self-worth comes from within—not from others.

• Finally, it's important to come to a relationship from a place of wholeness, not from a place of emotional neediness. If you're looking for an ideal partner, there's a good chance that you may be looking for someone to fill the voids in yourself and in your life. But you'll be in a much better position to live life on your own or to attract your ideal partner if you've filled those voids in yourself. That's the premise behind the idea of becoming the partner you seek.

Misguided Attempts to Fill the Voids

Patti Scialfi, a recording artist in her own right, has been married to Bruce Springsteen since 1991. They have three children together. Not long ago, she was interviewed on the radio about her new CD, and my ears perked up when I heard what she had to say about her marriage. "You know, I was a child of the '50s," she told interviewer Liane Hansen of NPR. "There was the idea that love is a simplistic promise of completion . . . that you're going to find the missing half, your lost twin, your soul mate. I don't think that you can look for something external to really complete you that way." She went on to say that her marriage had broadened her and given her a sense of fulfillment, but, she added, "You can't really look for that. And if you're looking for that, you're going to be disappointed."

I couldn't have said it better myself. One of the most common and widely accepted approaches to filling our personal voids is finding another person to make us feel happy, whole, and secure. But, in truth, relationships built on such premises tend to be conflict-ridden and unfulfilling. Why? Because if you're unconsciously seeking someone to fill your voids, you'll tend to attract someone who's also on an unconscious quest for wholeness. As a result, there will be more differences than similarities between the two of you. You'll both tend to be ill equipped to handle the conflicts inherent in such a relationship, which I call a "love battlefield" because the individuals eventually become intimate enemies. In contrast, in a healthy, interdependent relationship, the partners are integrated, whole individuals who have learned to meet their own needs and to communicate effectively. They come together out of conscious choice—not an unconscious drive to replicate old, familiar patterns.

There are all kinds of relationships that are built on default patterns or unconscious drivers that spring from our conditioning. I have a client who has been married twice. Although, outwardly, those men did not seem very similar, they were identical in two important respects. Both of her husbands seemed to adore her. When she split up with each of them, many of her friends were puzzled. "But he's crazy about you," they told her, in both instances. Yet, in private, both of these men were extremely demanding and critical. She had replicated the pattern of her family of origin in both her marriages. Her father adored her; he was unusually supportive of her goals, her independent nature, her spirit. Her mother, on the other hand, was critical of just about everything she did. My client found not one but *two* men who were embodiments of the dynamic she experienced with her parents. In each case, the chemistry—that initial attraction—was intense. Both times, she married in the wake of a whirlwind romance that lasted only a few short months. But both marriages were plagued by conflict. She spent many years trying to accommodate her demanding husbands—just as she had tried to accommodate her demanding mother—but the marriages were based on her default operating system. They were toxic relationships.

In *Getting the Love You Want,* Harville Hendrix illuminates how this process works. He maintains that in searching for the perfect mate, if you're like most of us, you're guided by "an unconscious image of the opposite sex" that you've been forming since you were born.[11] It's an image, he explains, that both resembles your caretakers and compensates for the repressed parts of yourself.[12] He calls this mental picture, this image that resides deep in your subconscious, the "imago." It represents a detailed composite of the positive and negative traits of the central people in your early life—parents, caretakers, siblings—and the experiences you had with them. According to Hendrix, the most powerful memories incorporated into the imago are the negative ones. Every time you meet a potential romantic partner, he asserts, you're sizing him or her up unconsciously against your imago. And when you experience that instant attraction, that thing we call chemistry, it's because you've found a match for your imago.[13]

I believe that chemistry takes a number of forms in these unconscious relationships. It can be a gut feeling that you've found the missing parts that are going to make you whole—your other half, as Patti Scialfi described it. Or it can be the recognition of the imago—the composite of your most intimate family histories coming to life, as Hendrix describes it. Or it may be that you experience a familiar dynamic with a romantic partner that you've had with your parents or, in some cases, haven't had—a missing piece that was never realized in your relationship with your parents. Any way you look at it, it's all about completion, and it's all about conditioning.

Let's say, for example, you're a woman who didn't feel safe, loved, and protected by your father. Without being aware of it, you might be looking for someone who makes you feel safe, loved, and protected, because, unconsciously, a part of you is missing those qualities and those feelings. Or maybe you're a man whose mother couldn't express her emotions, including affection. In response to your conditioning, you might be drawn to emotionally aloof women like your mother, thereby replicating your family dynamics, or, on the other hand, you might be attracted to affectionate, loving women who make you feel lovable and worthwhile. In either case, you're creating potential problems, because you aren't attracted to either of these women for who they really are—you're attracted to them based on an unconscious, hidden agenda driven by the past.

In romantic relationships, opposites tend to attract. Two people come together to fill the voids in each other. But such attractions are often problematic. Consider this example: Mary goes out with her friends on a Friday night and meets Brian. Outgoing and friendly,

Brian is a world traveler with a high-powered sales job and a magnetic personality. He's a dashing, interesting, charismatic person. They share a few drinks and a little conversation. She thinks he's fabulous and can't wait to see him again. Brian feels the same way. Mary is a nurse practitioner who has worked at the same hospital and lived in the same condo for ten years; he sees her as a solid, secure, dependable person. *Just the kind of woman I need,* he thinks. *Someone caring, giving, stable—someone to keep me grounded.* Mary, on the other hand, sees Brian as dynamic and exciting. He seems so worldly, so wise.

Mary is introverted, conservative, and security-oriented. Brian is eclectic, a bit of a Renaissance man, extroverted, and impulsive. At their first meeting, chemistry sparks. So they start a relationship, and over time, those very characteristics that initially attracted them to each other become sore points, sources of conflict. Mary starts telling her friends: "I don't trust Brian. He's always flirting with other women." Or "Brian can't hold down a job; he keeps hopping from one thing to another." Or "He's so irresponsible." They argue about money, about how they're going to spend their time. Their values are as different as their personalities. Over time, Brian starts to find Mary boring. "She has no spontaneity," he complains to his friends. "She's uptight." "Where's your sense of humor?" he asks her so often it becomes a running joke—only it's not so funny anymore.

Opposites attract for a reason—the very same reason that those relationships tend to fall apart. When a relationship is driven by conditioned patterns, when it's built on an unconscious need to replicate or compensate for your childhood experiences, it produces anger, resentment, disillusionment, and alienation. It erodes self-esteem. And it can lead to emotional and physical exhaustion because it takes a lot of energy to deal with the conflicts that arise again and again. Sometimes these relationships can go on for years, particularly if they represent a low level of dysfunction. Say two people marry at a young age because each embodies the other's lost parts. They strike a happy balance, finding a harmony that works. Maybe, despite their differences, they share similar values or enjoy the same close-knit community or derive pleasure from raising their children together. Then one partner hits a midlife crisis and it topples the precarious balance, or one partner dies. As a result of such unions, people can find themselves alone at some point, with big gaps in their lives—and in their selves.

Don't misunderstand me. It's quite possible for a couple to work through these issues within the context of a relationship, to learn and grow. When couples come to me for relationship coaching, I encourage them to work together to bring an unconscious relationship to a conscious level. But it's not easy. Both partners have to be committed to the process. Many people are ill equipped to handle the conflicts that arise in relationships because they've never learned how to communicate effectively. I attribute the high divorce rate to issues such as these. If you're not currently in a relationship, here's the good news: you have the opportunity to start from scratch to create a conscious, healthy relationship with *yourself* and to emerge whole—and better prepared for the possibility of a healthy, conscious relationship with someone else.

The First Step: Creating a Loving Relationship with Yourself

I first met Jenna when she came to me for relationship coaching. Her goal: to find a life partner. She was in her late 30s and desperate to fall in love, marry, and have a family. After the first couple of sessions, however, it became clear that before she could create and sustain a healthy and fulfilling relationship with another person, she first needed to develop a healthy and fulfilling relationship with herself.

Jenna's father had abandoned her family when she was two years old. An only child with no extended family, Jenna was raised by a highly critical and self-centered mother who controlled every aspect of her life—how she dressed, how she wore her hair, how she behaved, her school work and activities, what and how much she ate, and who she could and could not see. With no other relatives or friends to either support or serve as a buffer between them, Jenna and her mother developed an unhealthy, codependent relationship that revolved almost exclusively around each other.

Given that her mother exerted a high level of control and made all the decisions for her, Jenna became extremely dependent and was terrified that her mother, too, might leave. As is common among children who are abandoned, Jenna grew up believing that her father had left because she had been a bad daughter, and so she worked very hard to be perfect so her mother wouldn't leave too. Despite her vigilance, however, nothing Jenna did ever seemed good enough, and she was constantly subjected to her mother's criticism.

As a result, Jenna adopted the role of the Lost Child and became a classic people-pleaser. Driven by an ever-present fear of rejection and abandonment, she became a master at anticipating and meeting other people's needs as a way of keeping them in her life. At the age of 16, she began a series of brief encounters with men, a pattern that continued into her 30s. She sought their approval by acceding to their wishes, essentially playing the role of doormat again and again and again. By the time she came to me, she was not only trapped in this pattern of unsatisfying relationships, but she was living dangerously—having unprotected sex with men, many of them married, on a routine basis. Her core beliefs: *I'm worthless. I'm powerless. And if I don't do what others want, they'll reject or abandon me.*

The work that Jenna and I did together involved helping her identify her core limiting beliefs and override her fears. She began to transform into an independent, assertive, self-confident woman able to meet her own needs. But the cornerstone of that transformation involved changing her relationship with herself. Because she had never experienced unconditional love within her family of origin but *had* experienced the deep loss associated with abandonment, Jenna was driven to self-destructive behavior that centered on her relationships with men. Because she didn't love and respect herself, she didn't treat herself well.

Very few of us survive the conditioning process with our self-esteem intact—truly loving and appreciating ourselves. How do you restore a loving relationship with yourself? By activating your *Inner Nurturing Parent*. An Inner Nurturing Parent is someone who stands up for you, who loves you unconditionally, who comforts you, and who treats you with care and respect. It's the parent many of us never had, and it's a powerful way to silence the voice of the Inner Critical Parent we may have internalized from childhood. In my practice, I've found this to be a powerful tool to help my clients learn how to love and trust themselves.

Activating your Inner Nurturing Parent is also like having a loving life partner inside of you—a part of you that appreciates who you are, a part that stands up for you and doesn't allow others to mistreat you, a part that honors and nurtures you. Jenna, in effect, needed someone in her corner, and she had to find that someone inside. I believe we all can uncover that someone within ourselves and begin to treat ourselves in ways that we would want an ideal partner to treat us. When you do the next exercise, you'll be taking an important step toward mastering the art of aloneness.

Exercise: Developing Your Inner Nurturing Parent

To begin developing your own Inner Nurturing Parent, close your eyes and see yourself as a small child. If you have difficulty remembering what you looked like when you were little, then instead of closing your eyes, look at a photograph of you as a child. Imagine that this child is your own child, a child you love and feel tenderly toward. Someone is talking to that child using the harsh words of the inner critic. Your job is to protect the child. What would you say to the child to protect him from the hurtful words of the critic? For example, if your critic tells the child, "You're stupid and incompetent," then you, as the nurturing parent, may say,

"You are a very capable person and you can do anything you put your mind to; I'm here to support you and help you every step of the way." If the inner critic says, "You should be spending more time at work; you're not working hard enough," the nurturing parent would say, "It's good and important for you to take time to rejuvenate yourself." Whenever you feel your inner critic surfacing, step back and ask your Inner Nurturing Parent for love and support.

Another way to activate your Inner Nurturing Parent is by making a habit of asking yourself: *What do I need?* Then take action to meet those needs. For example, if you're feeling lonely and disconnected from people—if you feel you need human connection—you might go and get a massage. That's a wonderful way to experience the comfort and nurturance of another's touch. If you've been working hard or just met a difficult deadline at work, maybe you need a special treat. You can love and nurture yourself by sending yourself flowers along with a loving card, cooking yourself a favorite meal, taking yourself out to the movies, or preparing a luxurious, candlelit bath for yourself. Think about how you would want to be treated by a loving partner and instead of waiting for someone else to do those things for you, start doing them for yourself on a regular basis.

Conscious Versus Unconscious Relationships

You're reading this book for a reason. Whatever your innate nature and family history may be, you've arrived at this point because of your life experiences. Chances are you've had relationships in your life that reflect some of the patterns I've described in this chapter. You may have already begun to see the ways in which your own conditioning has influenced your expectations of a mate. Maybe you've even played out these expectations in relationships that didn't work. I believe that most relationships are built on default patterns. Very few people have moved beyond the powerful patterns of their conditioning and the power of the imago that Harville Hendrix describes. I see it all the time in my workshops and in my coaching practice. Here are just a few examples:

- A man tells me he was drawn to his ex-wife because she seemed so independent; he wanted someone who could take care of herself. After they married, she continued to pursue a career but announced that she wanted to have children. That wasn't at all what he had in mind. His own family had struggled financially, and his father had been an unhappy man with five children to support and a sickly wife. His core belief: *Women and children are a burden.*

- A young woman tells me that every guy she falls for is a high achiever; they work long hours and travel all the time. Eventually, she exits the relationships because she's lonely. Her father was the CEO of a major corporation, and he was absent through most of her young life. Her mother, depressed and absorbed in her own problems, paid little attention to her. She keeps replicating her childhood experiences over and over, driven by her core belief: *There's no one there for me.*

- A young man tells me he's unable to be faithful to any woman. He sabotages every relationship he's in by cheating. His father was an alcoholic and a womanizer. His mother was withdrawn and unhappy. They fought all the time, but they stayed together. He grew up feeling unwanted and unloved. He continually replicates his parents' conflict-ridden relationship. His core belief: *I'm unworthy and undeserving of love.*

- A woman tells me that she and her live-in boyfriend argue about money all the time. He grew up in a working-class home where money was an issue; she comes from an upper-class background where her mother stayed home and raised the kids. When she and her boyfriend moved in together, they talked about splitting everything 50–50. She has a great job, but she still resents not being financially taken care of by her boyfriend. Her core belief: *I'm entitled to have someone take care of me.*

The central lesson of these stories: by reclaiming your wholeness, reintegrating the parts of you that were lost during your life conditioning, and becoming aware of the habitual patterns that drive your relationships, you'll be in a better position to enter into a healthy, conscious relationship with another person. What is a conscious relationship? It's one in which both people have reclaimed their innate wholeness and are relating from their authentic selves. They can effectively function independently, but *choose* to share a relationship where there is a healthy balance between independence and interdependence.

Here are what I believe to be the basic requirements for a conscious relationship:

- The relationship is built on a partnership model versus a traditional model based on stereotypes. That means the partners don't fall unconsciously into prescribed roles—a pattern, for example, where all the house-hold and child-rearing responsibilities fall only to one person and all the financial responsibilities fall to the other. They share responsibilities in a way that meets each individual's needs and personal vision. And, like a healthy family system, the roles are flexible and fluid.

- From the very beginning, both partners approach the relationship in a conscious manner. They talk about the kind of life they want to share. Instead of operating from their default modes, they deliberately build a relationship based upon their values, what's important to each of them, and what's going to work for both partners.

- Both people have a similar level of self-awareness, self-love, self-respect, and emotional maturity. They're able to respect each other's needs, interests, and desires and to honor each other's differences.

- Each partner has well-developed interpersonal skills. They have the ability to effectively communicate and manage conflict, as well as the capacity for empathy and forgiveness. In other words, they possess emotional intelligence.

- They are equally committed to their own growth and the partner's growth. They view the relationship as an opportunity for greater learning and development and as a safe place to express their authentic selves.

By referring to this kind of relationship as conscious, I don't mean to suggest that there's no romance or chemistry involved. People in conscious relationships still share the experience of falling in love; their endorphins still kick in; they still experience a deep attraction. But here's the difference: when they experience that initial attraction, they're aware that they're not getting a complete picture of the other person; they understand that it takes time to get to know someone. The truth is, at the beginning of any relationship, it's impossible to see and understand all the dimensions of another person. People reveal different aspects of themselves as a relationship unfolds. When you're in a conscious relationship, you take the time to get to know the other person and to assess the level of compatibility and fit. That's how you can get a sense of whether or not the relationship can work. You come to a point where you understand where the similarities and differences lie and whether the differences can be managed effectively. You might discover that the differences between you are deal-breakers—differences that make the relationship unworkable. Or you might find that the differences are ones that are easily managed. If you aspire to a healthy, conscious partnership or marriage, mastering the art of aloneness and becoming the partner you seek are important prerequisites.

Defining Your Ideal Partner

The first step toward becoming your ideal partner involves defining very precisely what you're looking for and how those attributes relate to the life you want to create for yourself. The exercises that follow are an effective way to help you begin to clarify:

- The personal qualities and life circumstances you want for yourself

- The personal qualities and life circumstances you currently have

- The gaps between where you are today and where you want to be

Before you begin, prepare the environment by turning off your phone and sitting comfortably in a quiet room where you won't be disturbed. There is no right or wrong way to do a visualization exercise, and it's a different experience for each person. Some people are more visual than others; you may get more of a feeling than a clear picture. Just do the best you can and allow the experience to unfold naturally, instead of trying to control or direct it. If you notice that you're trying to force it, just let go and focus on allowing versus directing the experience. I suggest either recording the exercise beforehand, so you can follow your own voice with your eyes closed during the exercise or asking a trusted friend to guide you through it. As you read through the exercise, be sure to use the word "he" or "she" where appropriate.

Exercise: Ideal Partner Visualization

Sit back and relax in a comfortable chair. (You can also do this exercise lying down, as long as you don't fall asleep.) Inhaling through your mouth, take a deep breath in and slowly release it. Take another deep breath in and as you release it, allow your shoulders to relax and your belly to go soft. Notice whether there are any places of tension in your body, and allow those parts to let go and relax.

Imagine you're walking along the street, on your way to the home of your ideal life partner. Notice the street on which you're walking and the area around you. Are you on a city street, out in the country, or in a suburban neighborhood? Notice what the homes are like. Are they apartments, condominiums, or stand-alone homes? And now, see yourself standing in front of the home of your ideal partner. What does it look like? Is it an apartment, a condominium, or a stand-alone house? What color is the building and what style is it?

Now see yourself walking up to the doorway and knocking on the door. See the door open. Standing before you is your ideal life partner. The first thing to notice is his physical appearance. What does your ideal partner look like? How tall is he? What's his hair color? How is it cut or styled? Is it long or short? What kind of clothes and shoes is he wearing? How would you describe his body type? What is his facial expression?

See yourself stepping into your ideal partner's home and notice what it looks like. Is it small or large? How is it decorated? What kind of furniture is in it and what, if anything, is on the walls? How would you describe the style? Is it funky bohemian, eclectic, traditional, or, perhaps, contemporary? What is the environment like? What colors permeate your ideal partner's home?

And now, notice the personal qualities of your ideal partner. What words would you and others use to describe her personality? Is this person outgoing, or more on the quiet and reserved side? What other adjectives would describe her inner qualities? How does your ideal partner behave? With you? Around others? Toward herself? What words would describe the way she behaves? What are your ideal partner's interests and passions? How does she like to spend her leisure time?

Now notice what this person does professionally. Is he employed, or does he have his own business? What is your ideal partner's annual income? What is his work schedule? How does he feel about the work he does? Or is your ideal partner retired?

And now, notice the life circumstances and lifestyle of your ideal partner. Does she have a large or small network of friends, social contacts, and family members? What, if any, types of sports, exercise, or recreational activities does your ideal partner do? To what, if any, clubs or social, charitable, or religious organizations does she belong? How often and to what kinds of places does your ideal partner like to go out to socialize? Does she take vacations on a regular basis? If so, how often and where?

Now notice if there is anything else about your ideal partner that I didn't ask. Take your time. When you're finished with the visualization, slowly let the image of your ideal partner fade and begin to bring your awareness back into your body. Take a deep breath in and notice what, if any, emotions were evoked during this exercise. Slowly open your eyes, get your journal and pen, and complete the following exercise.

Exercise: Ideal Partner Attributes

Drawing from the Ideal Partner Visualization, write down the qualities of your ideal partner for each of the categories below. Try to be as specific as you can. If some of the answers weren't clear in your visualization, just write down what you think you would like in an ideal partner. The descriptions below are provided as examples, just to give you guidance on the types of answers that fit each category.

- *Physical appearance:* How does your ideal partner look and dress? Examples: stylish, casual, sophisticated, physically fit, attractive, athletic, professional.

- *Personal qualities:* What personal qualities does your ideal partner possess? Examples: kind, warm, outgoing, reserved, powerful, fulfilled, enthusiastic, self-aware, honest, self-confident, accomplished, joyful, dependable, energetic, intelligent, creative, strong.

- *Behaviors:* Describe how your ideal partner behaves. Examples: treats others with
  respect, consideration, and kindness; honestly communicates thoughts and feelings;
  follows through on commitments; maintains
  a healthy diet and lifestyle.

- *Passions:* What does your ideal partner care
  deeply about? Examples: helping others,
  social justice, work/life balance, spiritual-
  ity/religion, health and wellness, personal
  growth, the environment.

- *Interests:* What are your ideal partner's interests and leisure activities? Examples: travel,
  antiques, kayaking, ballroom dancing,
  music, cooking, movies.

- *Home and living environment:* Describe your
  ideal partner's home and environment. Does
  he own his own home or rent? Examples:
  rents an apartment in the city filled with
  art and modern furniture, uncluttered and
  elegant; owns a house in a small town filled
  with family photographs and books, comfy
  and homey, with overstuffed sofas, wicker
  everywhere, and a beautiful garden.

- *Profession:* What kind of work does your ideal
  partner do? Is she employed, does she have
  her own business, or is she retired? Some
  examples: self-employed with a flexible work
  schedule; a successful executive working in

a large corporation; works in a nonprofit, mission-driven organization, and has a nine-to-five work schedule; or retired, with plenty of time to travel.

- *Financial/lifestyle:* What is the annual income of your ideal partner? What kind of lifestyle does he have? Examples: earns $250,000 per year, drives a new Mercedes, eats out at fine restaurants three times a week, rents a beach house at the Hamptons for four weeks every summer; or earns $75,000 per year, drives a motorcycle, enjoys cooking and eating in, spends three weeks backpacking in South America every spring.

- *Other:* List any other life circumstances of your ideal life partner that surfaced during your visualization exercise or that are important to you. Examples: has a Labrador retriever; has a large, loving extended family that lives nearby; shares close relationships with a small circle of friends; has an active social life.

Exercise: Identifying the Gaps

Remember, this book is about mastering the art of aloneness—not finding your ideal mate. Look carefully at your Ideal Partner Attributes list, with an eye toward determining the differences between your life and the life of your ideal partner. Whatever you're looking for in an ideal partner is a piece of your puzzle—a key to understanding what you're seeking in your own life. Instead of looking for a partner to complete you, you're engaged in the process of completing yourself.

To complete this exercise, look at all the information you uncovered about your ideal partner. You may find that your ideal life partner is similar to you in many respects. But, at this point, you're going to focus on identifying the *differences*. Now circle all the personal qualities, behaviors, passions, interests, and life circumstances of your ideal partner that you *do not* currently possess in *your life*. The attributes you've circled represent the gaps between the life you seek and the life you are living today. On a new page in your journal, write "My Ideal Partner Gaps" at the top. Under that heading, list all of the attributes you circled—the gaps between your current life attributes and those of your ideal partner. We'll revisit this exercise later in the book when you begin to clearly define your Life Vision.

CHAPTER 8

CREATING YOUR LIFE VISION

When I attended my first personal-development workshop back in 1982, I was introduced to the concepts of visualization and affirmations. I also discovered that I had very low self-esteem and, as a result, I had developed the habit of keeping people at an emotional distance and always trying to appear perfect. In an effort to build my self-esteem and deepen my connections with others, I wrote an affirmation that said, "I am loving myself and sharing my heart with others." I hung this affirmation all around my house. I memorized it, and, just as I was taught to do in the workshop, I said it aloud a hundred times a day. "I am loving myself and sharing my heart with others." I repeated these words over and over to myself every day for more than a year. I gained a lot of valuable lessons in that workshop, including increased self-awareness. Yet no matter how many times I repeated those words to myself, I continued to struggle with feelings of unworthiness and inadequacy.

Visualization involves imagining something to which you aspire—a desired future state or life circumstance. A vision statement or affirmation is a clear and concise description of that future state or circumstance, written or spoken in the present tense, as if it were already true—as in "I am loving myself and sharing my heart with others." Visualizing helps you to clarify what it is that you want, and a vision statement or affirmation helps you stay focused on achieving it. For years, I tried unsuccessfully to use visualization, affirmations, and vision statements to change myself and my life. While I've learned that these techniques are powerful tools for change, I've also learned that it's not enough to simply visualize a future state, write down an affirmation, or say a vision statement aloud. It was only years later, when I went through the process of identifying my self-defeating behaviors and the core limiting beliefs that were driving them—and created and implemented an action plan to help me develop new, self-supporting beliefs and behaviors—that I was finally able to achieve and sustain the personal transformation to which I aspired.

To *realize* the affirmation, "I am loving myself and sharing my heart with others," I had to identify and activate *the behaviors* and *action steps* that would actually make me feel more loving toward myself and experience greater emotional connection with others. Why? Because, by failing to identify and take the necessary actions to generate the results I wanted, I was *at the mercy of my subconscious impulses*. In other words, my *default operating system* was still in the driver's seat. So, even though I was repeating my affirmation over and over, I was still living from my conditioned self, based on the old, self-defeating patterns I learned in childhood.

Until I became aware of my core limiting beliefs and habitual behaviors and developed a set of actions that would enable me to change them, I was powerless. No matter how many times I told myself, "I am loving myself and sharing my heart with others," my new vision wasn't going to become a reality. Instead of simply reciting my affirmation, here are some of the *action steps* I could have taken to bring that affirmation to life:

- Invoking my Inner Nurturing Parent whenever I bumped up against one of my human flaws or made a mistake

- Making a list of my positive qualities and the things I'd accomplished and focusing on that list every time I started to feel bad about myself

- Practicing self-care and self-nurturance by eating healthy food and making healthy lifestyle choices in every moment

- Identifying, honoring, and expressing my real feelings to others, even when I felt afraid of what they might think of me

- Expressing my needs to others and setting healthy boundaries regarding what was and was not okay for me

- Seeking out and building relationships with people who shared my values and were loving and supportive

- Doing something special for myself once a week, such as buying myself flowers, getting a massage, or treating myself to a lovely dinner out

The Next Steps: Creating and Activating Your Life Vision

At the end of this chapter, you're going to do a visualization exercise to define and articulate your Life Vision. You already have many of the tools you need to bring that vision to life. We spent a lot of time in Part I of this book focused on the past: your family of origin, your conditioned self, and the influences that have shaped who you are and the life you have today. We've talked about ways to begin to change your habitual patterns by living more deliberately, by managing your emotions and your communications more effectively, and by treating yourself differently—with compassion, nurturance, and love. We also began the process of cutting through the layers of your conditioning to uncover the authentic self—identifying your innate nature, your personal qualities, your interests and passions, and the contribution you'd like to make in your life. At this point, I hope you have a much clearer sense of who you are and have begun to take a more conscious and deliberate approach to your day-to-day life. Now, as we move forward with the work of Part II, you'll begin to identify the attributes of your ideal life and, as we move into the next chapters, you'll begin to activate that Life Vision by developing your support systems and an action plan to help get you where you want to go.

Developing and activating a Life Vision is something most people don't do because they never learned
how to do it. So most people just stumble through life,
drifting along on the wave of happenstance, driven by
circumstances they perceive to be beyond their control.
They feel as if life happens to them, that their fortunes
or misfortunes are just a matter of luck—that they are
powerless to determine the course of their lives. When
you begin to recognize that it's your default operating
system that's controlling the events in your life—not
forces beyond your control—you'll find that it gives you
an incredible sense of freedom and power.

Here are the steps you'll be taking to identify and
define your Life Vision:

- Becoming aware of your conditioned self,
  the core limiting beliefs from your subconscious that are driving your habitual behaviors. That's the work we began in Part I.

- Determining the new results you want to
  have in your life and the new beliefs and
  behaviors that will produce those results.
  That's the work of this chapter, which
  involves visualizing your ideal life. A Life
  Vision is a tool for changing your core limiting beliefs and behaviors, and creating and
  living the life you want to have.

- Beginning to activate that Life Vision by
  developing an action plan that incorporates
  the steps you need to take to change your
  limiting beliefs and behaviors, along with the

inner and outer support systems that will help you get there. You'll be using the exercises from earlier chapters to help guide you.

- Finally, becoming conscious of everything you do as it relates to your Life Vision. You'll develop "the observer"—the part of you that watches what you think and how you behave in each moment. Buddhists refer to this as practicing mindfulness, which is another way to say: being vigilantly aware of yourself *in every moment.*

Marshall's Story

Marshall's story illuminates this process at work. I first met Marshall, an energetic and engaging man, in the spring of 2005 when he came to me for career coaching. He was 29 and had begun his adult life as a professional tennis player. He loved the game, but he left the pro tennis circuit after only a few years for a variety of reasons: he was tiring of the competition, he wanted more of a mental challenge, and, as he put it, he was "aging out of the game." He came to me because he was looking for new career options that could provide the same kind of pleasure and satisfaction he'd experienced as a tennis player. He'd developed a pattern of jumping from one job to another, first exploring jobs in sports-related organizations, and then turning to nonprofits and private foundations. But none of these jobs made him happy.

He was certain of one thing: he wanted a career that wasn't "all about making money"—one that was meaningful and enabled him to make some kind of contribution to the world. When he began his work with me, he was actually making very little money, giving private tennis lessons at a local indoor facility and working in the development department of an education-related foundation. He'd been there for three months, and he was unhappy yet again. The work, he said, had become boring; it wasn't challenging enough, and he was depressed. In addition, because he kept hopping from one job to another, he was always new on the job, so he never moved beyond an entry-level salary.

During our first visit, I learned that Marshall had an undergraduate degree in marketing and management, and that his pattern of quickly losing interest in one job after another predated his tennis career. For example, immediately following graduation, he'd found a job in the marketing department of a major sporting-goods company. But he'd quit within three weeks because it wasn't as interesting as he'd expected. Now, approaching 30, he had no idea what he wanted to do with his life. Keenly aware that something was out of whack, he told me he wanted to "figure this thing out once and for all." He wanted to clarify his skills and interests, the direction he wanted to go, and whether or not he should go back to school. He wanted me to help him develop a strategy for achieving his new career goals—once we figured out what they were.

During our work together, we identified his family role and core limiting beliefs; his skills, passions, and interests; and, ultimately, his ideal career. We also discovered a clear connection between the limiting beliefs about money he'd adopted from his family and his pattern of job-hopping. Marshall comes from a family in which, due to a small inheritance, no one ever felt the need to work. Not only did he get the message that it wasn't necessary to work to earn a living, he even picked up on an underlying disdain for it. In fact, every time Marshall left a job he didn't like, his parents were always supportive. Yet the inheritance was insufficient to support generation after generation, and the money Marshall received from his family was not enough to meet his monthly expenses. His only other source of income was whatever he was able to earn. Marshall's limiting belief—*working for a living is unnecessary and bad*—was undermining his ability to move forward in his career and to adequately provide for himself financially.

In order to help Marshall begin to change his beliefs and behaviors around work and money, we did a reality check. I guided him through a visualization exercise to identify the attributes of his ideal life and then figured out exactly how much that ideal life would cost him annually. When he heard the number, Marshall was flabbergasted—and frustrated. "This is a complete waste of my time," he insisted. "I'll never earn that much money." In fact, it was three times what he was earning at his foundation job. "I want to love what I do," he said. "No one who makes that much money loves what they do." He was amazed by my response: "I love what I do, and I make more than that." It was the first time Marshall realized that he could love his work and make a good living—enough to support the life to which he aspired.

Marshall's next major revelation—and the point at which he very nearly abandoned the entire process—occurred during our voice dialoguing session. You'll recall that voice dialoguing is the technique developed by Drs. Hal and Sidra Stone through which the different parts of a client can be expressed. Two things occurred during that session. First, it became clear to Marshall that he had a lot of different aspects. There was a part of him

that was fulfilled by tennis and a part that really wanted
to make a contribution to the world; a part that craved
intellectual stimulation and a part that was excited by
change and the prospect of doing new things. He'd gone
through life believing that a job should satisfy every part
of him; when it didn't, he'd leave. He'd also fallen into
a pattern of taking jobs that were routine and uninspir-
ing, jobs where he would quickly lose interest. Marshall
realized he needed a job that engaged him in a variety of
different ways to fulfill his need for change and stimulation; but he also recognized for the first time that he
might be asking too much by expecting his career to fulfill every part of him. That recognition gave him a tremendous sense of freedom. He was empowered by it.

But something else happened during the voice
dialogue. A recollection from Marshall's past triggered
feelings of anger, which he had difficulty expressing. I
suggested that we take some time to address his anger.
But Marshall couldn't understand how his inability to
express anger related to his career goals. "What does this
have to do with my career?" he asked. My answer: "If
you don't figure this out, you'll just be continuing the
old patterns driven by your conditioning, and that, in
turn, will continue to limit your ability to fully realize
your professional potential."

He agreed, and we did more work on exploring the
anger issue, concentrating on the role he played in his
family of origin. The process gave him more valuable
information. Growing up, Marshall lived in a household
that was full of drama. His parents fought a great deal.
He had two older sisters, both of whom were outgoing
and quite outspoken. They tended to steal the limelight.
So Marshall became the observer of what he calls "all this
craziness." He became the quiet one, the good child, the

approval-seeker—he took on the role of the Lost Child. As a result, he grew up feeling invisible and unimportant—and keeping a lot of anger and resentment bottled up inside. Through this work, he saw how he had replicated this dynamic by taking jobs in which he felt undervalued and undercompensated, and how, instead of addressing those concerns, he simply quit and moved on to something else. This was another valuable piece of Marshall's puzzle. Everything started to fit together.

When Marshall saw how the role he had adopted in his family also connected to his career choices, he began to feel better about himself. He stopped judging himself and seeing himself as a victim. He began to take responsibility for his own life. Through that recognition, he gained a new confidence.

As we began to focus more directly on the issue of work—his strengths and interests, what he wanted and didn't want—he began to gain a better perspective on his options. Ultimately, Marshall realized he wanted to create his own business, one that would promote the importance of fitness to the next generation. In researching possibilities, he learned about a new national program promoting fitness in schools, and he contacted them to find out more about it. The directors of the program were intrigued by Marshall's experience as a tennis pro and how they might work together. Through those discussions, Marshall saw an opportunity to create a business that lined up professional athletes who would travel around the country talking to students about health and fitness and promoting fitness events for kids. Then we developed a step-by-step action plan for bringing his vision to life—one that included a strategy for segueing from his current job into his new work, developing a strategic business plan, and negotiating an initial contract with this national organization. He decided to start small, at the local level, and grow from there.

At one point, while he was visualizing his ideal life, Marshall imagined an auditorium full of kids listening to him talk about health and fitness. He imagined organizing a series of tennis instructional events linking kids and sports professionals. He imagined working with a network of athletes committed to the common goal of promoting youth fitness—all from an office in his apartment. And he imagined traveling all over the country. The purpose of that visualization exercise was to help Marshall find his focus. Today, he is a consultant who promotes youth fitness. Marshall's new career provides him with the variety and stimulation he craved and offers new challenges every day.

Marshall is working toward earning a living that can sustain his ideal life; he's living in alignment with his authentic self, and he approaches every day with energy and enthusiasm. Marshall didn't arrive where he is today though visualization alone. He did the work of identifying the core limiting beliefs and habitual behaviors that had been holding him back; he explored his innate nature to discover his untapped need for stimulation, variety, and challenge. He had to find his focus, and then he had to create an action plan to bring his new vision to fruition. Visualizing his dream job was just one step in the process of finding professional fulfillment. For you, visualizing your Ideal Life is just one step in the process of mastering the art of aloneness. That's the step you're about to take.

Finding Your Focus

In order to create—and live—the life to which you aspire, you first need to become clear about what that life looks like. This exercise is not unlike the Ideal Partner Visualization exercise you did earlier, only this time, you're the subject of the visualization: your ideal home, lifestyle, personal qualities, passions, and interests. The Ideal Life Visualization is an effective way to begin to clarify the personal qualities you want to have, the behaviors you want to activate in your relationship with yourself and others, and the experiences and circumstances you want to have in your personal and professional life. Before you move into the meditative part of this exercise, I want to remind you that this exercise is about visualizing the ideal life you could create and sustain *on your own—that is, with or without a partner.*

Exercise: Ideal Life Visualization

Before you begin, prepare the environment by turning off your phone and sitting comfortably in a quiet room where you won't be disturbed. There is no right or wrong way to do this exercise, and it's different for each person. Again, I suggest either recording the exercise beforehand, so you can follow your own voice with your eyes closed during the exercise, or asking a trusted friend to guide you through it.

Sit back and relax in a comfortable chair. (You can also do this exercise lying down, as long as you don't fall asleep.) Inhaling through your mouth, take a deep breath in and slowly release it. Take another deep breath in, and as you release it, allow your shoulders to relax and your belly to go soft. Notice if there are any places of tension in your body and allow those parts to let go and relax.

Imagine that you are walking someplace in nature, along a beautiful path. As you come to the end of the path, you come to a clearing that leads to an open field full of wildflowers. Off in the distance, in the middle of this field, is a large, white movie screen. As you make your way to the movie screen, it suddenly snaps to life, and you see that there is a movie playing on the screen. It is the movie of your ideal life, in which you are the star—you as your authentic self, expressing your fullest potential in every part of your life.

The first thing to notice in this ideal life movie is your physical appearance. As your optimal self, what does your physical form and body look like? What kind of clothes are you wearing? How is your hair cut or styled? What kind of expression do you have on your face?

Where are you? Notice your ideal physical environment. Do you live in a city, a small town, out in the country, or in a suburb? See yourself arriving at your home. Notice what the exterior of your ideal home looks like. Is it a freestanding home, an apartment, or a condo? What is its style? Now open the door and go inside. How does it feel? Look around you. How is it decorated? What's on the walls? What color is it? What kind of furniture surrounds you? Are the rooms large and airy, or small and cozy? Walk around. Open doors. Look in the rooms. What do you see?

Do you have any pets? What kind? Any musical instruments? Is there anything around you that you cherish or a space that you particularly appreciate? What's special to you?

Now allow the scene to change and see yourself at work. What kind of environment do you work in? Do you work outside your home, or do you work at home? Notice the physical surroundings. What does the space look like? Are you working alone or with others? Are you employed or are you your own boss? Notice what you're doing in your work. What kinds of activities, tasks, or projects are you doing? What is your work schedule like? What skills, talents, and abilities are you using? What is your annual income? What is the contribution you're making in your work? How do you feel about the work that you do?

Now notice what kinds of personal qualities you possess as your optimal self. What words would describe how you feel inside yourself and in your life? Joyful? Loving? Confident? Energetic? You choose the words that best describe the kind of person you are. Imagine the words others might use to describe your personal qualities.

In this ideal movie, what kind of relationship do you have with yourself? How do you treat and behave toward yourself? What's your daily routine like? How do you take care of yourself? What's your exercise regimen? What's your day-to-day life like? What do you do to love and nurture yourself?

Now notice the way your ideal self behaves with other people. How do you act when you're around them? What kinds of words do you use? How do you treat others? How are you treated by them?

What kind of people do you have in your ideal life, and what kind of relationships do you share? Do you have a large circle of friends you spend time with or, perhaps, a smaller circle of good friends? What are your friends like? What kinds of activities do you share with them? What kinds of words describe your relationships? Supportive? Accepting? Caring? Do you go out with friends? Do you have them over to your house? When you do, is it formal or casual? Do you share any activities—such as sports or community events or volunteer work?

In your ideal life, how do you spend your personal time? Your evenings? Your weekends? Your vacations? What are your interests and passions? What do you enjoy doing?

Is there anything else about your ideal life that's important to you? Take your time and continue to visualize your ideal life. When you're finished, slowly let the image of your ideal life fade and begin to bring your awareness back into your body. Take a deep breath in, and notice what, if any, emotions were evoked during this exercise. Slowly open your eyes, get your journal and pen, and complete the following Ideal Life exercises.

Exercise: Ideal Life Attributes

Take out your journal and, drawing from the Ideal Life Visualization, complete each statement below. If you do not have a clear picture of how to complete some of these statements based on your Ideal Life Visualization, just complete this section based on the attributes you'd like to have in your ideal life. Take your time and be as specific as you can be.

In my ideal life . . .

- Words that describe my physical appearance are:

- The kind of home and environment I live in is:

- Words that describe the personal qualities I possess are:

- The ways I behave toward myself are:

- My professional work, contribution, and income are:

- The ways I behave toward others are:

- Words that describe the qualities of my relationships with others are:

- The things I do in my leisure time are:

- My passions and interests are:

- Other aspects of my ideal life are:

Exercise: Ideal Personal Qualities, Behaviors, and Life Circumstances

Now you're going to begin to focus on the specific personal qualities, behaviors, and life circumstances that will move you forward in mastering the art of aloneness. The purpose of this exercise is to identify all the attributes—the personal qualities, behaviors, and life circumstances—that you would like to bring to reality in yourself and in your life but that *you do not yet possess*. You'll be using the information gleaned from the Ideal Life Attributes exercise you just completed, as well as from earlier exercises. You may want to refer back to your journal for the insights you gained from your Retrieving the Authentic Self exercises and Defining Your Ideal Partner exercises, particularly the items you circled in Identifying the Gaps. Let all these exercises be your guide as you hone in on the personal qualities, behaviors, and life circumstances to which you aspire in your ideal life. Remember, you'll be identifying attributes of your ideal self and ideal life that you *do not already possess*.

Personal Qualities

Open your journal and write "My Ideal Personal Qualities" at the top of a new page. Now make a list of all the personal qualities you aspire to in your ideal life *but do not already possess*. Below are some examples of personal qualities, but feel free to write down any personal qualities that are important to you:

Compassionate	Resourceful
Loving	Strong
Creative	Intelligent
Flexible	Adventurous
Authentic	Inspiring
Self-confident	Intuitive
Charismatic	Peaceful
Accepting	Gentle
Passionate	Physically fit
Self-disciplined	Healthy
Playful	Balanced
Spontaneous	Energetic
Generous	Nurturing

Behaviors

Now write "My Ideal Behaviors" in your journal. Beneath that heading, list all the behaviors that you aspire to in your ideal life but *do not already possess*. Again, I've provided some examples to help guide you, but feel free to write down any behaviors that are important to you.

Authentically express my thoughts, needs, and feelings to others	Be adventurous and take new risks
Be compassionate and forgiving with myself and others	Resourcefully address conflict with others
Unconditionally accept myself	Practice self-discipline
Be loving and caring to others	Be mindful and conscious in every moment
Trust and follow my intuition	Be playful and spontaneous
Express my creativity	Set and follow through on my goals
Eat healthy foods and take good care of myself	Take time to relax and create balance every day
Build and share healthy relationships with others	Communicate effectively with others
Choose love and compassion in each moment	Exercise on a regular basis
Inspire and motivate others	Develop and practice healthy lifestyle habits

Life Circumstances

Now write the heading "My Ideal Life Circumstances" in your journal, and then record all the life circumstances you aspire to but *do not already possess*. I've listed some examples below as a guide, but include any life circumstances that are important to you.

Live in a beautiful home and environment	Feel accomplished and fulfilled in my work
Share close, loving, and supportive relationships with others	Be self-sufficient and able to provide for myself
Enjoy financial abundance	Feel whole and happy on my own
Own a home that I love	Enjoy optimal energy and well-being
Enjoy a healthy work/life balance	Have a sense of inner peace and contentment
Actively pursue my interests and passions	Enjoy being physically fit and healthy
Enjoy a meaningful and fulfilling job	Be recognized and rewarded for my contributions

CHAPTER 9

BUILDING AN
INNER AND OUTER
SUPPORT SYSTEM

I have a friend who is a freelance graphic designer. Barbara lives alone and works out of her home, a lifestyle that can be isolating and challenging. But she has developed a system of inner and outer supports that are essential to her sustenance. She belongs to a professional group that meets once a month for lunch to talk about everything from new graphic design technology to how to deal with clients. Through that group, Barbara has not only gained valuable insights into and inspiration for her work, but has also made invaluable friendships. Several other members of the group have become close friends; she sees them for lunch, dinner, movies, or trips to the local museum. When Barbara gets bogged down in work, she often turns to a handful of colleagues she's known for years; she talks to them regularly on the phone from her in-home office about design, about the creative process, about whatever is on her mind. And she makes it a point to meet friends or colleagues for lunch at least twice a week. When she feels drained and over-worked, she'll sneak off to a movie or nearby exhibit in the afternoon by herself.

Although Barbara doesn't have a romantic partner, she has an active social life. She and another friend formed a dinner group made up of singles and couples who get together three or four times a year to talk about the arts, culture, and politics. Through her professional and dinner groups, she has gotten to know new people who share her interests and her creative energy. Because Barbara works for herself, she can move her schedule around so she sees people when they're most avail-able—if an interesting activity comes up during the day, she can work at night, and vice versa. Flexibility allows her to see people she wouldn't see if she had a nine-to-five work schedule.

Even so, Barbara sits in front of a computer eight hours a day, so she has to make a special effort to get plenty of exercise. She lives near a public park in a big city and walks two or three miles a day. She has two walking buddies who join her once or twice a week, so these walks provide not only exercise but also compan-ionship. She also belongs to a nearby gym, and that gets her out of the house, around people, and gives her a workout. Barbara is a reformed smoker; she relied on a support group to kick the habit, and she attends a meet-ing every Saturday to keep her on track. At any given moment, you'll find an inspirational book on her night table. She told me recently, "I just read a few pages a night, but I find it uplifting, and it keeps me focused on my personal goals." When she feels low or is struggling with a personal issue, she uses a journal to work through her feelings. Barbara relishes the time she spends alone, designing, absorbed in her work and her life, but, like all of us, she needs the love and support of others. Her challenge is to stay inspired, energized, and engaged while she's living and working alone—and the people in her life help make that happen. The walking, the journaling, the inspirational books, the workouts, the trips to the movies and museums—all are part of a strong inner support system. But her outer support system—the walking buddies, the professional and dinner groups, her weekly support group, the regular lunches out, and the deep professional and personal friendships she's developed—is just as important to her.

Personal transformation begins with learning how to self-support—how to rely on yourself for your physical, emotional, and financial well-being. But there are many aspects of outer support that are just as important. For one thing, your outer support system provides the connection and tenderness of other human beings, which are essential for living a rich, full life. We all need reassurance that others share our feelings and experiences; the enrichment that comes with learning from and engaging with others; and the assistance with life's day-to-day challenges that other people can provide.

Earlier on, I defined personal-development work as a process that involves deep self-examination and awareness of who you are, how you behave, and the results your actions generate. With greater awareness comes *a more conscious choice* of who you want to be and how you want to behave and interact with others. It involves *conscious, deliberate decisions* about the results we want to achieve in our lives and in our relationships. Personal transformation requires a high level of consciousness in your day-to-day life. It means living deliberately so that you can override the negative patterns of your life conditioning, change your limiting beliefs and behaviors, and bring your Life Vision to reality. Part of this chapter is devoted to developing positive, supportive relationships. In addition, I address the issue of enlisting professional support when you need it, including therapy and coaching.

As you embark on the process of building your inner and outer support systems, you'll want to check in with yourself on a regular basis to determine whether you're effectively addressing the areas of your life that need the most focus. At first, incorporating these support systems into your daily life will involve discipline and determination. But gradually they'll become part of your day-to-day routine and, over time, an integral part of your life. These are the questions you'll want to ask yourself every day:

- Am I loving and nurturing myself?

- Am I pursuing activities that are in alignment with my passions and life goals? Activities that inspire and motivate me?

- Am I engaged in supportive, uplifting, fun relationships that enrich my life?

- Am I taking action to create the physical health and emotional well-being, career path, financial security, experiences, relationships, and circumstances I want to have in my life?

You develop an *inner support system* by identifying and incorporating specific activities and actions into your life that you can do *on your own* as a way to replenish your inner resources and maintain your emotional, physical, and mental health. An *outer support system* refers to people and environments that support who you really are and help you achieve your goals.

Developing an Inner Support System

Every weekday morning a busy executive gets up and jogs for 30 minutes. Then she showers, has breakfast, and heads off to work. Three evenings a week, she sets aside an hour to play the cello. It's a routine that both energizes and inspires her. A college professor who struggled with his weight for many years follows an intensive exercise regimen four times a week at his gym; he meditates every evening before dinner and schedules a massage or takes a sauna once a week to relax; every weekend, he fills his freezer with scrumptious sugar-free muffins so he can have an occasional treat. A newspaper reporter who's under intense deadline pressure every day starts her mornings with a nice, quiet walk through the woods with her cocker spaniel; it replenishes her and gives her a sense of calm that helps her cope with her high-pressure workdays. She loves mystery novels, so she keeps one by her bedside table and reads 10 or 15 pages every night before she goes to sleep; she finds it inspiring and comforting. She's found a yoga class near her office and is committed to going three times a week; it helps her stay focused. Each of these individual routines is different, but they have one important thing in common: they are *conscious,* active ways these people love, nurture, and care for themselves on a daily basis.

The inner support system you're about to develop must meet two specific criteria: these are activities that are *part of your routine*—you do them on a regular basis—and they are all things you can do *independently of anyone else.* Beyond that, your inner support system is uniquely yours; the activities you do and actions you take reflect your interests, your passions, your personal preferences. What relaxes you? What inspires you? What gives you a sense of renewal and reduces stress? What quiets you? What helps *you* stay on course? By building your inner support system, you'll be developing the inner resources you need to achieve your Life Vision. So, in developing your inner support system, you'll want to look closely at the specific challenges and opportunities you've identified, the elements of your default operating system that you want to address, and, most importantly, your Life Vision.

Here's an example. If your Life Vision includes "I am a fit, energetic person," you'll need to develop specific action steps that will help you achieve this goal. You'll not only want to exercise, but you'll need to start eating right. If you don't know a lot about nutrition, it's time to find out more, because having a high level of energy depends on putting healthy foods in your body. You'll also need to address any habitual thoughts or behaviors that may sabotage your ability to achieve your goals. Let's say, for example, you use food to comfort yourself when you're upset. If something goes wrong, you head straight for that carton of ice cream in your freezer or right over to the grocery store to pick up a box of cookies. You need to find another way to comfort yourself. It may be through deep breathing exercises or a regular meditation practice. It may be by going for long walks or working out at the gym to release tension. You may need to seek help to build your inner resources—such as a support group for overeaters, a life coach or psycho-therapist, an acupuncturist, or massage therapist. In the next chapter, you'll begin to formulate a plan and a set of specific action steps. Whatever route you ultimately take, this is the point to start thinking about the actions that can help you move forward in your life.

By developing your inner support system, you'll be practicing self-love and building a sense of self-worth. As you experience the benefits of your efforts—whether it's a sense of inner peace, a healthier body, higher energy, or greater self-confidence—it will reinforce the value of what you're doing. In addition, you'll be mastering the art of aloneness by taking responsibility for creating your own well-being, instead of depending on others to provide it.

You'll want to develop a set of activities that addresses each of the broad headings: *Health and Wellness, Relaxation and Your Inner Self,* and *Inspiration and Motivation.* The following lists of possible actions and activities are far from complete. They're designed to give you some examples, ideas, and insights into ways to build your inner support system. Just as importantly, these are all areas that will help you build confidence and have the energy you need to move forward. Here are a few guidelines to help you as you proceed:

- *Be mindful.* Approach each day consciously and deliberately, with awareness that you are actively engaged in moving beyond your conditioned self and mastering the art of aloneness.

- *Keep a daily journal.* If you have specific exercise goals, write them down. If you're monitoring what you eat, write it down. Keep track of how you're doing. The most successful systems for achieving personal goals all incorporate *writing down goals and day-to-day achievements* as a powerful tool. This will help you live more consciously and stay on course.

- *Be flexible.* If something's not working, change it. As an example, I have a client who wanted to incorporate jogging into her daily routine. At the outset, she was jogging every afternoon after work. But she found she had little energy late in the afternoon, and she needed an afternoon snack to get through the day. It was uncomfortable for her to run with food in her stomach. She found she just wasn't able to meet her goals. So she switched her jogging routine to first thing in the morning, and it worked much better for her. When something doesn't work, instead of giving up, just course-correct. Try a different approach.

- *Check in regularly with your intuition.* Adding new activities involves moving outside your comfort zone. Remember to use your intuition to check in with your authentic self. For example, maybe everyone you know loves yoga, so you give it a try. But, the first few times, you don't enjoy it, and the entire process makes you uncomfortable. When

you feel as if something isn't right for you,
stick with it long enough to get a real sense
of what's going on and examine it carefully.
Does your discomfort spring from a fear?
Is it just a question of inexperience? Or is
the problem a practical one? Examine these
kinds of issues closely before you discontinue
it. But if you find, over time, that an activity
just doesn't sit well with you, then try something else that feels more suitable.

Health and Wellness

- *Eat a healthy diet.* There's a wealth of information about nutrition available online and in
  books and magazines. How you feel relates
  directly to what you consume. By eating a
  healthy diet, you feel better, you look better,
  and you have the energy you need to live a
  full and active life. This is crucial to mastering
  the art of aloneness.

- *Reduce or eliminate caffeine, refined sugar,
  white flour, and alcohol.* Minimize the use of
  substances that can affect your moods and
  energy levels.

- *Exercise regularly.* Do something. Do anything. Walk, jog, play tennis, ride a bike, go
  to a health club—but be sure it's something
  you enjoy. It will pump endorphins into
  your system, help you look and feel better,

and build your confidence. The more you stick with a good exercise regimen, the more confident you'll feel about your ability to effect change in your life.

- *Address your addictions.* If you overeat, smoke, drink too much alcohol, overspend, or use drugs, find a way to address your addictions. This is a very complex and personal issue, and it is covered more fully in the section that follows on outer support systems.

Relaxation and Your Inner Self

I talked earlier about the link between your soul and your intuition. There are numerous techniques that promote greater awareness of that connection—that can help you relax and reduce stress, live in the moment, achieve a greater sense of peace, and live more authentically. In her book *Eat, Pray, Love,* writer Elizabeth Gilbert talks about connecting with an inner voice through a journal—this "calm, compassionate, affectionate, and infinitely wise voice (who is maybe me, or maybe not exactly me) is always available for a conversation on paper at any time of day or night . . . Maybe what I'm reaching for is God," she writes, "or maybe it's my Guru speaking through me, or maybe it's the angel who was assigned to my case, or maybe it's my Highest Self, or maybe it is indeed just a construct of my subconscious."[1] In *Power, Freedom, and Grace,* Deepak Chopra writes about the "internal source of joy—our connection to our Creator, our source, our inner self . . . If you have lost touch with your internal source of joy, if the happiness you experience always originates in circumstances outside yourself, then you are at the mercy of every situation and every stranger you meet. This kind of happiness is always elusive."[2] I call this inner voice your intuition— the part of you that connects you to your higher self or soul. Here are a few examples of practices you can pursue on your own to develop it:

- Pray, meditate, or engage in a spiritual practice as part of your daily routine.

- Practice yoga or other relaxation techniques such as deep breathing exercises.

- Take a daily walk in nature. Be conscious of the stillness, beauty, and the world around you.

- Consciously take time to sit quietly and be still within yourself. Sit by a fire, look at the stars, or take a candlelit bath to rest quietly. Stillness is restorative.

- Keep a journal of your thoughts and feelings, and turn to it when you feel restless or troubled, or just want to reconnect with yourself.

- One more thing: make room in your life for laughter. Invite it into your home. Cultivate it in your friendships. Seek it out in your entertainment.

Inspiration and Motivation

Find ways to keep yourself inspired and motivated. That will help you stay on course and enrich your life in immeasurable ways. Here are some activities that have proven valuable to my clients:

- Read inspiring books or listen to positive, uplifting CDs. The Resource Guide at the back of this book includes some recommendations.

- Visit museums, galleries, and art events.

- Attend ballet and musical performances, or go to the theater.

- Visit a botanic garden or grow your own garden.

- Hang inspiring pictures and your Life Vision statement on walls and mirrors.

- Surround yourself with beautiful things that enrich your environment.

- Find creative outlets for self-expression such as singing, dancing, drawing, painting, writing, photography, or playing a musical instrument.

- Listen to beautiful music and watch uplifting films.

Exercise: Inner Support Assessment

Take out your journal and write "My Current Inner Support System" at the top of a new page. Think about what your inner support system currently comprises. Then list any activities and practices you currently do *on your own* that sustain and inspire you and help you build your inner resources. One note before you proceed: you may not have a long list of inner supports. Most of us were never taught to develop such a system. If you have few inner supports or none at all, don't beat yourself up about it. At this point, you're just looking for information that will help you move forward.

Developing an Outer Support System

There's no one who is alone who hasn't been encouraged by well-meaning friends and family members to join clubs and organizations to meet friends or, of course, to find a mate. One of my clients, who is spiritually attuned but not drawn to organized religion, has been told a dozen times to join a church. "That's the best way to meet new people," his friends and family advise. A mother tells her daughter, "Go to baseball games. That's where all the men are." A friend reports that his father went so far as to advise him to switch from one political party to another: "Join the Democratic Party. Democrats have much more fun." The truth is, the more you do, the more you get out, the more people you meet, the greater the opportunities you have to enrich your life. But there's no value in randomly joining clubs and organizations, or making new friends if they don't hold your interest or engage you in some way.

And there's little value in amassing friends who don't offer you the support you seek. The key is to develop a set of outer supports that genuinely enrich your life and provide support for the expression of your authentic self.

Building Supportive Relationships

Consider the example of Marie, a woman who recently attended one of my weekend workshops. Bright, energetic, and outgoing, Marie is in her 60s and has been divorced for 15 years. During that time, she's built an active social life by joining various groups, and she currently belongs to three singles groups in the Philadelphia area. Although Marie has many friends, most of these friendships are lopsided. She has always tended to be the one who reaches out, the one who offers support and nurturance, the one who takes care of other people. During a recent Mastering the Art of Aloneness workshop session, she realized she was replicating the relationship dynamic she had with her parents. Marie's father was an alcoholic; her mother was depressed and addicted to food, and as an only child, Marie suppressed her own needs in favor of those of her parents. She was the caretaker, the Lost Child. Throughout her life, Marie has played out the same scenario in many of her friendships—giving and giving but getting back little in return.

Mastering the art of aloneness has a lot to do with relationships—your relationship with yourself and your relationships with others. As Ann Kaiser Stearns wrote in *Living Through Personal Crisis:* "The most self-loving action any of us performs in a lifetime is learning how to develop . . . close friendships."[3] Developing and engaging in caring relationships is an important aspect of personal transformation. As you move forward, the emphasis must be on developing a *supportive* network of friends—not just developing a network of friends.

Like Marie, we all tend to pull people into our lives who treat us the way we were treated during our formative years, replicating the relationship dynamics that are familiar to us. For example, it's quite common for people to fall into the Critical Parent role in relationships or to seek out Critical Parents among their friends. That's because so many of us *had* critical parents. Such relationships may feel familiar, but they're ultimately unhealthy, unloving, and unsupportive. In earlier chapters, I've talked about ways to begin to be more discerning in your friendships and to communicate your needs and boundaries more effectively so you can enjoy friendships that are mutually respectful and fulfilling. Now, as you consciously build your outer support system, it's time to take that process to the next level. Here, we're going to focus more thoroughly on how to create a network of loving, supportive people in your life. I encourage you to refer back to those early chapters as you work through this section.

Not all people have what it takes to be supportive, and not all unsupportive people can be avoided—for example, sometimes you can't escape family members and co-workers. But, the idea here is to begin to identify the qualities that support your transformational process, spend time with people who embody those qualities, and, as much as possible, avoid people who are detrimental to you and your personal development.

Attributes of a Supportive Person

A truly supportive person:

- Provides a safe space for expressing your thoughts and feelings

- Does not judge or blame you

- Acknowledges and respects your feelings and boundaries

- Is empathetic and compassionate

- Is loving and caring, without sexual overtones or hidden, self-serving agendas

- Helps you recognize and nourish your own strengths and inner power

- Appreciates your willingness to be open and vulnerable, and behaves likewise

- Is loving, caring, and sensitive in his communication

- Expresses impatience, anger, or frustration in a respectful manner

- Is honest and clear about her boundaries

- Is dependable and honors commitments

- Is trustworthy and maintains confidentiality

- Offers small acts of kindness, especially during difficult times

- Is willing to listen, offering honest feedback when asked for it

- Acknowledges and takes responsibility for his flaws and mistakes

A truly supportive person does not:

- Criticize or blame you

- Label you as "selfish," "nuts," "out of control," "over-emotional," "silly," or " overreactive"

- Break your confidentiality and trust

- Disrespect your boundaries and needs

- Continually break commitments

- Disappear during the difficult times

- Use your vulnerability to her advantage— that is, to make herself look better

- Constantly tell you what you "should" be doing

- Make everything about his own needs

- Judge, react defensively, or counterattack when you share your feelings

- Take without ever giving in return

There are many ways to cultivate supportive friendships. Here are a few of them:

- *Be a good sounding board.* When a friend wants to talk to you about something he's going through—a crisis or problem—the best approach is simply to *listen.* Don't offer advice without asking permission, because it may be that he just wanted to share his experience, or vent his anger or frustration about a situation. He may be looking for someone to validate his feelings. Understanding and compassion should be the order of the day.

- *Don't be judgmental.* It's important to avoid being judgmental—especially if your friend is sharing something that's in conflict with your own value system. Remember that other people are not you; take care not to impose your value system on someone else. Remember, *everybody's doing the best they can at any given moment.*

- *Avoid "shoulding" people.* I suggest refraining from telling your friends what they "should" or "shouldn't" do. I talked earlier about "shoulding" people—it reflects the Critical Parent ego state. If you're in a relationship with someone who has a habit of telling you what you should and shouldn't do, that's a red flag. Instead of listening, this person is basing their actions on assumptions about you or about the way you should be living your life.

- *Be empathetic.* Empathy is the act of putting yourself in another person's shoes. It's a trait you'll want to develop in yourself and a quality you should be looking for in others. Years ago, I had a teacher who told me: "If you could connect, just for an instant, with the deepest pain that your greatest enemy has experienced, you would never again want to do anything that would cause that person more harm." If someone tells you something painful, recounting a personal crisis she went through, or a difficult situation she faces, show compassion. The simple statement "I'm really sorry you had to go through that" can be the most supportive approach.

- *Practice emotional intelligence.* Look for, practice, and promote emotional honesty, maturity, and intelligence in your relationships. Here's an example. Say you've made plans with a friend to go out on New Year's Eve, but you have to cancel because you have the flu. A supportive friend may be disappointed, but will be understanding. She might even

offer to pick up some chicken soup or a
movie for you. But, if your friend gets angry,
it's a tip-off that you're not dealing with a
supportive and emotionally mature person.

- *Cultivate effective communication skills.* You'll
  encounter occasional conflicts with any
  friend. Those conflicts present you with an
  opportunity to determine whether you can
  meet each other on an emotionally mature
  footing. For example, I had a friend who
  snapped at me, very early in our relationship, when I called her at an inconvenient
  time. In response, I didn't blame her or
  counterattack; instead, I carefully composed
  an e-mail, saying: "I apologize again for
  disturbing you last night. I tend to be sensitive to harsh communication styles, and
  although it may not have been your intention, I experienced your response as harsh.
  When you feel upset with me, it would be
  great if you could communicate your feelings
  and needs in a more gentle way. I respond
  much better to that kind of communication." She responded by calling me and
  apologizing. She was able to say: "I can be
  abrupt, especially when I feel like my space
  is being invaded. I'm sorry I snapped at you,
  and I'll try to be more sensitive going forward." As a result, our relationship has continued to grow, and she has become one of
  my dearest friends.

- *Be emotionally honest.* Emotional honesty, which involves the willingness to be vulnerable, is central to sharing healthy, supportive relationships. For example, what if a friend says something hurtful to you? "You look like you've put on weight," or "I saw your ex-husband last night with his new girlfriend, and he looked really happy." It's important to tell that person how you feel. You might say: "I'm having a reaction to what you just said. It may not have been your intention, but I found what you said hurtful." Many people believe that vulnerability is a sign of weakness. I see it, instead, as having the courage to be authentic. By saying, "I'm feeling hurt," you're laying yourself wide open. But it's a gesture that shows other people that you care enough about them and the relationship to share who you really are, and you're inviting them to be who they really are. And, when you do, the other person's response speaks volumes. It will let you know whether or not this is a supportive person with whom you want to engage.

- *Know when to let go.* Every relationship hits bumps along the way, which is when effective communication becomes especially important. It helps you find out whether you can effectively work through a conflict and negotiate your differences with someone else. If you can't—if the other person is not emotionally mature enough, not far enough along in his own development—you may find it's better to let the relationship go. Then, rather than create an unpleasant drama, you can disengage in a respectful, emotionally intelligent way. You can say: "I don't think we're a good fit as friends." Or "I think our values or lifestyles are just too different to support a friendship." Or "We're experiencing a lot of conflict that we can't seem to resolve and this just doesn't feel good to me." The better you know yourself, the easier it is to assess whether people are a good fit as part of your outer support system.

Assessing Your Relationships

The best starting point for assessing the quality of any relationship in your life is through your feelings. First and foremost, notice how you feel around the other person. Ask yourself: *Do I feel good? Do I feel uplifted? Do I feel happy to be with her? Do I walk away feeling it was a joyful time with her? Do I feel respected? Do I feel understood? Do I feel valued? Supported? Accepted?* If not, then it's time to further assess the relationship using these tools that you learned earlier:

- *Check in with your intuition.* Get a sense of how you feel about the relationship deep down inside. *Is this relationship good for me? Is it in alignment with who I really am and in alignment with where I want to go in my life?*

- *Do a reality check.* Notice how the other person behaves toward you. Does she honor your confidentiality? Does she respect your feelings, needs, and boundaries? Review and check her behavior against the attributes of a truly supportive person from the list provided earlier in this chapter.

- *Weigh the pros and cons.* If it's still not clear to you whether or not a relationship is serving your best interests, do the pros and cons exercise. List all the positive aspects of the relationship—all the things you value about the person and the relationship. Then list all the things you don't like. Just as I outlined earlier in the book, once you have all the pros and cons listed, go back and rate the items on each list, using a scale of 1 to 10 based on their importance or value to you (1 having the least impact, 10 having the highest). Then add up the totals from each column and compare them. Are there more pros or cons? Are there any 10s on your cons side? If your cons outweigh your pros or you have any 10s on your cons side, it may be time to let the relationship go.

You can use this approach to assess new relationships or old ones, to decide whether to deepen a friendship or let it go. Assessing your relationships will help you change or eliminate those that are unhealthy and develop an outer support system that will help you transform your life.

Seeking Professional Support

Someone asked me at a recent workshop if it's possible to fully achieve personal mastery and move completely beyond the core limiting beliefs and habitual behaviors of the conditioned self. My response: *No.* Each of us is a work in progress. There's always another layer to explore—something new to discover, another quality or strength to develop, or a new lesson to learn about your life and the people in it. Your conditioned self grew out of your need to adapt to your own family when you were a young child. It's been the driving force in your life for many years, and it will remain a part of who you are for the rest of your life.

The challenge is to manage your conditioned self with compassion. When it starts to take over, treat it as you would a young child—with consistency and love. In truth, that's exactly what your conditioned self is—a part of you that was created during your formative years and still functions as the child within. I encourage my clients to embrace the conditioned self and to work with it in a loving and gentle way, but not to allow it to run their lives. Just as you wouldn't allow a young child to take the steering wheel and drive your car, it is your authentic self that needs to be in control of your adult life. You need to manage your conditioned self so it's not managing you.

Many people have regrets about choices they've made, how they've lived their lives, or the pain that they've experienced or caused. When my clients encounter those feelings, I encourage them to activate the Inner Nurturing Parent. Instead of judging, hating, or rejecting the conditioned self, I suggest extending love and compassion to it, just as you would to a young child who makes mistakes because he doesn't know any better.

"One famous Zen master actually described spiritual practice as 'one mistake after another,'" writes Jack Kornfield in *A Path with Heart*, "which is to say, one opportunity after another to learn. It is from 'difficulties, mistakes, and errors' that we actually learn. To live life is to make a succession of errors. Understanding this can bring us great ease and forgiveness for ourselves and others—we are at ease with the difficulties of life."[4] When my clients are experiencing emotional pain, I suggest they reframe it as something of tremendous value. Emotional pain gives us a reference point for what it's like to feel joy. Pain and adversity are mechanisms by which we learn, grow, and develop. Pain can also be an effective barometer for telling us when we're off course in our lives. As such, it can be a powerful catalyst for change.

Personal-development work poses many challenges. While it's a pathway to greater freedom, joy, and fulfillment, it's not an easy journey. For many of us, it involves confronting parts of ourselves, our lives, and our past experiences that are upsetting and painful. In this book, I've offered you guidance for following a path of personal transformation, but as you move forward I encourage you to seek professional support whenever you need it. Here are some examples of instances in which professional resources may be valuable or even essential:

- *Support for specific steps in your family-of-origin work.* It can be helpful to seek professional help when you're working through issues and feelings associated with your family of origin—pain, anger, and confusion. Learning to treat your conditioned self with love and compassion is a process, and you may struggle with feelings or issues that you cannot resolve by yourself. A trained professional can help you understand and move beyond the old patterns that prevent you from realizing your true potential and achieving the life you want to have. So don't hesitate to seek help when you need it.

- *Crisis and loss.* Experiencing a crisis or loss can activate your default operating system and trigger your conditioned self to take over. A death in the family, divorce, job loss, or other personal or job-related setback can make you fall into old patterns. I cannot emphasize strongly enough the importance of finding a supportive group and/or professional during the grieving and healing process and beyond. If you're newly divorced, a supportive group, therapist, or coach can be a valuable resource by serving as a safe haven where you can explore old, self-defeating patterns that block you from moving forward; a place to share the pleasures and pain of your new-found freedom; and a resource for survival strategies and new perspectives on single parenting.

- *Feelings of depression or anxiety or other emotional issues.* If you're plagued by deep feelings of sadness or emptiness and you can't seem to shake them; if you have difficulty getting out

of bed in the morning or you've lost interest in your normal, daily routine; if you have
a decrease or increase in appetite, you can't
sleep, or you feel listless and depleted—you
may be in the throes of depression. You'll
recall my experience after my children and
I returned to Boston from Germany—that
Labor Day Weekend when I felt I just couldn't
go on. I found a doctor who prescribed medication to help me manage the crisis point of
my depression, and then I connected with an
exceptional therapist and coach to work with
over an extended period of time. Remember
Rana? She spent her evenings curled up in the
basement, watching TV, avoiding her family
and friends. She was experiencing a depression that didn't ease up until we began her
personal-development work.

Depression is not uncommon among
people who are living out of alignment with
their authentic selves. But depression comes
in many shapes and forms. If you're experiencing an ongoing or severe depression, it's
important to seek help. You can consult your
medical doctor, a psychiatrist, or a psychotherapist. When seeking help for depression
and/or anxiety, it's particularly important
to see someone who is qualified to diagnose
the severity of the depression and determine
whether or not you need medication. Depression and anxiety can be symptoms of a chemical imbalance that may require medication
or a combination of medication and therapy.

- *Addressing an addiction.* Addictions—to alcohol, nicotine, sex, food, or drugs—are powerful and difficult to overcome. Addiction is not an issue that is easily addressed by yourself. In my practice, I work with clients to help them replace destructive, addictive behaviors with new, healthy habits. There are many ways of addressing addiction, including multi-modal approaches and alternative therapies such as hypnotherapy and acupuncture. Support groups have proven to be particularly valuable for people dealing with addictions for a number of reasons: for one thing, being held accountable to a group can be a strong motivator; in addition, the emotional support such groups can offer can be invaluable. The first step in addressing any addiction is acknowledging that you're addicted and seeking the help you need. If you suffer from an addiction, I encourage you to explore all the resources available. Check online and in your local newspapers for support groups in your area; explore available treatment centers; talk with your medical doctor or a therapist about treatment options; and seek counsel from trusted friends and family members. Be sure to find a group or professional that you're comfortable with, one that offers compassion, understanding, and support.

- *Support for achieving your Life Vision.* Don't hesitate to seek out professional resources to support you as you work toward mastering

the art of aloneness. For example, if you're
working on issues around what you eat and
how much, there are all kinds of outer supports that can be valuable resources. A good
nutritionist can help you develop a healthy
food plan. A support group can help you
sustain your resolve. You may want to hire
a personal trainer to help you get in shape,
or you may sign up for a yoga class. Or you
may want to work with a coach who can
help you sustain your motivation and hold
you accountable to your goals and action
steps. You have the option of exploring alternative therapies to help you reduce stress or
finding a psychotherapist to help you move
beyond your conditioning and retrieve your
authentic self.

Mastering the art of aloneness does not mean
addressing your challenges and issues all by yourself.
You may need a coach, psychotherapist, or other practitioner to help you do some of the work it requires. There
are all kinds of therapeutic approaches and modalities
from which to choose—both traditional and alternative.
When you're seeking professional help, I encourage you
to use all the resources at your disposal to find the right
person—someone with the skills and expertise to meet
your needs and a working style you're comfortable with.
Here are some resources that may help you:

- You'll find descriptions of many of the most
  common types of healing and personal-
  development modalities listed in the
  Resource Guide at the back of this book. For

recommendations, I encourage you to talk with friends, family members, and health professionals you know and trust. A personal referral is always valuable. And take the time to interview anyone with whom you'll be working.

- Check the Internet for national organizations and associations representing various disciplines and specialties—such as the American Holistic Health Association, Mental Health America (formerly the National Mental Health Association), and the American Association of Acupuncture & Oriental Medicine. Such sites offer information on how to locate qualified professionals in your geographic area. They can also provide valuable information regarding the professional requirements for specific specialties—certification, licensing, and training. The Resource Guide at the back of this book also provides detailed listings for organizations and associations around the world that address specific issues.

Mastering the tools and techniques presented in this book should give you valuable skills for assessing the kind of professional help you need, evaluating providers, and determining what works best for you. The better you know yourself and the more fully developed your intuition, the greater your ability to identify the resources that can provide the support you need. When you're evaluating a psychotherapist, coach, physician, or any other type of professional, ask about:

- *Qualifications:* What are your credentials? What is your training and professional background?

- *Experience:* How long have you been in practice? What's the primary focus of your work? What is your experience and success in working with the types of issues, challenges, and/ or goals I want to address?

- *Approach:* What's your approach or methodology? What does the process involve and how much time does it typically take?

- *Practical Information:* How long does each session last? How frequently do we meet? What are your charges and payment policies?

Most importantly, you're looking for someone who is supportive, caring, and nonjudgmental. During your interview, look for someone who is 100 percent present and focused on you and your concerns. Red flags include brusqueness, inflexibility, a rigid approach, or a sense of distance. This must be someone you can trust fully. Ask yourself: *Do I feel comfortable with this person? Will I feel free to tell him anything? Is this someone who is engaging with me in a human and real way?* If not, don't hesitate to find someone else.

When you're looking for a support group, the operative word is *support*—that is, finding an uplifting, caring, supportive environment. Not long after my separation, I found a support group in Germany for people who were separated and divorced. Most of the people who attended the sessions were angry and in pain, seeing themselves as victims and blaming their spouses for their situations. While moving through anger is an important part of the healing process, at the time, it wasn't what I needed. If you're considering a support group, interview the person who runs the group. The facilitator's attitude will be a good indicator of the character and quality of the group. Any group can only be as supportive as the facilitator and the people involved. Feel free to explore the group situation before you commit to long-term involvement. Check in with your intuition, and base your evaluation on whether the group culture is compatible with your authentic self, your personal goals, and your Life Vision.

Exercise: Outer Support Assessment

Take out your journal and write "My Current Outer Support System." Again, if your list is short or you have no outer supports, don't judge yourself. Most of us were not conditioned to develop a set of outer supports. Remember: you're looking for information that will help you move forward in your life.

Step One: Supportive Relationships
First, make a list of all the people in your life with whom you share supportive relationships. This includes supportive friendships and professional relationships. You may find it helpful to refer back to the list "Attributes of a Supportive Person" earlier in this chapter. In your journal, complete the following sentence:

The people with whom I share supportive personal and professional relationships are:

Step Two: Other Outer Supports

Now think about any other outer supports you currently have in place in your life. These might include support groups; classes you take regularly; memberships in gyms, clubs, community organizations, or professional associations; or any professionals who provide you with ongoing support—for example, a personal trainer, coach, or psychotherapist. In your journal, complete the following sentence:

Other resources for outer support I currently have in my life are:

CHAPTER 10

BRINGING YOUR VISION TO LIFE

At the beginning of this book, I talked about these three keys to mastering the art of aloneness: focus, strategy, and commitment. You've already laid the groundwork. You've connected the dots between your family of origin and your default operating system. You've uncovered your innate nature and begun reclaiming the wholeness of your authentic self. And you've identified the attributes of your ideal life. But you still have some important work to do. In this chapter, you'll be clarifying and defining your focus—your Life Vision—and developing a strategy that will guide you through your day-to-day life—your action plan. In the final chapter, I'll talk more about how to sustain your commitment.

This chapter is a little different from the preceding chapters. It's particularly exercise-intensive, so I encourage you to work through it over a period of days or weeks. You may start to feel a bit overwhelmed if you try to complete all these exercises in one sitting. This is where everything will start to come together for you. You're going to develop a strategy for achieving your Life Vision and living in greater alignment with your authentic self. You'll be creating a life in which you'll feel more whole and complete on your own. And, like the Jane Austen character depicted in the movie *Becoming Jane*, you'll be in a position to honor your truth, because you'll know exactly who you are and possess the freedom to act on that knowledge.

This is where the culmination of your personal-development work begins:

- In Exercise One, you'll *identify the most important attributes of your ideal life,* zeroing in on your top priorities as you move forward. You'll do this by referring back to some of the exercises you completed earlier in the book and creating a list of ideal attributes that will help you refine your focus.

- In Exercise Two, based on this list of ideal attributes—the personal qualities, behaviors, and life circumstances to which you aspire— you'll *write a Life Vision statement* that will serve as your guidepost and anchor as you move forward.

- In Exercise Three, you'll *identify the barriers you face*—the core limiting beliefs and habitual behaviors of your default operating system, as well as other sabotaging beliefs, thoughts, behaviors, and circumstances that hinder your ability to move forward.

- In Exercise Four, you'll use all the information you've gleaned from the preceding exercises to *identify three specific goals*—your top priorities in moving toward achieving your Life Vision.

- In Exercise Five, you'll *develop a set of action steps* that will help you achieve those goals.

- Finally, in Exercise Six, you'll begin to *create a new life structure,* incorporating your action steps into your daily and weekly schedule. This structure will help you adhere to the new routines that will build your inner and outer supports and help you follow through on your goals and commitments to yourself.

Before you begin, consider some of the people you've met in this book: a woman who wanted to expand her social circle but felt uncomfortable attending *Dance Free* alone. A high-achieving man who had played the Hero role for so long that he was unable to live the balanced life to which he aspired. A woman so afraid she'd be unhappy without a man in her life that she plunged into a marriage that was doomed from the start. Everyone puts his own imprint on this process. Each of you comes to it with your own unique fears and foibles, a distinctive set of core beliefs and habitual behaviors, your own innate nature, and a vision of an ideal life that's all your own. As such, the exercises in this chapter will take each of you down a different path.

To help guide you, I'm going to introduce you to two hypothetical people: Jane Doe and John Doe. Their purpose is to provide a frame of reference for the exercises that follow—or rather, two frames of reference. Although through our life conditioning many of us have adopted patterns that are based on gender stereotypes, that's not why I've chosen a man and woman. My goal is simply to present you with two multidimensional people whose hypothetical experiences can guide you as you take these crucial steps toward becoming a whole and complete person on your own.

Meet Jane Doe

Jane Doe is in her late 20s. In her relationships, she has a tendency to withhold how she really thinks and feels, allow people to treat her disrespectfully, and put other people's needs ahead of her own. She's a classic people-pleaser. Jane grew up in the Midwest, the only girl in a family of five. Her father worked in sales and traveled a lot. When he was home, he'd toss the football around with Jane's brothers or take them to a ball game, but he never paid much attention to Jane. He was also a demanding husband, snapping orders at Jane's mother, treating her like a subordinate. Jane's brothers had strong personalities; they were athletes with big personas, popular and outgoing. They dominated the household. Her mother was compliant and accommodating, a homemaker who waited on her husband hand and foot and was devoted to her three children. But she was preoccupied with her only daughter's appearance, frequently telling Jane to stop slouching, lose weight, and try to improve her looks by wearing makeup.

Jane was the quiet one in the family, the brainy one. She always did well in school, but her mother focused more on Jane's appearance than on her academic achievements, and she was discouraged from participating in athletics of any kind. Like Cinderella, Jane was the one required to stay home and help her mother with the cooking and household chores. She believed that, like her mother, she'd grow up and find a man to take care of her.

Today Jane is a librarian's assistant. Although she has a winning smile and a fresh, natural look about her, she's self-conscious about her body and hides herself in baggy clothes. She's interested in politics and history, but she has yet to realize her academic or career potential. Plagued by feelings of low self-esteem, Jane is terrified of spending the rest of her life alone. She has a tendency to overindulge with junk food to comfort herself, a legacy of her mother's food-focused child-rearing style. Jane's family role: the Lost Child. Her core limiting beliefs: *Others' thoughts, feelings, and needs are more important than my own. I'm ugly.*

Here are some of the things Jane discovered by working through the exercises I've described in the early chapters of this book. She uncovered the aspects of her authentic self that had been buried through her conditioning—including a desire to pursue her interest in history and politics, go back to school, and excel in her field. During her Ideal Partner Visualization, she imagined her ideal partner as an author or professor—an academic whiz. In her Ideal Life Visualization, she imagined living in a small town near a university and renovating an older home. She saw herself as a smart, sophisticated, independent woman living an active, politically engaged life in a close-knit community of intellectuals. She envisioned herself feeling accomplished and sharing supportive relationships in which she was able to express her needs and set healthy boundaries.

Through her personal-development work, Jane realized that she reinforced her core limiting belief that she was unattractive by hiding beneath baggy clothes. She had long ago lost touch with her authentic self: a bright, intellectually engaged person with a passion for ideas and politics. To master her aloneness, Jane needed to focus on building her self-esteem and finding ways to have healthy relationships with others. She also decided to go back to school and complete her master's degree in history and politics.

Meet John Doe

John Doe is 45 years old. He's been on a quest for the ideal mate since his divorce three years ago, but he can't seem to find the perfect woman. He's a high achiever, a Type A who works long hours as a creative director at an ad agency. Because of his work schedule, he doesn't take very good care of himself. He drinks a lot, exercises little, and lives with a fair amount of stress. Whenever he tries to get in shape, he can't seem to stick with it. He has a pattern of going to the gym for a few days or weeks, then dropping his new regimen when he gets a new project at work. He also has a habit of being critical and demanding in his relationships, a pattern that has promoted conflict in his marriage, work, and social relationships. Since his divorce, John has fallen into a pattern of jumping from one brief relationship to another, looking for someone younger, someone better-looking, someone with a smaller waist or a higher salary.

John is charming, funny, and very creative, but lately he's been feeling disenchanted with his work and plagued by feelings of loneliness and frustration. He grew up in an affluent family where being the best at what you did was the measure of your self-esteem and money was the measure of the man. His father was a perfectionist, critical and demanding—a pattern that played out in his relationships with his wife and his children. John replicated that same pattern in his own marriage. While he was always highly creative, rather than pursue his dream of being a painter, he found an outlet for his creativity in a high-powered career that would be acceptable to his family. At this point, there's something missing in his professional life, and he's become bored and unhappy at work.

John's Ideal Partner Visualization uncovered these attributes of his ideal partner: healthy, physically fit, and peaceful. In fact, he imagined her as a yoga instructor. John's own Ideal Life Visualization included his passion for painting—an interest he had in high school and college but didn't pursue. Now it's something he wants to explore to bring more meaning and joy into his life. Through his personal-development work, John came to see that his desire for the perfect mate was a manifestation of his habitual drive for perfection, rooted in his family of origin. And, by identifying the attributes of his ideal mate, he recognized that balance, creativity, and fitness represented voids in his life. To master his aloneness, he needed to focus on restoring balance to his life, addressing his workaholism, and recovering his lost passion for painting.

For your reference, Jane Doe's and John Doe's complete action plans appear in the Appendix.

Exercise One: Life Vision Attributes

You're about to create your Life Vision Attributes list. To help you complete the exercise, go back through your journal to the exercises you completed earlier in this book.

- Review the results of the Ideal Life Attributes exercise that you completed following your Ideal Life Visualization (page 235). What did you list in your journal as your ideal personal qualities, ideal behaviors, and ideal life circumstances?

- Refer back to the interests, passions, and contributions you listed in your journal at the end of Chapter 6, "Reclaiming Your Innate Wholeness" (page 186).

- Review the items you listed in your journal under the heading "My Ideal Partner Gaps"—the gaps between your attributes and those of your ideal partner, which you identified at the end of Chapter 7, "Becoming the Partner You Seek" (page 218).

Use the outcomes of those exercises to help you identify the personal qualities, behaviors, and life circumstances that are the *most critical* to you. Now, in your journal, write "My Life Vision Attributes" at the top of the page. Focusing on attributes that are particularly important—attributes that you *do not currently possess*—complete the following sentences:

- The personal qualities that will help me master the art of aloneness are: (List two or three.)

- The behaviors that will help me master the art of aloneness are: (List two or three.)

- The life circumstances that will help me master the art of aloneness are: (List one or two.)

To give you a sense of what these lists might look like, here are Jane Doe's and John Doe's lists.

Jane's Life Vision Attributes
- Personal qualities: *Confident. Powerful. Self-sufficient.*

- Behaviors: *Loving and respecting myself. Expressing my feelings and setting healthy boundaries with others.*

- Life circumstances: *A successful and fulfilling academic career in history and politics. Feeling whole and complete on my own.*

John's Life Vision Attributes
- Personal qualities: *Healthy. Fit. Energetic.*

- Behaviors: *Loving and respecting myself and others. Expressing my creativity.*

- Life circumstances: *A balanced and fulfilling life. My own home-based graphic design business and painting studio.*

Exercise Two: Crafting Your Life Vision

Your Life Vision describes the state you want to achieve within yourself and in your life. It provides you with a clear focus on what you want and serves as a guidepost for all the decisions you make in your day-to-day life. You'll be using your Life Vision later in this chapter to create your action plan. Your Life Vision should be specific, inspiring, written in the present tense, and between 25 and 40 words in length so you can easily commit it to memory.

Here are Jane Doe's and John Doe's examples:

Jane's Life Vision
I am a confident, powerful, and self-sufficient woman, loving and respecting myself, expressing my feelings and setting healthy boundaries with others, enjoying a successful and fulfilling academic career in history and politics, and feeling whole and complete on my own.

John's Life Vision
I am a healthy, fit, and energetic man, loving and accepting myself and others, enjoying a balanced and fulfilling life, and expressing my creativity in my home-based graphic design business and painting studio.

Now, open your journal and write "My Life Vision" at the top of the page. Using your Life Vision Attributes list, write a concise and inspiring statement that clearly articulates the personal qualities, behaviors, and life circumstances you want to manifest in your life on your own. Remember to keep it to 25 to 40 words in length, so you can memorize it, and to write it in the present tense, as if it were already so. Since clearly identifying what you want is the first step to bringing your vision to reality, it's important to be as specific as you can be. Take the time you need to refine your statement, finishing only when you have a Life Vision with which you're completely satisfied, one that that makes you feel genuinely inspired and excited.

When you're happy with your Life Vision statement, memorize it. Then you can repeat it to yourself when you're on a treadmill at the gym or driving to work in the morning or before you go to sleep at night. Write it on the front page of your daily planner, or frame it and hang it in a special place. Let it be a constant reminder of the path you're following and the new life you're creating.

As a further reminder, I also encourage you to find objects that inspire you, symbols of mastering the art of aloneness and of your Life Vision. For example, I have a statue of Buddha on my desk that's a visual cue; it reminds me to stay connected to my authentic self and to take time to relax and regroup every day. I also have a painting of a woman flying high above the rooftops. For me, it symbolizes the idea of soaring fearlessly beyond my boundaries and continuously expanding my comfort zone. Although your action plan is critical to bringing your Life Vision to reality, it's your focused commitment that will let you really soar. Your Life Vision is a powerful tool to help you sustain that focus.

Exercise Three: Identifying Your Barriers

In this exercise, you're looking for anything you've uncovered about yourself that could sabotage your ability to achieve your Life Vision—your barriers. Before you begin, you'll want to review what you've learned about yourself:

- The lists that appear in your journal under the following headings will be particularly helpful—"The Challenges in Mastering My Aloneness," "My Core Limiting Beliefs," "My Family Role," and "My Fears and Core Beliefs."

- Refer back to your list of inner supports and outer supports. This will help you identify where the weaknesses in your support systems lie.

- Be sure to take into account any addictions or feelings of depression or anxiety that need to be addressed, as these will undermine your ability to realize your Life Vision.

- Finally, remember any "Aha!" moments you experienced as you worked through this book—anything else you've uncovered about yourself that could sabotage your ability to achieve your Life Vision.

Step One

In your journal, complete the following sentences.

- My family role is:

- My core limiting beliefs are:

- My habitual behaviors are:

- Other sabotaging thoughts, feelings, patterns, or life circumstances are:

Step Two

In your journal, write "My Barriers." Based on the results from Step One, make a list of your barriers to achieving your Life Vision.

Jane's Barriers

Here is how Jane Doe completed Exercise Three:

- My family role is: *Lost Child.*

- My core limiting beliefs are: *Others' thoughts, feelings, and needs are more important than my own. I'm ugly.*

- My habitual behaviors are: *Putting other people's needs ahead of my own. Withholding my real thoughts and feelings.*

- Other sabotaging patterns or life circumstances: *Eating junk food for comfort. Staying
  up late watching TV and not getting enough
  sleep. Engaging in relationships in which I feel
  disrespected and unvalued. Lack of outer supports. Fear of being alone forever.*

Then she wrote this list of barriers in her journal:

- *The limiting beliefs that others' needs are more
  important than my own and that I'm ugly*

- *Putting others' needs ahead of my own*

- *Withholding my real thoughts, feelings, and
  needs from others*

- *Eating junk food and not getting enough sleep*

- *Engaging in relationships in which I feel disrespected and unvalued*

- *Lack of outer supports*

- *Fear of being alone forever*

Exercise Four: Identifying Your Goals

Using your Life Vision and your barrier list as your reference points, identify your *three* most important goals—your three top priorities, the goals you want to address first to move you closer to achieving your Life Vision. Be as specific as you can.

In your journal, write "My Three Goals" and record today's date. Then list your three goals, one by one, including a deadline by which you will achieve each one.

As an example, here's how John Doe's goals look:

- Goal #1: *Leave my job and work in my own home-based graphic design business and art studio by the end of this year.*

- Goal #2: *Lose 15 pounds and achieve greater physical fitness, health, and energy by June 30.*

- Goal #3: *Experience more loving, accepting, and peaceful relationships with myself and others by the end of this year.*

Exercise Five: Identifying Your Action Steps

Now you're going to formulate a specific set of action steps for each of your goals. As you develop your action plan, don't try to do too much. Stay focused on the three goals you identified. It's important to keep this process as uncomplicated and focused as possible so you don't overwhelm yourself. To complete this part of the exercise, you may want to refer back to the examples of inner and outer supports that appeared earlier in the book, as well as the Resource Guide at the back of the book. Use what you've learned about yourself to identify the action steps that will work for you.

I suggest you start with *no more than six* specific action steps for each of your goals. To formulate them, you'll want to ask yourself these questions for each goal:

- What are the most important initial action steps I need to take to achieve this goal?

- What inner supports do I need to help me achieve this goal or to move through my barriers to achieving it?

- What outer supports do I need to help me achieve this goal or to move through my barriers to achieving it?

Now, for each goal, write down no more than six action steps you will take toward achieving it. Record your three goals and their action steps in your journal. Whenever possible, set a deadline for completing each action step and build that date into the step. As you complete each step, you can add further steps and keep updating them until you've reached the goal.

Here is an example of the action steps Jane Doe developed for her second goal—"Build friendships with at least three new people who are uplifting, fun, and respectful by August 31." (Again, you'll find complete action plans for Jane Doe and John Doe in the Appendix.)

- *Renew my membership at the YWCA and start taking group exercise classes by February 15.*

- *Find and take a salsa dance class at the adult education center by March 1.*

- *Attend a class on effective communication at the adult education center by March 10.*

- *Find and join a book club by April 30.*

- *Check the calendar section of the paper; plan and do at least one social activity each weekend.*

- *Express my needs, feelings, and boundaries to others on an ongoing basis.*

Congratulations! Your new life is about to begin. Before you move on to the next exercise, you'll need to buy yourself a daily planner, one that provides enough space to record and schedule the activities and actions steps you'll be incorporating into your new life.

Exercise Six: Creating Your Life Structure

You've determined the direction you want to go. You've identified the first steps you need to take to get you there. Now you're going to incorporate your action plan into your daily and weekly life by using a daily planner. To complete this exercise, take out your daily planner and record the following:

- All the action steps and deadlines you've set for yourself (e.g., find a yoga class by February 15)

- All the daily and weekly activities you've committed to engage in (e.g., Weight Watchers group every Friday; gym every Monday, Wednesday, and Friday)

Your action plan is something you'll need to keep updating as you complete your action steps. As you add new action steps and activities to your daily and weekly routine, be sure to record them in your daily planner. This will help you follow through on your action steps, complete your goals, and bring your Life Vision to reality.

Next Steps

Mastering the art of aloneness is an ongoing process. Here are a few things to remember as you move forward:

- For each of your three goals, once you've completed your action steps, keep setting and completing new action steps until you have achieved that goal.

- Once you've accomplished a goal, you can replace it with a new goal and set of action steps, keeping the process going until you've achieved your Life Vision.

- If you find that taking on three goals at a time is overwhelming, prioritize your goals and focus on just one or two at a time.

- When formulating your goals and action steps, include specific deadlines whenever you can. This will help prevent procrastination and keep you on course.

CHAPTER 11

SUSTAINING YOUR COMMITMENT

You've done the hard work of identifying your authentic self and mapping out a strategy for mastering the art of aloneness. Now the fun is about to begin. As you take these steps toward achieving your Life Vision, you're going to begin an exciting journey that will be full of surprises. You'll be amazed by how your life will change, first in small ways and, ultimately, in dramatic new ways. You'll have more energy, more confidence, and a new enthusiasm for what's ahead. You'll stop focusing on finding your perfect mate and become a whole and complete person on your own. By loving yourself, living deliberately, and pursuing your own Life Vision and goals, you'll create the life to which you aspire. This final chapter is designed to help you sustain your commitment to mastering your aloneness and provide an overview of the tools you've acquired throughout this book to manage any pitfalls you may encounter along the way.

Common Pitfalls

As I said at the beginning of this book, as you engage in the process of mastering aloneness and living in alignment with your authentic self, you will slip up. After all, we're all human. The challenge is to get back on course. When you find yourself slipping back into old, limiting patterns, think of it as a process of course-correcting. Welcome the challenge—it means that you're taking charge of your life. Don't judge yourself. Instead, treat yourself with love and compassion.

Here are some of the pitfalls you may encounter as you continue your process—and some of the ways to address them:

- *Feeling overwhelmed.* Most likely, if you start to feel overwhelmed, it's because you're trying to address too many issues or make too many changes all at once. The best way to deal with this is to step back and look at your action plan. If you're doing too much, it's time to reprioritize. Maybe you need to work on two goals instead of three. Or maybe one of your goals requires a lot of steps, so it's taking up all your energy. To address the problem, identify the goals that are most important to you. If you need to, just focus on one goal at a time and don't move on to the next one until the first one is complete.

- *Feeling discouraged.* This happens when you're listening to the inner critic—the inner voice that says: "You'll never make it." "It's hopeless." "This is too hard." "You're not

moving fast enough." Whatever that voice
is saying, you need to articulate a response,
drawing from the part of you that feels
strong, confident, and optimistic. Be your
own cheerleader. Review your accomplishments; remind yourself of what you're capable of doing and being. Instead of focusing
on and feeding the old voice that drags you
down, actively support the part of you that
believes that you can have a terrific life on
your own. Keep your inner critic at bay by
invoking your Inner Nurturing Parent.

- *Falling back into old patterns.* There are two
  ways to address this issue. First, be aware that
  you're more likely to slip up when you're trying to accomplish your goals *all by yourself.* It
  may be that you don't have an outer support
  system in place to help you maintain your
  focus and discipline and to give you the kind
  of outside encouragement everyone needs.
  Outer supports might include a trusted
  friend or family member, a coach or therapist, or an ongoing support group. To have
  a strong system of outer supports, you have
  to actively build, nurture, and sustain it.
  That involves reaching out to people instead
  of keeping yourself isolated and shutting
  yourself off from people. Second, if you're
  falling back into old patterns, it may be helpful to avoid situations that trigger your old
  behavior. For example, say Jane Doe tends
  to fall into her pattern of eating junk food
  when she's feeling isolated and lonely on the

weekends. That's her trigger. To avoid falling back into her old pattern, she has to be sure to schedule some activities on the weekend to help her bypass the old trigger.

- *Lack of energy.* Take good care of yourself—whether it's one of your three goals or not. A lack of energy typically relates to a failure to sustain your inner support system, which provides the physical, emotional, and mental energy needed to achieve your goals. If you're eating poorly, neglecting your health, or living a high-stress lifestyle, you're depleting your inner resources. That will make it difficult to maintain the energy you need to participate fully and actively in your life—which is central to achieving your Life Vision and mastering the art of aloneness.

- *Lack of motivation.* If you don't have a loving and caring relationship with yourself, it's hard to sustain the motivation to take action and make good choices for yourself. Building and sustaining a healthy, loving relationship with yourself is absolutely crucial to mastering the art of aloneness. Loving yourself compels you to make lifestyle choices that make you feel good and generate the results you want. If you begin to feel unmotivated, revisit your relationship with yourself. Invoke your Inner Nurturing Parent. Make a conscious effort to treat yourself with respect, kindness, love, and compassion.

Overriding Your Conditioned Self

As you engage in the process of mastering aloneness, be aware that your limiting beliefs and habitual behaviors will resurface again and again. When they do, you'll need to *consciously redirect your thoughts and behaviors* in a way that supports your authentic self. This act of consciously redirecting your thoughts and behaviors is central to achieving your Life Vision—and to mastering the art of aloneness. It means living in a state of continual aware-ness, consciously living your life in each moment. When you fall back into the old thought and behavior patterns of your conditioned self, consciously replace those old, conditioned beliefs and behaviors with the new beliefs and behaviors you've identified—those articulated in your Life Vision. Over time, your new beliefs and behav-iors will become part of your new operating system. But that's a process that takes time and requires *relentless but gentle perseverance.*

Your conditioned self is and will always be a part of you. Your default operating system—your core beliefs and habitual behaviors—are deeply ingrained. By living deliberately, you'll be actively engaged in *overriding your conditioned self.* Let me explain why this is so important. According to a variety of psychological models, from clas-sic Freudian theories to new mind-body therapies, the unconscious—or subconscious—mind is the part of us that holds our repressed memories. It's the place where our core beliefs reside; it's the home of your conditioned self. When you're operating from your conditioned self, your unconscious mind is in the driver's seat—running you and your life. The premise of Sigmund Freud's theory of the unconscious, or subconscious, mind is that some past experiences are too painful to remember, so the mind pushes them down into the subconscious, thereby protecting us from emotional pain. Although these painful memories and associations are repressed, Freud believed they still played a significant role in determining human behavior.[1] Subsequent psychological theories teach that it's not only traumatic memories that are stored in the subconscious but also our core beliefs and habitual patterns.

Not long ago I ran across an article by Bruce Lipton, Ph.D., entitled "Mind Over Genes" that echoes many of my own theories. He explains that during the first six years of life, a child unconsciously not only "acquires the behavioral repertoire needed to become a functional member of society," but also "downloads beliefs relating to the self,"[2] and that it's our biology that enables this process. As babies, we are hardwired to absorb lessons from our families and culture and store them in our unconscious mind. During our early years of development, he writes, our brains are operating at low EEG (electroencephalography) frequencies, so we are all functioning in what he calls a hypnogogic state: "While in this hypnotic trance, a child does not have to be actively coached by its parents for they obtain their behavioral programs simply by observing their parents, siblings, peers, and teachers."[3]

The unconscious patterns of our conditioned self are set in place during early childhood and remain powerful drivers of our behavior into adulthood. Lipton writes that "as neuroscientists emphasize, the conscious mind provides five percent or less of the cognitive activity during the day. Ninety-five to ninety-nine percent of our behavior is directly derived from the subconscious."[4] That's an astounding number. We're on autopilot at least 95 percent of the time! That's why I call it the default operating system; it's the one we fall back on again and again. When we're relying on our default operating system, we're relying on messages from the subconscious mind—powerful, deep-seated messages of which we're totally unaware. So overriding those messages represents a tremendous challenge.

As you implement your action plan and pursue your Life Vision, you'll be taking the idea of living deliberately to the next level. You'll be engaged in the process of overriding your conditioned self and allowing your authentic self to take charge of your life. That requires constant vigilance, because, as Bruce Lipton points out, "the moment you lapse in consciousness, the subconscious mind will automatically engage."[5] And when that happens, your old patterns will automatically kick back in.

Creating a Life Vision and identifying specific goals and action steps for achieving it are powerful tools. You'll be engaged in replacing your default operating system with one that allows you to live a more joyful and fulfilling life. You'll need to stay mindful of your default operating system so you can recognize when it starts to kick in and take over. And you'll need to maintain a relentless commitment to observing and course-correcting yourself, so you can override your conditioning and create the life you want to have.

Your Solemate Tool Kit

As you move forward, *all* the tools you've acquired in this book are crucial elements in your arsenal of support—essential for improving your relationships, managing your fears, building your self-esteem, and, most importantly, nurturing your relationship with yourself.

Using these tools will help you override your habitual patterns and behaviors, stay focused on your Life Vision, and accomplish the action steps needed to achieve it:

- *The Five Steps to Managing Fear (page 94)*— This is a valuable technique to help you address specific fears and help you step outside your comfort zone.

- *Weighing the Pros and Cons (page 97)*—You'll want to use this exercise to help you make decisions about your life and your relationships.

- *Reality Checks (page 98)*—This is a valuable tool for helping you overcome self-doubt when you're embarking on any new experience or making a decision about your life. Checking in with reality is a way of overriding your default operating system and moving out of trance states.

- *Honoring Your Intuition (page 136)*—Your intuition is your connection to your authentic self, a valuable tool for helping you live in alignment with your Life Vision.

- *Developing Your Inner Nurturing Parent (page 122)*—Loving and nurturing yourself is the surest route to building and sustaining a healthy relationship with yourself. This is a good way to silence your inner critic, which represents one of the greatest barriers to your success.

- *Practicing Emotional Intelligence (page 130)*—
  Live with deliberateness. Develop your ability to manage your emotions effectively. This
  will support your efforts to improve your
  relationships with others.

- *Enlisting the Power of Thought (page 131)*—
  Align your thoughts with your Life Vision.
  Stay focused on what it is that you want.

- *Taking Responsibility (page 109)*—Remember
  the three levels of creation: creating, promoting, allowing. When you feel yourself blaming others, look closely at the role you play
  in situations as they arise.

- *Communicating Effectively (page 170)*—By
  communicating effectively from your
  authentic self, you build better relationships,
  are more likely to get the results you want,
  and reinforce the power of your authentic
  self.

Be the Change You Want to See in the World

By engaging in the personal-development work
you've done throughout this book, I hope you've already
begun to integrate many of these tools into your life and
are seeing some of the transformative results. As you
embark on your new life, I encourage you to refer back
to the book again and again, using it as a resource for
addressing the specific barriers you face in realizing your

Life Vision, or any time you find yourself needing extra support. Think of it as your tool kit for developing a loving, healthy relationship with yourself—for transforming your life by becoming your own solemate.

Your journal and action plan are powerful resources for staying on course—for tracking your progress, celebrating your accomplishments, and setting new goals that will continually expand your comfort zone. I also encourage you to share your transformational process with others, learning from those who can help you move forward, and using where you've been and what you've learned to help others. Mahatma Gandhi said that to induce change out in the world you have to first *become* that change. It is my hope that this book has helped you to find greater joy and peace in the sacred space of your aloneness, rediscover the magnificent and powerful person you are, and become the change you want to see out in your world.

ACKNOWLEDGMENTS

There are many people who contributed to the creation of this book. First and foremost are: Susan Dynerman, whose brilliant help and unflagging support played a major role in bringing this book to life. My literary agent, Molly Lyons, the first to catch the vision and whose call to action moved mountains. My editor, Patty Gift, for her unerring editorial instincts, creative vision, and unobtrusive support. And Joelle Delbourgo, for her encouragement and resourcefulness. Thanks to Laura Koch, Anne Barthel, Jacqui Clark, Reid Tracy, Margarete Nielsen, Nancy Levin, Carina Sammartino and the entire Hay House team for making this experience such a joy. I'm grateful to Shawna Carboni, Robert Kiess, M.D., and Roger Abdell for reading and providing feedback on book chapters. I thank my clients who generously agreed to let their stories grace the pages of this book, and I thank Pamela Hamilton for her research and fact-finding expertise.

I extend my heartfelt gratitude to Terry Kellerman, Ursula and Walter Friedl, Karen Köbel, Silvia Roell, Erika Marshall, Anita Landa, Debra Sherman, Joyce Cousens, Carol and David Krentzman, Betsy Peck, Lidia and Rick Sylvia, Mary Jane Golden, Deb and Bruce Holden, Maria Kogan, and Matt and Lindsay Oberman, all of whom provided support in a thousand different ways.

305

I'm indebted to the many people who have been sources of inspiration and whose work has informed my own. These include Carl Jung, Milton Erikson, Gregory Bateson, Murray Bowen, Braulio Montalvo, Virginia Satir, Salvador Minuchin, Alexander Lowen, Stephen Wolinsky, Harville Hendrix, Louise Hay, John Bradshaw, and Insight Seminars founders John Roger and Russell Bishop.

And finally, I want to thank my children, to whom I also dedicate this book, for being the incredible, resilient, loving human beings that you are.

Appendix
Sample Action Plans

Jane Doe's Action Plan

Life Vision:

I am a confident, powerful, and self-sufficient woman, loving and respecting myself, expressing my feelings and setting healthy boundaries with others, enjoying a successful and fulfilling academic career in history and politics, and feeling whole and complete on my own.

Barriers:

- *The limiting beliefs that others' needs are more important than my own and that I'm ugly*
- *Putting others' needs ahead of my own*
- *Withholding my real thoughts, feelings, and needs from others*
- *Eating junk food and not getting enough sleep*
- *Engaging in relationships in which I feel disrespected and unvalued*
- *Lack of outer supports*
- *Fear of being alone forever*

Goal #1: *Build a stronger inner support system by the end of this year.*

Action Steps:

- *Start a new routine of going up to bed by 9:30 P.M. on weeknights, reading for 30 minutes, and going to sleep by 10:00 P.M. by February 10.*

- *Find a psychotherapist and start weekly therapy sessions by February 10.*

- *Read three books on nutrition and develop and start adhering to a new, healthy eating plan by February 25.*

- *Develop my Inner Nurturing Parent by saying positive and loving messages to myself on a daily basis.*

- *Write in my journal every morning and record my feelings and progress.*

- *Go through the Five Steps to Managing Fear whenever my fear of being alone surfaces.*

Goal #2: *Build friendships with at least three new people who are uplifting, fun, and respectful by August 31.*

Action Steps:

- *Renew my membership at the YWCA and start taking group exercise classes by February 15.*

- *Find and take a salsa dance class at the adult education center by March 1.*

- *Attend a class on effective communication at the adult education center by March 10.*

- *Find and join a book club by April 30.*

- *Check the calendar section of the paper and plan and do at least one social activity each weekend.*

- *Express my needs, feelings, and boundaries to others on an ongoing basis.*

Goal #3: *Complete my master's degree within the next three years.*

Action Steps:

- *Research master's programs in history and in political science by May 1 of this year.*

- *Prepare for and take the graduate entrance exam by September 1 of this year.*

- *Check with Human Resources at work about their Tuition Reimbursement Program by June 1 of this year.*

- *Complete and submit my school applications by November 5 of this year.*

John Doe's Action Plan

Life Vision:

I am a healthy, fit, and energetic man, loving and accepting myself and others, enjoying a balanced and fulfilling life, and expressing my creativity in my home-based graphic design business and painting studio.

Barriers:

- *The limiting beliefs that I have to be perfect at all times and that I'm unworthy and undeserving of love*
- *Being very critical, impatient, and unforgiving with myself and others*
- *Working 12-hour days in a job that I hate*
- *Fear of not making enough money if I leave my current job*
- *Using alcohol to manage stress*
- *No time to exercise*

Goal #1: *Leave my job and work in my own home-based graphic design business and art studio by the end of this year.*

Action Steps:

- *Meet with my financial advisor to discuss my plan to start my own business by February 1.*

- *Read books on starting your own business and talk to people I know who have done it.*

- *Donate the old furniture stored in my upstairs loft by March 1.*

- *Hire a decorator to help me turn my loft into an office and art studio by March 1.*

- *Refurbish and paint the loft as needed by March 31.*

- *Complete a strategic business plan by May 1.*

Goal #2: *Lose 15 pounds and achieve greater physical fitness, health, and energy by June 30.*

Action Steps:

- *Find a new gym that I like, hire a personal trainer, and start working out three times a week by February 5.*

- *Join Weight Watchers and start attending weekly meetings by February 5.*

- *Learn about different meditation practices, find one that I like, and start meditating 20 minutes a day by March 1.*

Goal #3: *Experience more loving, accepting, and peaceful relationships with myself and others by the end of the year.*

Action Steps:

- *Buy and read books on spirituality, forgiveness, and compassion.*

- *Invoke my Inner Nurturing Parent and say loving messages to myself each time my inner critic comes up inside of me.*

- *When I feel judgmental toward others, remind myself that the other person is doing the best he can in that moment.*

- *Be aware of which ego state I'm communicating from in each moment, and move out of the Critical Parent and into the Adult ego state when I slip into my old pattern.*

- *Treat myself to a massage at least once a month starting February 2.*

NOTES

Chapter 2

1. Sam Roberts, "It's Official: To Be Married Means to Be Outnumbered," *The New York Times,* October 15, 2006.
2. Ibid.
3. Sam Roberts, "51% of Women Are Now Living Without Spouse," *The New York Times,* January 16, 2007.
4. Ibid.
5. U.S. Census Bureau press release, "Facts for Features," July 19, 2004, http://www.census.gov/Press-Release/www/releases/archives/facts_for_features_special_editions/002265.html.
6. U.S. Bureau of the Census, *Current Population Reports,* Series P-20, No. 372, "Marital Status and Living Arrangements: March 1981" (Washington, D.C.: U.S. Government Printing Office, 1982).
7. U.S. Census Bureau press release, "Facts for Features," July 19, 2004, http://www.census.gov/Press-Release/www/releases/archives/facts_for_features_special_editions/002265.html.
8. Jason Fields and Lynn M. Casper, "America's Families and Living Arrangements: Population Characteristics," *Current Population Reports,* U.S. Census Bureau, March 2000.

9. BBC News, "Living Alone is 'The Norm,'" January 11, 2002, http://news.bbc.co.uk/1/hi/uk/1754824.stm (accessed November 11, 2007).

10. Linda Hantrais, *Family Policy Matters: Responding to Family Change in Europe* (Bristol: The Policy Press, 2004), 62.

11. William J. Cromie, "Why Women Live Longer Than Men," *The Harvard University Gazette*, October 1, 1998, http://www.hno.harvard.edu/gazette/1998/10.01/WhyWomenLiveLon.html (accessed January 15, 2008); Jennifer Jones, "Around The Globe, Women Outlive Men," *Population Today*, August/September 2001, http://www.prb.org/Articles/2001/AroundtheGlobe-WomenOutliveMen.aspx (accessed November 10, 2007).

12. U.S. Census Bureau press release, "Facts for Features," July 19, 2004, http://www.census.gov/Press-Release/www/releases/archives/facts_for_features_special_editions/002265.html.

13. Bella DePaulo, *Singled Out: How Singles Are Stereotyped, Stigmatized, and Ignored, and Still Live Happily Ever After* (New York: St. Martin's Press, 2006).

14. See, for example, the following articles: Lea Winerman, "Helping Men to Help Themselves," *Monitor on Psychology* 36, no. 6, American Psychological Association (June 2005), http://www.apa.org/monitor/jun05/helping.html (accessed November 20, 2007); Willow Lawson, "Boys Don't Cry," *Psychology Today*, July/August 2004.

Chapter 3

1. *Faces & Voices of Recovery Public Survey.* Washington, D.C.: Peter D. Hart Research Associates, Inc., and Coldwater Corporation, May 4, 2004, 1.
2. Bridget F. Grant, "Estimates of US Children Exposed to Alcohol Abuse and Dependence in the Family," *American Journal of Public Health,* 90 (1), Washington, D.C.: American Public Health Association, January 2000, 112–15.
3. http://www.aamft.org/families/Consumer_ Updates/ChildrenandDivorce.asp (accessed November 10, 2007).
4. J. Bailey Molineux, "Dysfunctional Families Can Be Loving," *Helena Independent Record,* September 4, 2007.
5. John Bradshaw, *Bradshaw On: The Family* (Deerfield Beach, FL: Health Communications, Inc., 1988).
6. Ibid., 33.

Chapter 4

1. Stephen Wolinsky, *The Dark Side of the Inner Child* (Putney, VT: Bramble Books, 1993).
2. Ibid., 1.
3. Harville Hendrix, *Getting the Love You Want* (London: Pocket Books, 2005), 13.

Chapter 5

1. Daniel Goleman, *Emotional Intelligence* (New York: Bantam Books, 1997), 43–44.
2. Ibid., xii.
3. Wayne W. Dyer, *The Power of Intention* (Carlsbad, CA: Hay House, 2004), 71.
4. Sharon Jayson, "Power of a Super Attitude," *USA Today*, October 12, 2004, http://www.usatoday.com/news/health/2004-10-12-mind-body_x.htm?bc=interstitialskip (accessed November 11, 2007).
5. Ibid.
6. Lauran Neergaard, "Study Verifies Power of Positive Thinking," *Associated Press*, November 28, 2005, http://www.livescience.com/health/ap_051128_placebo.html (accessed November 11, 2007).
7. Ibid.
8. Ibid.

Chapter 6

1. Joseph Campbell, ed., *The Portable Jung*, trans. R. F. C. Hull (New York: Viking Penguin, Inc., 1971), xxvi.
2. Lawrence Wright, "A Reporter at Large: Double Mystery," *The New Yorker*, August 7, 1995, 45–62.
3. Thomas J. Bouchard, Jr. and Matt McGue, "Genetic and Environmental Influences on Human Psychological Differences," *Journal of Neurobiology* 54, no. 1 (2003): 4–45.

4. American Automobile Association Foundation for Traffic Safety, "Aggressive Driving: Three Studies" (1997), http://www.aaafoundation.org/resources/index.cfm?button=agdrtext (accessed November 14, 2007).

5. Daniel J. Levinson, *The Seasons of a Man's Life* (New York: Knopf, 1978), 199.

Chapter 7

1. Colette Dowling, *The Cinderella Complex: Women's Hidden Fear of Independence* (New York: Summit Books, 1981), 16.

2. Ibid., 46.

3. Ibid., 16.

4. Leslie Bennetts, *The Feminine Mistake* (New York: Voice, 2007), 102.

5. Ibid., xxiv.

6. Ibid., 120.

7. Ibid., 117–120.

8. Ibid., xxiv.

9. Ibid., 120.

10. Ibid., xxiv.

11. Hendrix, *Getting the Love You Want,* 36.

12. Ibid., 36.

13. Ibid., 36–39.

Chapter 9

1. Elizabeth Gilbert, *Eat, Pray, Love* (New York: Viking Penguin, 2006), 53.
2. Deepak Chopra, *Power, Freedom, and Grace* (San Rafael, CA: Amber-Allen Publishing, 2006), 7.
3. Ann Kaiser Stearns, *Living Through Personal Crisis* (New York: Ballantine Books, 1985), 69.
4. Jack Kornfield, *A Path with Heart* (New York: Bantam Books, 1993), 72.

Chapter 11

1. The Skeptic's Dictionary, entry on "Unconscious Mind," http://skepdic.com/unconscious.html.
2. Bruce Lipton, "Mind Over Genes," 2005, www.brucelipton.com/article/mind-over-genes-the-new-biology (accessed December 6, 2007).
3. Ibid., 3.
4. Ibid., 4.
5. Ibid., 4.

GLOSSARY

This is a compilation of some of the terms I use in the book, including some that I've developed and some developed by other people in my field.

Action plan: A written document that includes one's *Life Vision* and the goals and action steps one needs to take to achieve that vision.

Action steps: Actions that need to be taken to achieve one's goals.

Affirmation: A written statement that clearly and concisely describes something one aspires to be, achieve, have, or experience (e.g., personal qualities, behaviors, and/or life circumstances).

Authentic self: The person you were born to be—the true self—composed of one's innate personality traits, wholeness, and strengths. *Living from the authentic self* means living in alignment with one's innate nature, wholeness, and intuition, and developing and living from an operating system made up of beliefs and behaviors that activate one's innate potential.

Comfort zone: The boundary one lives within that comprises all that is known and familiar (education, job,

relationships, income, life experiences, life circumstances, etc.).

Conditioned self: The person one becomes as the result
of the life conditioning process. Living from *the conditioned self* means habitually and unconsciously living
from one's *default operating system* rather than from *the
authentic self.*

Constructive family system: A family system in which there
is a healthy state of homeostasis; family roles are fluid
and interchangeable (that is, the system's needs are met
by members assuming different roles at different times);
each member's innate nature is allowed expression; and
each member's innate wholeness remains intact.

Core beliefs: The conclusions about oneself and the world
that are unconsciously internalized during one's formative years. Although core beliefs usually reside in the
subconscious, they are the underlying drivers of human
behavior.

Core limiting beliefs: The conclusions about oneself and
the world, unconsciously internalized during the formative years, that prevent or limit expression of one's innate
nature, wholeness, and potential (e.g., "I'm unworthy
and undeserving.").

Default mode: Living on autopilot instead of with conscious intention.

Default operating system: The internal operating system
rooted in the subconscious that's composed of the core

limiting beliefs and habitual behaviors adopted during the formative years.

Dysfunctional family system: A family system in which there is an absence of balance and stability; family roles are fixed and rigid; parts of members' innate nature become submerged (those that threaten the family norms); the innate wholeness of individual family members is eroded; and some or many of the family system requirements are not met.

Dysfunctions and pathologies: Patterns of thought and behavior that prevent or limit expression of the authentic self.

Family of origin: The family one grows up in.

Family role: The primary role each family member unconsciously adopts within the family as part of the natural dynamic of homeostasis.

Family system: A group made up of family members who interact within the context of certain defined relationships and according to a set of accepted ways of thinking and behaving (family "norms").

Family system homeostasis: A natural and unconscious dynamic of human interaction in which the family system continuously moves toward a state of balance and stability to meet its collective needs.

Family system requirements: The conditions and environment needed for a family system to function in a healthy, constructive manner and for each member to retain and express his or her innate nature and wholeness.

Goal: A clear and concise written description of a desired result one wants to achieve.

Innate nature: The unique personality traits each person is born with.

Innate wholeness: The capacity to access and express the innate personality traits and natural range of human emotions each person is born with.

Inner Critical Parent: The inner voice that is self-critical and reprimanding and hinders the full activation of one's innate potential. Also referred to as the inner critic.

Inner Nurturing Parent: The inner voice that sends loving and supporting messages to the self and is a source of love, support, and encouragement from within.

Inner support system: The activities one does alone on a routine basis to build and sustain one's health and inner resources and to achieve one's *Life Vision.*

Intuition: The instinctive knowing that comes through one's "sixth sense" rather than through rational thought.

Life conditioning: The shaping of one's identity as the result of external influences such as the family of origin; environment; social, cultural, religious, and educational influences; and the life experiences and circumstances to which one is exposed during one's formative years.

Life Vision: A written statement that clearly and concisely synthesizes the attributes of one's ideal self and life.

Limiting behaviors: Patterns of behavior that are not part of the *default operating system* developed in childhood, but serve as barriers and limitations in one's adult life (e.g., compulsive shopping and overspending).

Limiting beliefs/thoughts: Patterns of thought that are not part of the *default operating system* developed in childhood, but serve as barriers and limitations in one's adult life (e.g., "I can do meaningful work or make a good living, but I can't have both").

Limiting habitual behaviors: The patterns of behavior unconsciously adopted during the formative years that prevent or limit expression of one's innate nature, wholeness, and potential (e.g., always making others' needs more important in an effort to be loved).

Observer: The part of the self that watches what one thinks and how one behaves in each moment. Buddhists refer to this form of observation as practicing mindfulness. Developing the observer is key to living deliberately.

Outer support system: The external resources one utilizes as a means of support for one's health and well-being and to achieve one's *Life Vision.*

Visualization: The process of using the mind to imagine a desired future state or result.

INNER AND OUTER
SUPPORT RESOURCES

Books

Bradshaw, John. *Bradshaw On: The Family*. Deerfield Beach, FL: Health Communications, Inc., 1988.

Cameron, Julia. *Transitions: Prayers and Declarations for a Changing Life*. New York: Tarcher/Putnam, 1999.

De Angelis, Barbara. *Confidence: Finding It and Living It*. Carlsbad, CA: Hay House, 2005.

Dowling, Colette. *The Cinderella Complex: Women's Hidden Fear of Independence*. New York: Summit Books, 1981.

Dyer, Wayne W. *The Power of Intention*. Carlsbad, CA: Hay House, 2004.

Flanigan, Beverly. *Forgiving the Unforgivable*. Hoboken, NJ: Wiley, 1994.

Ford, Debbie. *Spiritual Divorce: Divorce as a Catalyst for an Extraordinary Life*. New York: HarperSanFrancisco, 2001.

Hay, Louise. *You Can Heal Your Life*. Carlsbad, CA: Hay House, 1984.

Hendricks, Gay, and Kathlyn Hendricks. *Conscious Loving*. New York: Bantam, 1990.

Hendrix, Harville. *Keeping the Love You Find*. New York: Pocket Books, 1992.

Kavanaugh, Philip. *Magnificent Addiction: Discovering Addiction as Gateway to Healing.* Fairfield, CT: Aslan Publishing, 1992.

Keirsey, David, and Marilyn Bates. *Please Understand Me: Character & Temperament Types.* Del Mar, CA: Gnosology Books, Ltd., 1978.

Levinson, Daniel J. *The Seasons of a Man's Life.* New York: Knopf, 1978.

Mackler, Lauren, Jack Canfield, Stephen Covey, and Ken Blanchard. *Speaking of Success.* Sevierville, TN: Insight Publishing, 2007.

Mellody, Pia, Andrea Wells Miller, and J. Keith Miller. *Facing Codependence.* New York: Harper & Row Publishers, 1989.

Orman, Suze. *The Laws of Money, The Lessons of Life: Keep What You Have and Create What You Deserve.* New York: Free Press, 2003.

Real, Terrence. *I Don't Want to Talk About It: Overcoming the Secret Legacy of Male Depression.* New York: Simon & Schuster, 1997.

Robbins, Anthony. *Unlimited Power.* New York: Fireside, 1986.

Ruiz, Don Miguel. *The Four Agreements: A Practical Guide to Personal Freedom.* San Rafael, CA: Amber-Allen Publishing, 1997.

Schaef, Anne Wilson. *Co-Dependence: Misunderstood— Mistreated.* New York: HarperSanFrancisco, 1992.

Sharma, Robin. *Who Will Cry When You Die?* Carlsbad, CA: Hay House, 2002.

Sheehy, Gail. *Understanding Men's Passages: Discovering the New Map of Men's Lives*. New York: Ballantine Books, 1999.

Smith, Alan. *UnBreak Your Health: The Complete Guide to Complementary & Alternative Therapies*. Ann Arbor, MI: Loving Healing Press, 2007.

Stearns, Ann Kaiser. *Living Through Personal Crisis*. New York: Ballantine Books, 1985.

Stone, Hal, and Sidra Stone. *Embracing Our Selves*. Mill Valley, CA: Nataraj Publishing, 1989.

Storr, Anthony. *Solitude: A Return to the Self*. New York: Ballantine Books, 1989.

Weil, Andrew. *Eating Well For Optimum Health: The Essential Guide to Bringing Health and Pleasure Back to Eating*. New York: Random House, 2000.

Williamson, Marianne. *The Age of Miracles: Embracing the New Midlife*. Carlsbad, CA: Hay House, 2008.

Wolinsky, Stephen. *The Dark Side of the Inner Child*. Putney, VT: Bramble Books, 1993.

Zukav, Gary. *The Seat of the Soul*. New York: Simon & Schuster, 1989.

Audio Books and CDs

Dyer, Wayne W., and Deepak Chopra. *Creating Your World the Way You Really Want It to Be*. Carlsbad, CA: Hay House, 2002.

Hay, Louise. *How to Love Yourself: Cherishing the Incredible Miracle That You Are*. Carlsbad, CA: Hay House, 2005.

Jeffers, Susan. *Feel the Fear and Do It Anyway: Dynamic Techniques for Turning Fear, Indecision, and Anger into Power, Action, and Love*. Carlsbad, CA: Hay House, 2007.

Myss, Caroline. *Finding Your Sacred Contract*. Carlsbad, CA: Hay House, 2003.

Northrup, Christiane, and Mona Lisa Schulz. *Igniting Intuition: Unearthing Body Genius*. Carlsbad, CA: Hay House, 2005.

Personal-Development and Psychotherapy Approaches

There are many types of traditional and alternative mental-health and personal-development modalities and practitioners, including clinical social workers, clinical psychologists, psychiatrists, mental-health counselors, mind-body psychotherapists, and life coaches. This is a partial list.

Bioenergetic Analysis: Founded by Alexander Lowen, bioenergetic analysis is a form of psychotherapy rooted in the work of Wilhelm Reich. It involves working with both the body and the mind to help resolve emotional problems and is viewed as a way of understanding personality in terms of the body and its energetic processes. Bioenergetic analysis focuses on the expression of feelings and the reestablishment of energy flow in the body to enhance pleasure and joy in living.

Cognitive-Behavioral Psychotherapy: This is typically a short-term therapy focused more on changing current, problematic thoughts and behaviors, and less on addressing underlying past issues. The practitioner helps the client identify unhealthy, negative beliefs and behaviors, and replace them with healthy, positive ones. Treatment may include stress management, biofeedback, and relaxation techniques.

EMDR: EMDR, or Eye Movement Desensitization and Reprocessing, is a psychotherapeutic technique that is typically used as part of a comprehensive treatment plan. It is a neurological therapy used to treat psychological trauma, phobias, and personal and professional performance issues.

Humanistic Psychotherapy: Founded by Carl Rogers, humanistic psychotherapy focuses on supporting the client's inherent capacity for growth, rather than dwelling on past events or on the therapist's ideas of how the client should change. It's based on the premise that people have within themselves the resources and capacity for self-awareness and development. The goal of therapy is to create a safe place for that self-discovery and growth to take place.

Hypnotherapy: By allowing clients to access the unconscious mind, hypnotherapy helps them learn how to react differently to certain situations. A trained therapist guides a person to remember events that have brought about dysfunctional or problem-causing responses or memories and then reconstruct those events with new, healthier associations. Hypnosis is used to relieve many conditions that have an emotional or psychological component. Studies have shown that hypnosis may improve immune function, decrease feelings of stress and anxiety, and lessen pain.

Life Coaching: Coaching is a resource for people who want to improve their personal or professional lives or achieve specific goals such as creating healthier relationships, making a career change, improving business results, gaining greater self-awareness, or living more deliberately. Although there are no regulatory or training requirements for becoming a coach, the necessary skills and qualifications are similar to those of a psychotherapist. However, life coaching differs from therapy in that it focuses more on the present and future and on achieving specific goals and objectives, than on the past. When choosing a life coach, it's important to inquire about training, credentials, and methodology.

Mind-Body Psychotherapy: Mind-body psychotherapy is a holistic approach that combines traditional talk therapy with other, less traditional approaches to engage the client at all levels—mental, emotional, and physical. Mind-body approaches and techniques vary from therapist to therapist, but practitioners usually have training in traditional psychology as well as in nontraditional modalities such as breath therapy, hypnotherapy, bioenergetics, or voice dialogue.

Psychoanalysis: A long-term, intensive therapy that often involves several sessions a week for several years, this practice evolved out of theories developed by Sigmund Freud. Psychoanalysis involves examining dreams, memories, and past events to understand current feelings and behavior. It's based on the premise that childhood events and biological urges create an unconscious mind that drives how we think, feel, and behave. In formal psychoanalysis, the therapist sits out of sight behind the patient, who typically lies on a couch.

Psychodynamic Psychotherapy: Based on the theories of psychoanalysis, this approach focuses on increasing the client's awareness of the subconscious and using those insights to resolve inner conflicts and issues. Generally, the patient and therapist sit face to face. Meetings generally occur less often than during psychoanalysis—usually once a week—and the entire therapeutic process usually lasts a year or less.

Voice Dialogue: Voice dialogue is a therapeutic technique developed by two American psychologists, Hal and Sidra Stone. Rooted in Jungian psychology, this work is based upon the premise that we have myriad selves living inside us, each with its own interests, needs, thoughts, feelings, and opinions. These selves, referred to as subpersonalities, or "voices," influence our lives and life choices. Voice dialogue is used to help the client gain greater awareness of the parts that are dominant in his life, better manage the parts that limit him, and further develop the state of consciousness known as the "aware ego."

Approaches for Physical Health and Well-Being

Acupressure: Based on the principles of Oriental medicine, acupressure predates acupuncture but is similar in that treatment involves contact with the same key points on the surface of the skin. When these points are pressed, it relieves muscular tension and heightens blood circulation. The practitioner uses hands and fingers to apply pressure to stimulate the meridian system, those pathways along which the body's energy force is believed to flow. Acupressure is used to relieve pain and stress and to promote overall good health by supporting the body's own curative properties.

Acupuncture: Acupuncture is a Chinese medical practice dating back more than 5,000 years. It involves inserting needles at points on the surface of the body to increase or decrease the flow of energy—or *qi*—throughout the body. This energy is believed to travel along special pathways known as meridians. The acupuncture points are those locations where the meridians come to the surface of the skin and are more easily accessible. Acupuncture is used to treat a variety of illnesses, relieve pain, promote relaxation, and address addictions.

Applied Kinesiology: The word *kinesiology* refers to a branch of science that studies the human body's anatomy, physiology, and mechanics of movement. Founded in 1964 by the American chiropractor George Goodheart, applied kinesiology is primarily a diagnostic tool that evaluates health problems through muscle tests. It is a holistic approach to balancing the movement and interaction of a person's energy systems and is used to enhance physical, mental, emotional, and spiritual well-being.

Aromatherapy: Aromatherapy is the therapeutic use of essential oils, which are concentrated plant extracts. These oils are complex, fragrant, and volatile compounds that are believed to be easily absorbed so that they penetrate deeply into tissues, bloodstream, and organ systems. They are used in skin care, massage, and simple inhalation to promote natural body functioning, well-being, and vitality. This approach was first documented in the 13th century in Britain.

Ayurveda: Recognized as one of the most ancient medical systems, Ayurveda originated in India. Ayurveda is a comprehensive system of health care that employs lifestyle interventions and natural therapies including herbs, nutrition, special cleansing, massage, breathing, and meditation. The actual diagnostic and healing process varies from one practitioner to another. Ayurveda seeks to prevent disease, increase life span, and restore and rejuvenate the body and body systems by emphasizing the integration of body and mind and each person's union with nature, the self, and the universe.

Biofeedback: Biofeedback is the process of monitoring physiological signals (such as muscle tension or brain waves) and making the results available to the person being treated. The patient then uses this information to learn how to self-regulate and control physiological functioning. Biofeedback has been found to be helpful in treating a wide variety of conditions including asthma, headaches, and high blood pressure.

Breath Therapy: A practice based on both ancient Eastern and modern Western disciplines and methods, breath therapy employs a number of specific breathing techniques and exercises. Each of these is designed to achieve a particular end—for example, correcting breathing patterns, promoting relaxation, increasing inner awareness, and enabling emotional release. Full and correct breathing helps the body heal itself and is believed to provide renewal of body, mind, and spirit.

Chiropractic Medicine: Originally developed in the 19th century, chiropractic medicine involves the hands-on manipulation of the spine in order to maintain the integrity of the spine and nervous system. Spinal manipulation, to realign the vertebrae and relieve pressure on the nerves, is believed to be an effective treatment for a number of health-related problems including muscle spasms of the back and neck, and tension headaches. While many patients seek out a chiropractor for the relief of pain, the chiropractor's aim is to restore and promote the overall health of the patient.

Craniosacral Therapy: This is a form of therapy that uses gentle touch to both evaluate and affect the craniosacral system—the cranium or skull, the spinal column, and the membranes and cerebrospinal fluid that surround and protect the brain and spinal cord. Craniosacral therapy is believed to affect all aspects of the body by promoting general health, reducing stress, and improving brain and spinal cord function. It is used to treat problems such as chronic pain, scoliosis, coordination issues, postoperative care, sports injuries, depression, birth trauma, hyperactivity, and hormonal imbalances.

Herbal Medicine: Based on the use of plants and plant extracts, herbalism is perhaps the most ancient form of medicine. According to the World Health Organization, herbal medicine is three to four times more commonly practiced worldwide than conventional medicine, and 25 percent of modern medicines are made from plants. Herbs can be administered in many forms, including tinctures (alcoholic extracts of herb), tisanes (hot water extracts of herb), topical application, whole-herb consumption, and inhalation. Herbalism is a holistic approach that treats the patient as a whole and not the disease as such.

Homeopathy: Founded in the late 18th century by German physician Samuel Hahnemann, homeopathy is based on the principle that "like cures like"—the idea that the best remedy for an illness is a substance that produces symptoms similar to the disease. Homeopathy seeks to stimulate the body's defense mechanisms and processes to prevent and treat illness, and treatment is tailored to the individual. That is, homeopathic practitioners use the total picture of the patient—including symptoms, lifestyle, emotional and mental state, and other factors—to select remedies.

Massage Therapy: Massage is one of the oldest healing arts, dating back thousands of years and used by the ancient Chinese, Hindus, Persians, and Egyptians. It involves the application of various manipulation techniques to the muscular structure and soft tissues of the human body, which has the effect of reducing stress and fatigue and improving circulation. Massage therapy is used to treat many conditions including back pain, arthritis, bursitis, high blood pressure, diabetes, depression, suppressed immunity, and tension.

Meditation: There are several forms of meditation, most of which can be grouped into two basic approaches: (1) focused or concentrated attention and (2) mindfulness. Meditation moves one toward balance and harmony and is often used as a pathway to self-knowledge. The practice may well be as old as humankind. It is particularly conducive to relaxation, which allows the body's self-healing capabilities to work, and can be used to relieve stress-induced physiological and psychological problems and to strengthen the immune system.

Naturopathy: A holistic approach that addresses the whole patient—mind, body, and spirit—naturopathic medicine is a system based upon the healing power of nature. It employs a variety of techniques, such as nutrition, herbal medicine, acupuncture, and homeopathy, both to support the body's own healing abilities and to enable individuals to make lifestyle changes necessary to achieve good health. Used primarily to prevent diseases, naturopathy may also be used to treat illness and chronic conditions.

Nutritional therapy: Nutritional therapy targets diet as a treatment for health problems. Toxic overload, food allergies or intolerances, and the inability to assimilate food properly are some of the issues nutritional therapy addresses. The nutritional therapist works with each individual to determine what that person's particular dietary needs and problems may be. Different types of diets, herbs, and supplements may be prescribed to alleviate symptoms and treat problem conditions.

Osteopathy: Osteopathic medicine is a complete system of medical care that treats the whole person—not just the symptoms. It is concerned with the relationships of structure and function and attempts to use the body's self-curative abilities. Osteopathy regards true health as total physical, mental, and social well-being, rather than just the absence of disease. Osteopaths use treatment with the hands or mechanical means to restore proper relationships among the various parts of the body and correct defects in the musculoskeletal system.

Reiki: Reiki is a Japanese technique that promotes healing, stress reduction, and relaxation. It is a holistic approach that has its roots in ancient Buddhist teachings. It is based on the idea that there is a life-force energy—the *ki* (in Chinese, *qi*) that flows through us and that this life force can be harnessed for the purpose of healing. When this energy is high, we are able to feel healthy and happy; and when it is low, we are more likely to become ill and to feel stress. The Reiki practitioner channels the ki by means of a "laying on of hands" to the patient, activating the body's natural ability to heal itself.

Yoga: Yoga is an ancient Indian practice focused on the creation of balance in the body through the development of both strength and flexibility. Yoga involves the use of poses or postures that promote harmony of mind, body, and spirit. During the performance of these postures, the discipline of breathing and concentration helps the yoga practitioner achieve greater tranquility and heightened awareness.

Other Resources

ALCOHOL ABUSE

United States

Al-Anon/Alateen
Al-Anon Family Group Headquarters
1600 Corporate Landing Pkwy.
Virginia Beach, VA 23454-5617
(888) 4AL-ANON (425-2666)
www.al-anon.alateen.org

Alcoholics Anonymous (AA)
General Service Office
475 Riverside Dr., 11th Fl.
New York, NY 10115
(212) 870-3400
www.aa.org

Center on Addiction and the Family
164 W. 74th St.
New York, NY 10023
(646) 505-2060
(800) 359-COAF (359-2623)
www.coaf.org

Mothers Against Drunk Driving (MADD)
511 E. John Carpenter Frwy, Ste. 700
Irving, TX 75062
(800) GET-MADD (438-6233)
www.madd.org

National Association for Children of Alcoholics (NACoA)
11426 Rockville Pike, Ste. 100
Rockville, MD 20852
(301) 468-0985
(888) 55-4COAS (554-2627)
www.nacoa.net

National Clearinghouse for Alcohol and Drug Information (NCADI)
(800) 729-6686
www.health.org

National Council on Alcoholism and Drug Dependence (NCADD)
244 E. 58th St., 4th Fl.
New York, NY 10022
(212) 269-7797
(800) NCA-CALL (622-2255—24-hour hotline)
www.ncadd.org

Women for Sobriety
P.O. Box 618
Quakertown, PA 18951
(215) 536-8026
www.womenforsobriety.org

United Kingdom

Alcohol Concern
020 7264 0510
www.alcoholconcern.org.uk

Alcoholics Anonymous
General Service Office
PO Box 1, 10 Toft Green
York YO1 7NJ
01904 644026
www.alcoholics-anonymous.org.uk

Drinkline
0800 917 8282

Canada

Alcoholics Anonymous
www.aa.org

Al-Anon/Alateen
(800) 714-7498

Canadian Centre on Substance Abuse
75 Albert St., Ste. 300
Ottawa ON K1P 5E7
(613) 235-4048
www.ccsa.ca

CODEPENDENCY

Co-Dependents Anonymous
P.O. Box 33577
Phoenix, AZ 85067-3577
(602) 277-7991
www.codependents.org

DEATH/GRIEVING/SUICIDE

United States

AARP Grief and Loss Programs
(888) OUR-AARP (687-2277)
www.aarp.org/griefandloss

Grief Recovery Institute
P.O. Box 6061-382
Sherman Oaks, CA 91413
(818) 907-9600
www.grief-recovery.com

National Hospice and Palliative Care Organization
1700 Diagonal Rd., Ste. 625
Alexandria, VA 22314
(703) 837-1500
www.nhpco.org

Suicide Awareness Voices of Education (SAVE)
8120 Penn Ave., Ste. 470
Bloomington, MN 55431
(952) 946-7998
www.save.org

Suicide National Hotline
(800) 273-8255

United Kingdom

The Compassionate Friends
53 North St.
Bristol BS3 1EN
0845 123 2304 (helpline)
0845 120 3785 (administration)
www.compassionatefriends.org.uk

Winston's Wish
Westmoreland House
80-86 Bath Rd.
Cheltenham GL53 7JT
0124 251 5157 (general inquiries)
0845 203 0405 (helpline)
www.winstonswish.org.uk

Canada

Canadian Hospice Palliative Care Association
Annex B, Saint-Vincent Hospital
60 Cambridge St. North
Ottawa, ON K1R 7A5
(800) 668-2785
www.chpca.net

Grieving Children at Seasons Centre
38 McDonald St.
Barrie, ON L4M 1P1
(705) 721-KIDS (721-5437)
www.grievingchildren.com

Centre for Suicide Prevention
Ste. 320, 1202 Centre St. SE
Calgary, AB T2G 5A5
(403) 245-3900
www.suicideinfo.ca

DRUG ABUSE

United States

Cocaine Anonymous International Referral Line
(800) 347-8998
www.ca.org

Cocaine Abuse Hotline
(800) COCAINE (262-2463)

Drug and Alcohol Treatment and Prevention Services
www.drughelp.org

National Institute on Drug Abuse (NIDA)
National Institutes of Health
6001 Executive Blvd., Rm. 5213
Bethesda, MD 20892-9561
(301) 443-1124 (for information)
(800) 662-HELP (662-4357—for referrals)
www.nida.nih.gov

Narcotics Anonymous World Service Office, Inc.
P.O. Box 9999
Van Nuys, CA 91409
(818) 773-9999
www.na.org

United Kingdom

National Drug Helpline
0800 77 66 00
0800 917 8765 (textphone)
www.talktofrank.com

The Centre for Recovery
Cyswllt Ceredigion Contact
49 North Parade
Aberystwyth
Ceredigion SY23 2JN
01970 626470
www.recovery.org.uk

Narcotics Anonymous, UK Region
0845 FREEDOM (373 3366—helpline)
020 7730 0009 (helpline)
www.ukna.org

Canada

Canadian Assembly of Narcotics Anonymous
CANA/ACNA
P.O. Box 25073 RPO West Kildonan
Winnipeg, MB R2V 4C7
www.canaacna.org

Canadian Centre on Substance Abuse
75 Albert St., Ste. 300
Ottawa, ON K1P 5E7
(613) 235-4048
www.ccsa.ca

EATING DISORDERS

United States

Focus Adolescent Services
(410) 341-4216
(877) 362-8727
www.focusas.com/EatingDisorders.html

Overeaters Anonymous
World Service Office
P.O. Box 44020
Rio Rancho, NM 87174-4020
(505) 891-2664
www.oa.org

United Kingdom

Eating Disorders Association
103 Prince of Wales Rd.
Norwich NR1 1DW
0845 634 1414 (adults)
0845 634 7650 (youth)
www.b-eat.co.uk

Canada

National Eating Disorder Information Centre
ES 7-421
200 Elizabeth St.
Toronto, ON M5G 2C4
(866) 633-4220
www.nedic.ca

HEALTH ISSUES

United States

American Chronic Pain Association
P.O. Box 850
Rocklin, CA 95677
(800) 533-3231
www.theacpa.org

American Holistic Health Association
P.O. Box 17400
Anaheim, CA 92817-7400
(714) 779-6152
www.ahha.org

The Chopra Center
2013 Costa Del Mar Rd.
Carlsbad, CA 92009
(760) 494-1600
(888) 424-6772
www.chopra.com

The Fetzer Institute
9292 W. KL Ave.
Kalamazoo, MI 49009-9398
(269) 375-2000
www.fetzer.org

Hippocrates Health Institute
1443 Palmdale Ct.
West Palm Beach, FL 33411
(800) 842-2125
www.hippocratesinst.com

Hospice Education Institute
P.O. Box 98
Machiasport, ME 04655-0098
(207) 255-8800
(800) 331-1620 (Hospicelink)
www.hospiceworld.org

Institute of Noetic Sciences
101 San Antonio Rd.
Petaluma, CA 94952
(707) 775-3500
www.noetic.org

Benson-Henry Institute for Mind-Body Medicine
151 Merrimac St.
Boston, MA 02114
(617) 643-6090
www.mbmi.org

National Health Information Center
Referral Specialist
P.O. Box 1133
Washington, DC 20013-1133
(301) 565-4167
(800) 336-4797
www.health.gov/NHIC

Optimum Health Institute
6970 Central Ave.
Lemon Grove, CA 91945
(619) 464-3346
(800) 993-4325
www.optimumhealth.org

Preventive Medicine Research Institute
Dean Ornish, M.D.
900 Bridgeway
Sausalito, CA 94965
(415) 332-2525
www.pmri.org

United Kingdom

National Health Service (NHS) Direct
0845 4647 (24-hour nurse advice line)
www.nhsdirect.nhs.uk

Canada

Health Canada
(613) 957-2991
www.hc-sc.gc.ca

MENTAL HEALTH

United States

American Psychiatric Association
1000 Wilson Blvd., Ste. 1825
Arlington, VA 22209-3901
(703) 907-7300
(800) 35-PSYCH (357-7924)
www.psych.org

Anxiety Disorders Association of America
8730 Georgia Ave., Ste. 600
Silver Spring, MD 20910
(240) 485-1001
www.adaa.org

Depression and Bipolar Support Alliance
730 N. Franklin St., Ste. 501
Chicago, IL 60654-7725
(312) 642-7243
(800) 826-3632
www.dbsalliance.org

American Psychological Association Help Center
(800) 964-2000
www.apahelpcenter.org

The International Society for Mental Health Online
www.ismho.org

The Substance Abuse and Mental Health Services Administration's National Mental Health Information Center
(800) 789-2647
www.mentalhealth.org

National Center for Post-Traumatic Stress Disorder (PTSD)
(802) 296-6300
www.ncptsd.org

National Alliance for the Mentally Ill (NAMI)
Colonial Place Three
2107 Wilson Blvd., Ste. 300
Arlington, VA 22201-3042
(703) 524-7600
(800) 950-NAMI (6264)
www.nami.org

National Institute of Mental Health
Office of Communications
6001 Executive Blvd.
Rm. 8184, MSC 9663
Bethesda, MD 20892-9663
(301) 443-4513
(866) 615-6464
(301) 443-8431 (TTY)
(866) 415-8051 (TTY)
www.nimh.nih.gov

United Kingdom

Mind (The National Association for Mental Health)
15-19 Broadway
London E15 4BQ
0845 766 0163
www.mind.org.uk

SANE
1st Floor Cityside House
40 Adler St.
London E1 1EE
020 7375 1002
0845 767 8000 (SANEline)
www.sane.org.uk

Canada

Canadian Mental Health Association
Phenix Professional Building
595 Montreal Rd., Ste. 303
Ottawa, ON K1K 4L2
(613) 745-7750
www.cmha.ca

Mood Disorders Society of Canada
3-304 Stone Rd. West, Ste. 736
Guelph, ON N1G 4W4
(519) 824-5565
www.mooddisorderscanada.ca

STRESS REDUCTION

United States

The Menninger Clinic
(A leading center for psychiatric treatment, including biofeedback and psychophysiology)
2801 Gessner Dr.
Houston, TX 77080
(713) 275-5000
(800) 351-9058
www.menninger.edu

New York Open Center
(In-depth workshops to invigorate the spirit)
83 Spring St.
New York, NY 10012
(212) 219-2527
www.opencenter.org

Omega Institute
(A healing, spiritual retreat community)
150 Lake Dr.
Rhinebeck, NY 12572-3212
(845) 266-4444 (info)
(800) 944-1001 (to enroll)
www.eomega.org

Center for Mindfulness in Medicine, Health Care, and Society
(Home of a mindfulness-based stress reduction program)
University of Massachusetts Medical School
55 Lake Ave. North
Worcester, MA 01655
(508) 856-2656
www.umassmed.edu/cfm

United Kingdom

International Stress Management Association UK
P.O. Box 491
Bradley Stoke
Bristol BS34 9AH
www.isma.org.uk

ABOUT THE AUTHOR

Lauren Mackler, an innovator in activating human potential, is a renowned coach, keynote speaker, teacher, and popular radio and TV talk-show guest. Over the past 25 years, she has been a psychotherapist, workshop facilitator, corporate consultant, and a leading authority in the areas of personal transformation, relationships, and professional performance. She is a fellow author of *Speaking of Success* with Jack Canfield, Stephen Covey, and Ken Blanchard and founder of the coaching and consulting firm Lauren Mackler & Associates.

Visit her Website at **www.laurenmackler.com**.

NOTE TO THE READER

Imagine a world in which each one of us is free to realize our fullest potential. A world where peace and kindness prevail and people treat themselves and others with dignity, love, and respect. Margaret Mead said, "Never doubt that a small group of thoughtful, committed citizens can change the world. Indeed, it is the only thing that ever has."

The information, skills, and tools I've compiled in this book have transformed my life and the lives of many others. I've often wondered how differently my life would have unfolded had I learned in my formative years that it is by our actions that we create the life we have, that it is by living deliberately and authentically that we activate our potential, and that to truly love and care for others we have to truly love and care for ourselves.

I encourage you to be one of the "committed citizens" who can change the world. Here are some suggestions for staying focused on your own transformational work and for sharing the information, skills, and tools in this book with others:

1. Form a *Solemate* Reading Group. This is a great way to go through the book and exercises with others, share your insights and growth, and give and receive support. To help you create and lead a *Solemate* Reading Group,

I've developed the *Solemate* Reading Group
Tool Kit, which can be ordered through my
Website at www.laurenmackler.com.

2. Suggest *Solemate* to a friend, family mem-
    ber, colleague, book club, women's or men's
    group, church, civic group, synagogue,
    mosque, university, or adult-education class.

3. Give a copy of the book as a gift to a friend
    or family member.

4. Find out if *Solemate* is in your local library.
    If not, either donate a copy or suggest that
    the library add the book to its inventory.
    Ask your friends or family who live in other
    states to do this, too.

5. Encourage your chain bookstore or local
    independent store to carry *Solemate*.

6. Write an online review of *Solemate* for Ama-
    zon, Borders, Barnes & Noble, or a blog.

7. Ask the book editor of your local radio or
    newspaper to consider reviewing the book.

8. Visit my Website, www.laurenmackler.com,
    for more information and events, or to join
    my online Life Keys community.

I wish you much love, peace, and joy as you continue your journey.

Lauren

Index

Hay House Titles of Related Interest

YOU CAN HEAL YOUR LIFE, the movie,
starring Louise L. Hay & Friends
(available as a 1-DVD program and an expanded 2-DVD set)
Watch the trailer at: **www.LouiseHayMovie.com**

AMBITION TO MEANING:
Finding Your Life's Purpose, the movie,
starring Dr. Wayne W. Dyer
(available as a 1-DVD program and an expanded 2-DVD set)
Watch the trailer at: **www.DyerMovie.com**

THE AGE OF MIRACLES: Embracing the New Middle Age,
by Marianne Williamson

THE POWER OF INTENTION:
Learning to Co-Create Your World Your Way,
by Dr. Wayne W. Dyer

All of the above are available at your
local bookstore, or may be ordered by
contacting Hay House (see next page).

We hope you enjoyed this Hay House book.
If you would like to receive a free catalogue featuring additional
Hay House books and products, or if you would like information
about the Hay Foundation, please contact:

Hay House UK Ltd
292B Kensal Rd • London W10 5BE
Tel: (44) 20 8962 1230; Fax: (44) 20 8962 1239
www.hayhouse.co.uk

***

Published and distributed in the United States of America by:
Hay House, Inc. • PO Box 5100 • Carlsbad, CA 92018-5100
Tel.: (1) 760 431 7695 or (1) 800 654 5126;
Fax: (1) 760 431 6948 or (1) 800 650 5115
www.hayhouse.com

Published and distributed in Australia by:
Hay House Australia Ltd • 18/36 Ralph St • Alexandria NSW 2015
Tel.: (61) 2 9669 4299; Fax: (61) 2 9669 4144
www.hayhouse.com.au

Published and distributed in the Republic of South Africa by:
Hay House SA (Pty) Ltd • PO Box 990 • Witkoppen 2068
Tel./Fax: (27) 11 467 8904 • www.hayhouse.co.za

Published and distributed in India by:
Hay House Publishers India • Muskaan Complex • Plot No.3
B-2 • Vasant Kunj • New Delhi – 110 070.
Tel.: (91) 11 41761620; Fax: (91) 11 41761630.
www.hayhouse.co.in

Distributed in Canada by:
Raincoast • 9050 Shaughnessy St • Vancouver, BC V6P 6E5
Tel.: (1) 604 323 7100; Fax: (1) 604 323 2600

***

Sign up via the Hay House UK website to receive the Hay House
online newsletter and stay informed about what's going on with
your favourite authors. You'll receive bimonthly announcements
about discounts and offers, special events, product highlights,
free excerpts, giveaways, and more!
www.hayhouse.co.uk